The Idea of Progress in Classical Antiquity

The
IDEA of PROGRESS
in
CLASSICAL
ANTIQUITY

by Ludwig Edelstein

The Johns Hopkins Press, Baltimore, Maryland

In memory of E. J. E.

*"Die Regentropfen Allahs
Gereift in bescheidener Muschel"*—
Goethe, *West–Oestlicher Divan*

FOREWORD

At the meeting of the American Philosophical Society in the autumn of 1955, Ludwig Edelstein read a paper entitled "The Idea of Progress in Antiquity." He did not publish this paper, undertaking instead to write a detailed and carefully considered history of the subject and to carry it down to the sixth century after Christ.

When he died in August, 1965, Professor Edelstein had not yet written the last four chapters of the eight he had planned; but he had completed the introduction and the first four chapters, which cover the idea of progress through what is conventionally called the Hellenistic Age, i.e., down to 30 B.C. (see chapter IV, note 1). Since this much has a unity of its own and exists in the author's definitive version, it is published here with a title appropriately altered to suit the part of the larger work that death prevented Professor Edelstein from finishing.

The manuscript was made available to The Johns Hopkins Press by Harold Cherniss, who found it among the papers bequeathed to him by Professor Edelstein. The Press gratefully acknowledges the assistance given by Professor Cherniss in preparing it for publication.

JACK G. GOELLNER
The Johns Hopkins Press

TABLE OF CONTENTS

INTRODUCTION

In this book I propose to narrate the fortunes of the idea of progress in Greek and Roman times; or, to put the matter more concretely and precisely and to forestall misunderstanding of the ambiguous word, "progress," I intend to analyse the ancients' belief that "an appraisal both of the historic process in general and of the predominant trend which was manifested in it" leads to the recognition of "a tendency inherent in nature or in man to pass through a regular sequence of stages of development in past, present and future, the latter stages being—with perhaps occasional retardations or minor regressions—superior to the earlier."[1]

Such an enterprise, I am well aware, may easily appear to be a defense of a lost cause. For in recent years it has become commonplace to assert that the Greeks and Romans were entirely innocent of a belief in progress in this sense of the term. No one will deny, of course, that they took cognizance of advances actually made in the past and in the present; but the "bearing on the future" from which the concept of progress derives "its value, its interest and its

[1] This is Lovejoy's definition of "the law of progress" or "what is usually meant by the 'idea of progress' in contemporary usage." Arthur O. Lovejoy and George Boas, *Primitivism and Related Ideas in Antiquity, A Documentary History of Primitivism and Related Ideas* (Baltimore [Md.], 1935), I, 6. (Cf. also p. ix, where there is an outline of the general problem to which the concept of progress, among others, provides a solution.) J.B. Bury, in *The Idea of Progress* (London, 1920), p. 7, says: "This idea means that civilization has moved, is moving, and will move in a desirable direction." Cf. also G.H. Hildebrandt in the introduction to his revision of F.J. Teggart, *The Idea of Progress* (Berkeley [Calif.], 1949), p. 4.

power," the expectation of still better things to come was, it is usually maintained, alien to ancient thought.[2] Any precedents of such a notion in earlier ages are said to be found, if at all, in the teachings of the Jewish prophets and of the first Christian writers, in religious tenets of a revealed faith, and not in the rational doctrines propounded by the pagans.[3] So firmly has this dogma of the ancients' ignorance of the concept of progress become entrenched that at the moment it is the unquestioned and unquestionable truth. That there could be any doubt of it is no longer even mentioned by the majority of historians of ideas or historians of antiquity.[4]

This modern attitude is the reverse of that which obtained during the nineteenth century and the first two decades of the twentieth, although the thesis now taken as obvious was then not unknown, for it had been formulated by A. Comte, the apostle of the modern idea of progress, as early as 1839, and had in the second half of the nineteenth century been accepted by some French writers and by such outstanding philosophers and historians as John Stuart Mill and Wilhelm Dilthey.[5] In general, however, it was held that to the Greeks "it was given to create the Principle of progress"; the concept was said to be attested "throughout antiq-

[2] Bury, *op. cit.*, pp. 6 ff.

[3] Cf. John Baillie, *The Belief in Progress* (New York, 1951), pp. 57 ff.; 67 ff., where the recent literature dealing with the Jewish–Christian background of progressivism is surveyed. Baillie ascribes a certain progressive outlook to the religion of Zarathustra also (cf. p. 94); but "it is, of course, entirely from the Old Testament . . . that this conception has been fed into the later history of Western thought." (p. 59.) Bury is one of those who deny the influence of Christian philosophy on later concepts of progress.

[4] See, for instance, Baillie's interpretation of antiquity, *ibid.*, pp. 6 ff.; or Harold Mattingly, *Roman Imperial Civilization* (New York: Anchor Books, 1959), pp. 212 ff.

[5] For Comte, see *Cours de philosophie positive* (3d. ed.; Paris, 1869), IV, 230, 240–43. On the situation in France and the works of Pierre Leroux, cf. J. Delvaille, *Essai sur l'Histoire de L'Idée de Progrès* (Paris, 1910), p. 3, and note 1; on Mill, cf. Bury, *The Idea of Progress*, p. 308. For Dilthey, see "Einleitung in die Geisteswissenschaften," *Gesammelte Schriften* I[3] (Leipzig, 1933 [originally published in 1883]), 330 f. and 334. Dilthey does not refer to Comte here, but he is most likely indebted to him for his understanding of progress, as his whole analysis of the moral sciences takes its departure from Comte's philosophy and the logic of Mill, which are of special importance for the "Konstitution der Theorie der gesellschaftlich–geschichtlichen Wirklichkeit" (p. 23, note 1).

uity."[6] In fact, so much did the interpretation of ancient culture emphasize the rational and optimistic aspects that other philosophies of history current among the Greeks and Romans were neglected until E. Rohde, in 1876, contrasted their progressive outlook to the theory of decay and insisted that the belief "in a development *in peius*" had been more popular. Rohde wrote under influence of that disillusionment with the progressivist creed which had begun to grip the *avant-garde* of European intellectuals, and he was strongly influenced by Nietzsche's discovery of the deep-seated pessimism of the Greeks—a pessimism Nietzsche extolled in contrast to the shallow optimism of his own century.[7]

The insight thus gained was to set the pattern for the subsequent debate on the problem. If there was an issue, it was concerned with the relative strength of the progressive and regressive tendencies.[8] According to some, the two opposing views had held each other in balance, both in the judgment of the educated in the ancient world and in the minds of the common people. Most interpreters, however, followed in the footsteps of Rohde;[9] and it was in his terms that in 1920 W. R. Inge in his famous Romanes Lecture, "The Idea of Progress," summarized the attitudes of the ancients to progressivism without mentioning any challenge to their knowledge of it.

[6] The former quotation is from Sir H. S. Maine, the Rede Lecture of May 22, 1875, p. 38 (adopted as the motto of *Griechische Denker* by T. Gomperz [Leipzig, 1896]); the latter is from the first edition of R. Eucken's *Geschichte und Kritik der Grundbegriffe der Gegenwart* (Leipzig, 1878), p. 190, note 2.

[7] Rohde stated his verdict quite incidentally in his *Der Griechische Roman und seine Vorläufer*, p. 201, note 2 (1914³, p. 216, note 2).

[8] L. Schmidt, *Die Ethik der alten Griechen* (Berlin, 1882), II, 68, is exceptional in denying that "was der Moderne je nach seiner besonderen Betrachtungsweise Fortschritt, Erziehung des Menschengeschlechts oder Kommen des Reiches Gottes nennt" had any place in the consciousness of the Greeks of the classical age.

[9] The growing acceptance of Rohde's contention is illustrated by the fact that Eucken (cf. above note 6) in later editions of his work expresses himself more cautiously, saying that the idea of progress despite the predominance of the doctrine of permanence was not foreign to antiquity (*Geistige Strömungen der Gegenwart* [4. Auf.; Leipzig, 1909], p. 199, note 1). In opposition to Rohde, R. Hirzel ("Άγραφος Νόμος, *Abhandlungen der Sächsischen Akademie der Wissenschaften, Phil.–Hist. Classe*, XX, No. 1 [1900], 79, note 2; cf. also pp. 79 ff; pp. 87 ff.) insisted that the two historical views had been equal in strength.

That the Greeks had outlined a doctrine of progressivism was then the unquestioned and unquestionable truth.[10]

How was one certain truth replaced by another apparently as certain? In the very year in which Inge's essay appeared, J.B. Bury published *The Idea of Progress*, which revived the thesis of Comte and sought to make it impregnable against attack. Comte and his earlier followers had dogmatically asserted the ancients' ignorance of the idea of progress without scrutinizing the evidence in detail. Bury marshaled passages from ancient literature of different centuries and maintained that none speaks of trust in progress past, present, or future, not even those that had always been thought to manifest a belief in the continuous progress of the ages.[11] The authority of the eminent historian prevailed; and, whereas in the nineteenth century scarcely anyone denied the idea of progress to the ancients, today very few remain who contend in agreement with Rohde that some Greek and Roman thinkers did have the notion of continuous progress, though it languished because it did not suit the "climate of opinion" prevailing in antiquity. It is still less frequently said that discussions of progressivism pervade Greek philosophical writings, or that infinite progress was acknowledged in Roman times.[12]

Does the truth lie with the majority or with the minority? Bury's analysis of the texts had not failed to arouse objections. He was charged with citing the Roman testimony out of context or with neglect of contrary assertions made by the same authors, and he

[10] Even Delvaille, who emphasized the contribution of the Jewish prophets to progressive thinking (chap. I), did not minimize the "feeble presentiments" of later theories in the philosophy of the Pre-Socratics (pp. 13 ff. and 16) and did not fail to notice the resemblance between the Stoic view and that of Condorcet, for which see chap. IV, pp. 175 f. below.

[11] Cf. *op. cit.*, pp. 8–20. Even Seneca's observations on progress, which clearly imply "that increases in knowledge must be expected in the future" (p. 13), are "far from adumbrating a doctrine of the progress of man" (p. 15); they are, moreover, "unique in ancient literature." (*Ibid.*)

[12] For the latter view see R. Mondolfo, *La comprensione del soggetto umano nell' antichità classica*, trans. Livinia Bassi (Firenze, 1958), Pt. IV, chap. III, pp. 629–739; for the former, see F. M. Cornford, *The Unwritten Philosophy and Other Essays* (Cambridge, 1950), pp. 45 ff. The essay in question first appeared in 1935; and now William K. C. Guthrie, *In the Beginning* (Ithaca [N.Y.], 1957), chap. V.

was also said to have overlooked certain statements that unambiguously testify to the Greek belief in future advance.[13] These criticisms, offered *en passant* in books not directly concerned with the history of progressivism, made no impression. In my opinion, they are weighty enough to cast doubt on Bury's thesis, and other reasons for scepticism are not lacking either. One may grant Bury that some of the authors who have often been cited for an ancient doctrine of progress do not speak of the future improvement that a theory of progressivism must include, and it may be admitted further that certainty about the intent of some passages is beyond the reach of the interpreter. Nevertheless, not a few of the very statements which Bury rejects do testify to the ancient belief in progress as defined at the outset.[14] Moreover, if one collects the material in a more systematic way than either party to the dispute has hitherto done and does not rely on passages selected at random and discussed again and again, it becomes apparent that there is abundant and unimpeachable evidence for ancient progressivism. To reexamine the evidence and to appraise the share of the ancients in the history of the idea of progress is not to throw sand against the wind. So much may be maintained without fear of the outcome, though obviously the detailed proof of my claim must be left to the book itself.[15]

It has been said, however, not only that in ancient literature there is no discussion of the likelihood of future progress but also that general considerations make it impossible to suppose that either Greeks or Romans could have entertained such a notion, the

[13] Concerning Roman writers cf. E. K. Rand, *Founders of the Middle Ages* (Cambridge [Mass.], 1928), p. 14, and in general, Tenney Frank, "Changing Conceptions of Literary and Philological Research," *Journal of the History of Ideas* III (1942), 409–411. Concerning passages from Greek literature cf. A.W. Gomme, *A Historical Commentary on Thucydides* (Oxford, 1945–56), I, 232. (Rand expressly refers to Bury; Gomme does not mention him by name but certainly must have him in mind when he speaks of "those who deny to the Greeks the ordinary concept of progress.")

[14] Notably the statements of Seneca (see note 11 above).

[15] Concerning the collection of the material, cf. also below, pp. xxx ff. It is only fair to observe that what is considered to be the available evidence depends in part upon the definition of progress accepted (see below, pp. xxix f.) and upon the investigation's being restricted or not to passages where the word progress is used (below, p. xxx).

basic presuppositions of which were foreign to ancient thought. Naturally, if the view now predominant is controverted by the evidence, it cannot be upheld by arguments as to what is possible or impossible such as have been advanced in its support since the early nineteenth century. Yet I think it not amiss by way of introduction to deal with these arguments, for they raise certain fundamental problems that must be clarified in connection with a study of the history of the idea of progress, and their discussion may help to explain the approach of my own inquiry and the general point of view to which I am committed. If, in what I am about to say criticism of earlier work outweighs approval, I am not unaware that, as was recognized even by ancient believers in progress, one is indebted to one's predecessors equally for what in their opinions one accepts as right and rejects as wrong.[16]

As has been said, Comte was the first to deny that the ancients had the conception of progress. He contended that a "true" or "scientific" idea of progress is dependent on "positive philosophy" which "alone can indicate the final term which human nature will be forever approaching and never attaining"; and such a philosophy, he thought, had not been possible before the French Revolution, by which "the direction of the social movement had been determined." Before that, "the only rational ideas of continuous advance" were formulated in connection with the expansion of the positive sciences in the seventeenth century.[17] Comte considered that the turning point in the development of progressivism had been the *Querelle des anciens et des modernes*, which had begun almost simultaneously in Italy, France, and England about the end of the seventeenth century, for awareness of what is ancient and what is modern is a precondition for belief in progress and such awareness had been achieved in that famous debate. That is why it "constitutes a ripe event in the history of the human spirit, which

[16] Aristotle, *Metaphysics* II, 1, 933 b, 11–14.
[17] *Philosophie positive* IV, pp. 229 ff. and pp. 233 ff. (Teggart, *The Idea of Progress,* pp. 371 ff.). In agreement with his theory of the development of the sciences, Comte considered it significant that the "first ray of light" shines forth in one of the aphorisms of the mathematician Pascal; see below, chap. III, note 75.

thus for the first time declared that it had made an irreversible advance."[18]

Comte's thesis, which expresses the pride of the nineteenth century in being the century of science and scientific progress and in having freed itself once and for all from the shackles of the past, clearly contains the germ of the argument that was advanced by Bury to explain why the ancients were prevented from formulating a progressive view. Bury, to be sure, was not in full agreement with Comte. The idea of progress, he held, is not a "scientific" idea: belief in progress is "an act of faith"; it cannot be proved true or false; man does not know the destination toward which he is moving.[19] Nevertheless, he did believe that it is in the main derived from scientific understanding, for it is science that after a certain point in its development looks forward to ever greater achievements, and this point was reached only after the Renaissance when the discoveries were made that ushered in the era of modern science.[20] In antiquity, "there had been no impressive series of new discoveries, suggesting either an indefinite increase of knowledge or a growing mastery of the forces of nature." Consequently, no "vista into the future" was opened to the Greeks or Romans; and they did not learn to trust in man's continued advancement. The Greeks remained faithful to "that profound veneration of antiquity which seems natural to mankind." Even "the Athenians of the age of Pericles or of Plato, though they were thoroughly, obviously 'modern' compared with the Homeric Greeks, were never self-consciously 'modern' as we are."[21]

To take up the latter assertion first, consciousness of progress does presuppose a comparison of past and present, an awareness of continuity and discontinuity; and progressivism in the full sense of the word implies a distinction between the antiquated and the modern, which despite all its differences from the old has its roots in what precedes it. The battle of the ancients and the moderns was

[18] *Op. cit.*, pp. 234 ff.
[19] Cf. *op. cit.*, pp. 2–4. For Bury's judgment on Comte's own philosophy see pp. 306 ff.
[20] Cf. pp. 7 and 64 ff.
[21] *Op. cit.*, pp. 7 ff.

not fought for the first time, however, in the seventeenth century. The concepts of antiquity and modernity are familiar bywords of Greek literature at least from the end of the fifth century B.C., and of Roman literature almost from its beginnings.[22]

Secondly, Bury's characterization of ancient science followed from the conception of the Greek and Roman achievement which was current in his generation but which has been refuted by the work that, during the last few decades, has revolutionized the appreciation of ancient science and technology as a whole. In antiquity, science advanced far enough and new discoveries were numerous enough to permit belief in future progress. This need not be elaborated now; it will suffice to point out that Greek scientists themselves came to expect an ever greater future advance in their respective fields of research.[23]

Although disproved by the facts, the argument that Bury employed in agreement with Comte drew attention to the close connection of progressive thought with scientific advance and thereby provided a clue to the understanding of ancient progressivism. The history of the ancient idea of progress must indeed be written with the history of ancient science in mind. To the evidence almost exclusively adduced hitherto—that of philosophy and belles lettres—must be added an analysis of the scientific testimony and of the state of affairs within the sciences. I do not mean to imply that the idea of progress had its origin solely in scientific progress and that it depended on that alone. This is perhaps not true even of modern progressive thought. In antiquity, at any rate, many currents of thought and many circumstances, political as well as mate-

[22] See below, chap. II, pp. 39 ff. That the comparison of two historical periods or ways of life is an indispensable condition of progressive thought is observed by R.G. Collingwood in "Progress as Created by Historical Thinking," *The Idea of History* (Oxford, 1946), pp. 321 ff., esp. pp. 326, 328, 333. I doubt, however, that the comparison must necessarily be made by one who "can understand historically, that is, with enough sympathy and insight to reconstruct this [the two historical periods'] experience for himself" (p. 329). This surely was not true even in the seventeenth and eighteenth centuries, though it may be the ideal requisite of historical consciousness in the twentieth century.

[23] It is almost universally held that the principle of scientific progress is not attested before the Renaissance. The evidence which refutes such a thesis I have briefly noted in "Recent Trends in the Interpretation of Ancient Science," *J.H.I.*, XIII (1952), 575; see also chap. IV, p. 143, note 23 below.

rial, seem to have conspired to create and sustain a hope for improvement of all things; but the growth of the ancients' belief in general progress owed much to the expansion of science, just as undoubtedly the growth of modern progressive thought was furthered by the rapid scientific development after the Renaissance.[24]

To turn now to those who find the first glimmerings of progressivism in the Jewish-Christian experience, their reasoning too was foreshadowed in Comte's outline of the history of the idea of progress. For Comte was willing to admit that in early Christianity there could be found "the first general sketch of the concept, or rather of the feeling, of a progress of mankind." It was the recognition of the "fundamental superiority of the law of Christ over that of Moses" that led to the formulation of "this hitherto unknown idea."[25]

Comte's *aperçu* was first developed into a complete theory by Dilthey, who traced the idea of progress to the Christian conception of human history as a teleological process. Such an interpretation, he held, arose among the early Apologists and was fully expressed by Augustine. It was inspired by the Christian belief in "the education of mankind through God"; and, reshaped in the Middle Ages, it became the doctrine of the progress of the human race.[26] For the pagans, on the other hand, history was not a process

[24] A perusal of Bury's analysis of the modern history of the idea of progress will, I think, bear out the claim that the writers between the sixteenth and the eighteenth centuries were preoccupied with the progress actually made in science. See also R.V. Sampson, *Progress in the Age of Reason* (Cambridge [Mass.], 1957), who shows "how basic assumptions about the growth of modern science, and especially the empiricist approach to knowledge, contributed to the idea of progress." (*J.H.I.*, XVIII [1957], 607.)

[25] *Op. cit.*, pp. 231 ff.; Comte, by "early Christianity," understood the time of the first development of an organized church and an organized dogma, for he held the progressive attitude to be characteristic of Catholicism (p. 232) and rebuked Protestantism for its return to the "time of the primitive church" (p. 232, note 1), which he held to be as much responsible for its "antiprogressivism" as is its stress on the Jewish books of the Bible. Comte's view that Jewish religion is identical with the Mosaic Law was corrected only in the second half of the nineteenth century (below, note 28). The passages dealing with Comte's judgment of Christianity are quoted in K. Löwith's analysis of Comte in *Meaning in History* (Chicago [Ill.], 1949), p. 78, but unfortunately are omitted from Teggart's collection.

[26] *Gesammelte Schriften* I[3], 96–99, 334–40, 380–82; also V, 1 (1924), 45; III (1927), 211.

moving toward a goal, a development in time. The Greeks even in their evaluation of human actions were concerned with the contemplation of an eternal and unchanging truth; their vaunted substantialism carried over into historiography.[27]

In recent decades, the interpretation that Dilthey had propounded has usually been formulated in a slightly different form. The rôle played by the teaching of the Jewish prophets—their Messianism—has been stressed as the harbinger of modern progressivism;[28] and with regard to the contrast between Christian and pagan thought, the accent has been put not so much on the truly historical consciousness of the Christians and the lack of such consciousness on the part of the pagans as on the distinction between a Christian concept of time and a pagan one. For the Christians, it is said, time was the medium in which God's will is fulfilled and accordingly in which unique—that is, truly historical—events take place. Thus man came to be separated from nature; and human history, which is characterized by the singularity of acts and actors, came to be differentiated from the monotonous and repetitious course of natural phenomena. The pagan philosophers, on the contrary, are said to have been familiar only with the concept of cyclical time as the eternal recurrence of the same. Greek and Roman historians too traced the unchangeable patterns of human deeds.[29] This is said to be the reason why the idea of progress

[27] Cf. *Gesammelte Schriften* I[3], 252–54. Dilthey allows the Greeks only the concept of scientific progress (see below, chap. III, note 73); and in the first edition of his "Einleitung" he does not mention the Romans (but see his "Zusätze zum zweiten Buch" I[3], 423 ff.), to whom he later attributed an important share in progressive thought (*Gesammelte Schriften* II [1923], pp. 11, 15).

[28] See above, p. xii and note 3. In the general literature concerning progress the thesis in question seems to appear for the first time in Delvaille's *L'Idée de Progrès*, where it is based on Renan's studies of Jewish religion (pp. 7, note 1; 14, note 1; 26, note 4; 27, note 6; 29, notes 1–3; Delvaille was influenced also by the philosophical and historical work of Renouvier, the great critic of the modern theory of progress [*Esquisse d'une classification systématique des doctrines philosophiques; Philosophie analytique de l'Histoire*]). I find no influence of Dilthey's analysis on later writers on the subject.

[29] Cf. Baillie, *op. cit.*, pp. 57 ff., 67 ff., and pp. 45 ff. and 50 ff. (For the progressivist aspect of Zoroastrianism, see above note 3.) Since the modern literature on the Christian concept of time in contradistinction to that of the pagan is amply quoted in Baillie's book, I refrain from compiling names. For literature published after the appearance of Baillie's study cf. R.K. Bultman, *Presence of Eternity: History and Eschatology* (New York, 1957), pp. 17 f.

remained unknown to the ancients, why "it is Jewish–Christian futurism which opened the future as the dynamic horizon of all modern striving and thinking," for "within a cyclic *Weltanschauung* and order of the universe, where every moment of advance is at the same time a moment of return, there is no place for progress."[30]

Now, undoubtedly, a more profound understanding of time and of history resulted from the Jewish–Christian belief in creation, and especially from what Augustine calls the conviction that "once Christ died for our sins . . . He dieth no more . . . and we ourselves after the resurrection shall be forever with the Lord." But is Augustine right in his implicit contention accepted by modern writers that Greek philosophy knows only of "cycles of time," and that "the sound doctrine of a rectilinear course" of time through which alone "we can escape from I know not what false cycles discovered by false and deceitful sages" is a novelty of Christian origin?[31]

This question must be answered in the negative, I think. Time was considered to be noncyclical by many classical and Hellenistic philosophers as well as historians and scientists, and was so considered by many even in late antiquity.[32] Besides, a theory of cyclical time deprived events of uniqueness only if the cyclical movement denotes the recurrence of exactly the same events. If what repeats itself is only the pattern of events—if things are identical not numerically but only in kind—unique and individual events occur even from cycle to cycle of time; and the assumption of an identity in kind was certainly more usual in antiquity than was that of a numerical identity. Finally, even if the cycles have numerical identity, within any one of them the present moment does not necessarily fail to bring something new compared with the past or the future to bring something new compared with the present, so that these three aspects of time may stand to one another in the relation

---

[30] Löwith, *Meaning in History*, p. 111; cf. also p. 200, and note 33 below.

[31] Cf. Augustine, *De civitate Dei* XII, 13 (see Baillie, *op. cit.*, pp. 75 ff.).

[32] Cf. below, chap. II, pp. 46 f. Augustine's judgment was probably determined by the prevalence of the cyclical theory in his own time and by his awareness of its importance in Gnostic theory, to which he was as firmly opposed as was Origen in his *De principii* II, 3, 4 (see Baillie, *op. cit.*, pp. 74 ff.).

of progression—a relation that was denied by scarcely any ancient proponent of a theory of cyclical time. Even from this point of view, therefore, it is unwarranted to speak of an absolute antithesis of the pagan and Christian concepts of time, as it is becoming fashionable to do in philosophical and historical as well as theological literature.[33]

It is an oversimplification also to say that the ancient and the modern attitudes to historiography are diametrically opposed. To be sure, in antiquity the historian tried to detect in the world of politics man's unchangeable nature rather than human reactions varying in time and space. The same emotions and passions and the same moral law were supposed to obtain at all times and always to be engaged in a conflict that man has to resolve, for he is free to choose. Thus far historiography was permeated by eternalism.[34] It is questionable, however, whether "all the agencies that appear on the stage of history"—men and institutions or political entities such as Athens or Rome—were regarded as "ready-made," whether history as a whole was subject to an eternal law of decay of political fortunes that deprived the historical process of a goal lying in the future. It is safer to say that in this respect the judgment of the various writers differed;[35] and certainly, when the historian instead of speaking of wars and political strife or of human passions dealt with the sum total of the intellectual activities and creative accomplishments of man, who builds up a world of his own, he abandoned all substantialism. Here he acknowledged a development, discovered changes, and stressed the fact that things will not remain the same forever.[36]

Expressed more generally, there was besides political history an-

[33] The distinction between a Christian and a pagan consciousness of time is regarded as essential to an understanding of the respective phases of human thought even by such writers as Collingwood (*The Idea of History* [Oxford, 1946], p. 48) and E. Bréhier (*Histoire de la philosophie* I [Paris, 1931], 489 ff.).

[34] The same attitude is characterized by Collingwood (*op. cit.*, pp. 40–42) as "the humanism" and by others as the moralism that led ancient historians to neglect the importance of economic and material conditions in general.

[35] Contrary to Collingwood, *op. cit.*, pp. 42–45 (whom I have quoted in the text) and Löwith, *The Meaning of History*, pp. 6–9. (The latter stresses the belief in "the possibility of knowing the future" as distinguishing ancient from modern historical writings; but see below, chap. I, note 8.)

[36] This is true even of Thucydides (cf. below, chap. II, p. 47), who is often said to exhibit an awareness only of different conditions in the past (e.g., Baillie, *op. cit.*, pp. 7–9) and to typify the attitude of ancient historians (p. 9).

other field of historical studies, in which truly historical categories were employed by ancient writers. This is, as they said and as was still said in the eighteenth century, the realm of the arts and sciences and their "inventions" or contributions, the realm of all the kinds of organized knowledge that man has gathered for the sake of knowledge or for practical purposes; in modern terms, the realm of culture or civilization. The subject was often treated in works of political history, it formed part and parcel of philosophical inquiry and political theory, and it also was made the topic of special investigations;[37] and here the unity of history was taken to be constituted not by the will of a deity but by a pattern of improvement distinctive of humanity. The novel and unique events were regarded as steps that had been taken in the course of time to ameliorate conditions, and that would be taken to improve them still further. If at first the concern was primarily with the origin of culture, it shifted to an increasing degree to speculation on the future and the outcome of the development; for it was assumed that, whatever happens or may happen to one's native city, that other city of which man is a member, the community of mankind, continues to grow. Thus the separation of man from nature that Christianity achieved through the grandiose vision of a human destiny guided by God, paganism achieved through a conception of the history of human civilization which gives man a place of his own in the scheme of the world.[38]

There remains the third argument commonly advanced to prove the basic antiprogressivism of the ancients. "What they knew of

[37] Cf. below, note 58. In the eighteenth century Hume, for example, still dealt with the history of the arts and crafts in chapters of his *History of England* (New York, 1852–53), e.g., II, 508 ff.; cf. also his essay, "Of the Rise and Progress of the Arts and Sciences." (Cf. also the formulation of the question put by the Academy of Dijon and answered by Rousseau in his famous *Discours sur les sciences et les arts*.) The distinction between political and cultural history is usually not emphasized in modern literature, but I think that it is fundamentally important for the understanding of ancient historiography. I should say that here and in what follows "civilization" and "culture" are used interchangeably as they usually are in modern literature (cf. F. Gilbert, "Cultural History and Its Problems," *XI⁰ Congrès International des Sciences Historiques, 1960: Rapports* I, 40–58).

[38] G. Simmel observed that the unity of the historical process is necessarily presupposed by the concept of progress (*Die Probleme der Geschichtsphilosophie* [5. Auf., Leipzig, 1923], pp. 203 ff.). If, as he holds, the first condition of progress is the existence of an ideal to be realized in time (pp. 199 ff.), it would for the ancients be the ideal of culture itself; see below, chap. IV, 156.

the advance of human knowledge and technical skill," it is said, "had little if any qualifying effect upon their general pessimism, since they were without the conviction that such knowledge and skill could alter the essential conditions of human destiny. They believed the present trend of things, when viewed on any large scale, to be a downward one and to be heading for final, though it still might be far distant, disaster."[39] This is, of course, the reasoning of those who thought that the idea of progress had failed to gain ascendancy in antiquity because it was in conflict with a pessimistic philosophy of history. It is usually narrowed down to three more specific points: one, that the dream of a Golden Age, of an immemorial past which would perhaps one day return, could not be forgotten but haunted even the progressivists; then, that time to the ancients was the enemy of man and that the human race seemed to them to be constantly degenerating; and finally, that even for philosophers belief in future progress was prevented by the assumption of the periodic destruction of the world or at least of the human race and its civilization either in the near or distant future.[40]

As to the last point, I shall not attempt to discuss the intricate question how much time men must feel lies ahead of them before they find it worth their while to consider the future and to work for it; but the present has shown that belief in the "running down of the clock of the universe" does not of itself deter human beings from progressivism. What is more important, when one speaks of progress, one thinks of progress "within history"; and such progress is not rendered illusory by the fact that "history as a whole does not have the character of the definitive."[41] On the other hand, while it

[39] Baillie, *op. cit.*, p. 50. (He concludes his assertion of the pessimism of the ancients by pointing to their lack of hope in the Christian sense of the word [*ibid.*], but see below, chap. II, p. 46 and chap. III, p. 116.)

[40] Cf. Bury, *op. cit.*, pp. 8 ff.; pp. 17–19.

[41] Simmel, *op. cit.*, p. 203, note 1. The modern attitude to possible destruction of the world is well illustrated by the statement, "But we children of the dawn need give but little thought to the far-off sunset." (Sir James Jeans, *Eos, or the Wider Aspects of Cosmogony*, quoted by A. Toynbee, *A Study of History* [New York/London, 1947–57], I, 247 ff.) It used to be maintained generally and is sometimes still maintained that the conception of progress presupposes an infinite duration of the world. This contention is untenable in view of the modern situation (cf. M. Taylor, "Progress and Primitivism in Lucretius," *American Journal of Philology*, LXVIII [1947], 182 ff.) as well as on general philosophical grounds; see below, p. xxviii.

cannot be denied that by some Greek philosophers time was considered to be the enemy of man, it cannot be maintained that this was generally believed. Even when it was assumed that the world would end, it was not always supposed that the end would coincide with the final point of universal decay, for there were those who expected the end to be brought about by sudden catastrophe in the full bloom of things, as it were.[42] Again, it must be conceded that the belief in a Golden Age had a strong hold over the ancients. It did not tyrannize their thought, however; nor did the typical ancient theory of progress exhibit any admixture of this belief. Usually the process of amelioration was viewed as continuous; but, just as some ancient primitivistic theories did not entirely exclude progressivism, so a few progressivist theories betrayed a longing for the past. In neither case is the dominant attitude thereby invalidated. These so-called inconsistencies merely point to the phenomena that are admittedly contrary to the basic development. In the case of progressivism, it was acknowledged that along with the gains made there were losses. Examples of such a restricted or cautious belief in progress may be found throughout history.[43]

So much should have made it clear that the arguments for the inability of the Greeks to formulate a progressive creed are unfounded. Those who deny that the ancients had the idea of progress have by their arguments, however, illuminated the problem and given precision to the questions that should be put to the evidence, which is a considerable contribution, for their adversaries had usually treated the matter too lightly. The conception of a continuous advance of mankind is expressive of a world view, and

[42] Bury said in 1920 that the idea of progress "would lose its meaning and would automatically disappear" if it were certain that the earth would become uninhabitable in A.D. 2000 or 2100 (op. cit., p. 5); but Seneca thought that the destruction of the cosmos was "around the corner" and nevertheless persisted in his progressive outlook (see below, chap. IV, p. 172).

[43] As W.D. Wallis rightly observed, when Rousseau says that "iron and wheat have civilized man—and ruined him," he "is not paradoxical; rather, he is pointing to the paradox in that great step which led to so-called civilization. For iron and wheat gave man new power; and in giving him new power bestowed power for evil as well as for good." ("Progress and Power," Journal of Social Philosophy, II [1937], 344.) An adherent of progress may be aware of the dangers inherent in progress itself and therefore show some appreciation of more primitive conditions, just as for the adherent of primitivism the dream of a Golden Age "need not be, and often has not been, hostile to a certain faith in progress." (Lovejoy and Boas, op. cit., p. 192.)

this view itself in its many and diverse aspects must be taken into account if progressive thought is to be adequately understood.

What form should the inquiry take if the full justice is to be done to the importance of the topic? Hitherto, one of two procedures has ordinarily been adopted. The writings of the various authors have been analysed, and the philosophical systems in which progress is dealt with have been taken up one after the other in chronological sequence; or assertions of a progressivist outlook have been assembled from philosophers as well as poets and historians of the different centuries, they have been balanced against statements of the opposite tendency, and the numerical proportion has been roughly calculated.[44] In the former case, though an insight into the position taken by outstanding individuals is gained, nothing is learned about the general reaction to progressivism. In the latter case, the evaluation of the relative strength of the two parties remains a more or less convincing guess depending on the evidence the interpreter happens to quote; but progressivism and anti-progressivism are both given a rôle in the thought of antiquity as a whole, and this is no doubt the aim of what can properly be called an historical appreciation of the idea of progress. The question is not merely whether it was known to individuals but what its significance and importance were in the fabric of ancient thought.

Yet I cannot persuade myself that one all-encompassing answer could ever decribe adequately the attitude of a civilization that lasted for more than a millennium, or that the forces of progressivism and of antiprogressivism were constants to be computed by adding and comparing bits of evidence as if they were numerals and as if the views embodied in them were independent of time and circumstance.[45] It is true that there are *leitmotifs* in history. Nations like individuals seem to have an indelible character that sets

[44] The first method is that used by Delvaille in his *L'Idée de Progrès* and by Bury, though both, of course, observe the most general historical divisions. The second method is that of Rohde and his followers. Methodological problems are hardly ever discussed in the pertinent literature, which may be one of the reasons why the subject as a whole has not yet been satisfactorily treated. See A.O. Lovejoy, *Essays in the History of Ideas* (Baltimore [Md.], 1948), p. 12 and note 8.

[45] Thus Cornford (*The Unwritten Philosophy*) says "all ancient thought is haunted by regret for a Golden Age in the remote past. . . ." (pp. 45 ff.); see also Inge, *The Idea of Progress* (Oxford, 1920), p. 6. The same tendency to draw generalizations is to be found among the adherents of the more popular view. Bury,

them apart from others and gives a specific coloring to their intellectual as well as political and social history. The eternal realizes itself in time and in many different forms, however; and even the native pessimism of the Greeks appeared in various guises in various ages, and the native optimism of the Romans spoke louder in favor of progressivism in the Republic than it did in the Empire.[46] Moreover, ideas themselves, once they are formulated, have a life of their own. Their hold on man's imagination waxes and wanes in the course of history according to a rhythm that must be acknowledged even when it cannot be explained. The intellectual climate of which ideas form a part undergoes constant changes, gives birth to new shades of meaning, and thus transforms the relevance of the patterns of thought which constitute it. In addition to the changing climate of opinion there is a changing temper of the times which is shaped by political events, by the degree to which aims are achieved, and by the aim itself, whether self-fulfillment in this world or withdrawal from it, whether practical accomplishment or theoretical understanding.[47] So one may presume that the idea of progress, belief in it or distrust of it, has always been particularly susceptible to those alterations and vicissitudes that determine the sentiment prevailing in a generation or an era, for the future and the past are illumined by the light that the fleeting present seems to cast upon them, and the hope for things to come no less than the evaluation of what has been is shaped correspondingly.[48]

for example, talks of "the ancient climate of opinion" (*op. cit.*, p. 7; cf. p. 17 "no period of their history"; "in the mentality of the ancient Greeks"); others oppose Christianity to ancient thought as such.

[46] Even Dilthey, who noticed the influence of Roman thought on the development of progressivism (above note 27), made no attempt to discriminate between the attitudes of the Romans in the various centuries.

[47] On "the psychological character of the processes by which changes in the vogue and influence of ideas come about" see A.O. Lovejoy, *The Great Chain of Being* (Cambridge [Mass.], 1936), p. 20. Cf. in general G. Boas, "The History of Philosophy," *Naturalism and the Human Spirit*, ed. Y.H. Krikorian (New York, 1944), pp. 133 ff. On the climate of opinion, a concept not unknown to the ancients, see C.L. Becker, *The Heavenly City of the Eighteenth Century Philosophers* (New Haven [Conn.], 1932), chap. I; and on the relation of this concept to the history of ideas, cf. Theodore Spencer, "Review of A.O. Lovejoy, *Essays in the History of Ideas*," *J.H.I.*, IX (1948), 439–441; also Abraham Edel, "Levels of Meaning and the History of Ideas," *J.H.I.*, VII (1946), 335 ff.

[48] These brief remarks, self-evident as they must seem, will, I trust, be reinforced by later discussions of the presuppositions of the idea of progress and the general belief in it.

Thus, instead of following the approaches hitherto adopted, I have felt it necessary to choose the very concept of progress as my subject and to trace its gradual unfolding in ancient history. The various authors, even if they have much to tell about the issue, will not be interpreted for their own sake, and no unified accounts of their views will be given; but these views will be used as if they were windows through which to catch a glimpse of the opinions held by the generation of the writer, and those opinions will be related to the general intellectual climate and the general conditions of life which characterized the various periods that can with reasonable confidence be distinguished as separate historical units.[49]

In describing the background of the times I must depend upon the work done by others; but I consider it my special duty to elaborate the rôle of concepts connected with the idea of progress and of those opposed to it, such as the concept of renaissance and the so-called law of reaction, the theory of primitivism and decadence, and any other doctrine that may conceivably have had a particular bearing on the acceptance or rejection of progressivism.[50] Lastly, going beyond interpretation in the strict sense, I shall permit myself to conjecture how progressivism may have been influenced by the actual achievement in the arts and sciences with the development of which the idea of progress seems to be most intimately connected. For trust in the idea of progress is not dissociated from the subjective feeling of having advanced or regressed; and the subjective sentiment prevailing in a period or generation of the past can, I think, be reconstructed, whatever the difficulty the historian of today may have in determining the objective reality of progress throughout human history.[51]

[49] This unfortunately can be done only in the periodization of ancient history through the Hellenistic age. In the later centuries, for which no generally accepted categorization exists, the material must be arranged differently.

[50] For the literature on primitivism see below, note 60. Studies concerned with the other topics will be cited as they are discussed.

[51] Baillie clearly distinguishes between the history of progress and the history of the belief in it (op. cit., p. 4); and, though he considers the two largely independent, even he does not deny that the former influences the latter. Cf. also M. Ginsberg, The Idea of Progress (Boston [Mass.], 1953), p. 8: "If belief in progress is not to be a mere dream, it depends on progress actually made or assumed by a generation to have been made."

Within the historical framework that I have chosen, I shall, moreover, not only narrate the fortunes of the idea of progress, but also undertake to ferret out the manifold guises in which the law of progress has appeared in different times; for from the historical point of view this law contains only one proposition that is invariable and necessarily identical in all periods of history, the assumption of improvement in the past, the present, and the future. Without this there is, properly speaking, no theory of progress. All the other propositions that a complete law of progress implies are, as it were, accidental and not essential properties of this. Even the second proposition included in the definition of progress that I quoted at the outset cannot be stated in unqualified terms, for the agent directing and bringing about the upward movement can be either nature or man.[52] Which of these any era or generation supposes to be decisive the historian can only read off the record. The same is true of the standard by which the superiority to one another of the various stages in the development is to be judged, and also of the determination of the scope and the final outcome of the development. The criterion of improvement can be physical survival, the increase of material riches, or even novelty itself, moral advance, intellectual improvement, or greater happiness. Improvement can be looked for in all sectors of life or in a few alone. The goal can be one to be realized or merely to be approximated; improvement itself, whether finite or infinite, can be taken to be the goal. In all these regards progressivists of the various centuries have differed greatly without forfeiting their claim to belief in progress.[53]

In other words, the definition of progress with which the histo-

[52] Cf. above, p. xi.

[53] Simmel, in his analysis of the concept of progress, puts first agreement on the *Endzustand* by which the phases of the historical development are characterized as progressive (*Die Probleme der Geschichtsphilosophie*, pp. 198 ff.); but he is intent on a philosophical analysis of the structure of progressive thought, whereas I am concerned to formulate an historical definition (cf. above, pp. xxvi ff.). As an illustration of the various judgments concerning the scope of progress it may be noticed that Fontenelle believed there was progress in science but not in poetry, eloquence, or happiness (Bury, *op. cit.*, pp. 100, 104 ff.). He probably thought progress necessary, while others considered it only possible (pp. 109 ff.); he did not believe in the progress of society (pp. 110 ff.).

rian begins cannot be that of the philosopher. The latter defines the corollaries of the law of progress in addition to its first and basic principle. The initial definition of the historian must not prejudice its concrete specifications, for otherwise he would fail to detect the idea of progress where it is in fact adumbrated, or would believe that he had detected it where he had found only agreement with his preconceptions or with the prejudices of the day. He must instead first show that the basic principle of progress was recognized and then, what is no less important, must elucidate the nuances of progressivism by "listening to the word," by attending to the evidence and reporting it.[54]

This evidence is not limited to passages in which the word "progress" occurs. It was relatively late that the Greeks coined the word which in its Latin translation has become the archetype of the modern term. For a long period—roughly speaking from the end of the classical age to the early period of Hellenism—the Greek language conveyed the meaning of the idea of progress by means of other metaphorical expressions. At the very beginning—at the end of the sixth century and even in the fifth—no single word seems as yet to have embodied a theory of ascent. Nevertheless, one must begin at the point in time when men first envisaged what later centuries came to call progress, and the changes of linguistic usage must be treated as part of the subject, for in tracing the history of a concept one cannot be bound by lexicographical considerations but must look for identity of content. It follows, of course, that in the analysis of the early phase of the development one is sometimes

---

[54] The distinction between a philosophical and an historical analysis of the "Wesen" of "Subjektsbegriffe" is made in Dilthey's essay "Das Wesen der Philosophie" (*Gesammelte Schriften* V, 1 [1924], esp. pp. 340–345, 358, 363). The danger of overlooking this distinction is illustrated by G.C. Field's remark that "there is in the Greek language no word which really corresponds to our word Progress and no idea in Greek thought which corresponds to our idea of it" (*Plato and His Contemporaries* [London, 1930], p. 94), for "many of us in modern times seem ready to trust vaguely in something that we call Progress which will ensure that the unforeseen results of our actions will in general work out for the good, while the Greek normally preferred to see where he was going, and the idea that we are continually drifting along in a direction which we cannot foresee or control would have been abhorrent to him." To declare the past ignorant or disdainful of a concept when it is not in full agreement with the most recent understanding of the concept is to make of history "a pack of tricks we play on the dead."

constrained to use language that sounds strange to modern ears and often to speak in categories unknown to the ancients.[55]

As regards the span of time from which the evidence is drawn, the story should be followed down to the end of antiquity, that is to the sixth century after Christ; the Christian contemporaries of the late pagan authors should be included. Hitherto scholars, influenced by the classicistic prejudice, have refrained even from asking whether any contribution to progressivist thought could have been made as late as the third century, the period called the period of decay;[56] but, even if the answer is to be negative, the negative ought to be demonstrated. As for Christian writers, the first formulations of the Christian creed, its originality notwithstanding, were certainly shaped by controversy with pagan philosophy and pagan religion; and the Christian conception of progress, as was pointed out long ago, is no exception to this rule. The Christian evidence should therefore illuminate, if only by its polemic, that of the heathens.[57]

Two more remarks should be made concerning the evidence available. First, the extant material is not what one could wish for. No discussion survives in which the subject under consideration is set forth in principle and in such detail as it is in Bacon's *Novum Organum* and after that in modern times. In the preserved philosophical and historical or political works the treatment is incidental.[58] In fact, the evidence consists mostly of fragments, and it is fragmentary also in the sense that even the statements preserved in their original context are usually no more than a few brief sentences. In almost all cases the interpreter must set up his own

[55] The validity of this procedure has been emphasized by W. Jaeger ("Review of H. Merki, . . ." *Gnomon*, XXVII [1955], 573 ff.).

[56] Mondolfo seems to be the only writer to refer at all to the century of Plotinus (cf. above, note 12). Certain aspects of the problem have been touched upon in the literature on the Christian concept of progress, see e.g., Theodor E. Mommsen, "St. Augustine and the Christian Idea of Progress," *J.H.I.*, XII (1951), 346–374.

[57] While Comte had thought only of the Christian reaction to the Mosaic Law (cf. above, p. xix), Dilthey pointed out the interaction of Christian and pagan thought (*op. cit.*, I³, pp. 334 ff.).

[58] If I am not mistaken, no book entitled "On Progress" is extant or even mentioned. The writings that come closest to a treatise on the subject are Pre-Socratic essays on the beginnings of civilization and Dicaearchus' "Life of Hellas," see below, chap. II, p. 21 and chap. IV, p. 134.

scheme of categories for the analysis of the material. In order to get a general view, he must put the various pieces together as if they were parts of a lost mosaic. Since the ground-plan is missing, there inevitably remains an element of arbitrariness in the reconstruction, which can be justified not so much from the details as from the whole.

Secondly, the evidence is widely dispersed. The subject was obviously popular in antiquity and was treated on the stage and in song as well as by philosophers, historians, and scholars. A collection of the material as complete as possible is necessary; but, since no systematic collection of it has ever been made, it would be presumptuous of me to believe that I am myself acquainted with all the extant evidence.[59] The material could certainly be augmented by canvassing the fields of science and technology, which are so important for ancient thought about progress and which thus far have been largely neglected. The theories concerning the origin of civilization, in which the alternatives of progress and decay play an important rôle, have been thoroughly scrutinized, however; and the recent critical analysis of ancient primitivism takes account of certain aspects of "antiprimitivism" as well and draws attention to a number of passages that had escaped the notice of students of the idea of progress.[60] These studies in closely related fields permit me to feel more confident than I should otherwise feel about not having overlooked much essential evidence.

I am keenly aware of the fact that problems are involved about which one can speak only with diffidence, nor can I hope to avoid all the pitfalls lying in the path of one who tries to recapture the fullness of a life that is past and is reflected only in the biassed and incomplete comments of those who lived it. Nevertheless, the evi-

[59] W.A. Oldfather, who, as I learn from E.K. Rand (*The Building of Eternal Rome* (Cambridge [Mass.], 1943), p. 72, note 111), dealt with the idea of progress in his unpublished Sather lectures, may have brought together more material than had been compiled before.

[60] Lovejoy and Boas, *Primitivism in Antiquity* (see above, note 1). Of recent studies of the origin of culture I mention as especially important Woldemar Uxkull–Gyllenband, *Griechische Kultur–Entstehungslehren* (Bibliothek für Philosophie, XXVI [Berlin, 1924]); and Adolf Kleingünther, Πρῶτος Εὑρετής, *Philologus*, Suppl. XXVI, Heft 1 (1933).

dence will make it clear, I believe, that the ancient progressivists were not a negligible group of isolated thinkers out of touch with their own world but were the representatives of a movement that lasted almost from the beginning to the end of antiquity; and with this clarification it will be possible to make a more just and fair appraisal of the mediaeval and modern history of the idea of progress, for the ancients, it will appear, formulated most of the thoughts and sentiments that later generations down to the nineteenth century were accustomed to associate with the blessed or cursed word—"progress."

The Idea of Progress in Classical Antiquity

I

It is from the work of one of the Pre-Socratic philosophers, who wrote in the second half of the sixth century and the beginning of the fifth, that there has been preserved the first statement expressing, though not in modern terms, the principle underlying the belief in progress. "The gods did not reveal to men all things from the beginning," Xenophanes said, "but men through their own search find in the course of time that which is better." (Fr. 18, Diels–Kranz.)[1] The fragment—two lines quoted from a poem in a late collection of *sententiae*—is tantalizingly brief. It is not even known in what context it occurred.[2] It is clear, however, that Xenophanes envisaged an improvement of human life through the agency of men alone, for what they are "finding," that is "inventing," in the course of time, the better, is due to their efforts and not

---

[1] It is often assumed that the words "in the course of time" imply a "gradual," i.e., a step by step increase. This is not borne out by the text; cf. Harold F. Cherniss, "The History of Ideas and Ancient Greek Philosophy," *Studies in Intellectual History* (Baltimore [Md.], 1953), p. 26; and below, p. 5.

[2] The fragment is attributed to the *Satires* by Hermann Diels and Walther Kranz, *Die Fragmente der Vorsokratiker* (6. Auf.; Berlin, 1951–52), I. Diels himself in *Poetarum Philosophorum Fragmenta* (Berlin, 1901), p. 39, considered the possibility that it might have come from the work *On Nature*. The existence of such a book has been doubted, however: cf. J. Burnet, *Early Greek Philosophy* (London, 1930), pp. 115 ff.; W. Jaeger, *The Theology of the Early Greek Philosophers* (Oxford, 1947), pp. 40 ff.

to those of the gods;[3] and with the help of other fragments of Xenophanes' writings it can be shown that the assertion reflects more than a passing thought, that Xenophanes recognized the definite instances of progress and of progress, moreover, in all fields of human activity.

One of the things better now than before is knowledge about men and gods. For Xenophanes considered his "wisdom" (Fr. 2, v. 12), his moral teaching, to be "better," that is superior to the agonistic ideal prevailing among his contemporaries. He wished to substitute his doctrine of the gods for the "fictions of earlier men" (Fr. 1, v. 22), by which he meant especially those of Homer and Hesiod (cf. Fr. 11).[4] An earlier step in intellectual advance had been taken by Thales, his predecessor, whom Xenophanes "admired" for predicting the eclipse of the sun. Eudemus, the ancient historian of astronomy, explained this admiration on the part of Xenophanes as the result of his belief that Thales was "the first" to accomplish such a feat (Fr. 19).[5] Material things also, however, are included in his notion of invention. Xenophanes said that the Lydians were the first to coin money (Fr. 4). And in blaming them for the "dainty and unprofitable ways" that his fellow countrymen, the people of Colophon, "learned" from them (Fr. 3, v. 1), he shows that for him social customs were no less human in origin than the data of scientific knowledge and of economic life.

The evidence makes it clear that Xenophanes in talking of man's finding the better was not thinking only of a mythical past but

[3] As the contrast between "from the beginning" and "in time" shows, Xenophanes meant to eliminate the share of the gods altogether; he did not mean to say that they gave men a start, as it were; cf. Kleingünther, *op. cit.*, p. 41; also Uxkull, *op. cit.*, p. 4.

[4] Xenophanes' "wisdom" must be understood as including both his "knowledge" and his "poetic art"; cf. C.M. Bowra, "Xenophanes and the Olympic Games," *A.J.P.*, LIX (1938), 257 ff.

[5] Kleingünther (p. 41, note 4) dismisses the claim as untrue because Herodotus, mentioned in the source of Fr. 19 together with Xenophanes as one who "admired" Thales, does not attribute the first prediction of an eclipse to the latter (I, 74). Yet it is unlikely that the historian would have mentioned Thales' feat at all had he not considered it to be one of the "great deeds of man" that he proposed to record, and it is almost certain that he would have held it to be such only because it was the first "scientific" prediction known to him. (Heraclitus, Fr. 38 [Diels–Kranz], and Democritus, Fr. 115 a [Diels–Kranz], are said to have looked upon Thales as the first astronomer.)

4

thought of progress as continuous up to his own time. This is apparent from what he says of his own wisdom or that of Thales. The fragment last quoted shows in addition that in his opinion improvement is not a forward movement without interruption or deviation. Occasional regressions do occur, as when the Lydians corrupted the men of Colophon with their inventions. Xenophanes, then, can have meant only that *on the whole* things are "getting better."[6] Did he also mean that progress will continue in the future? The verses expressing his trust in the improvement of man's estate have the ring of a comprehensive statement which may cover all dimensions of time. His thesis therefore could well be more than a theory regarding the origin of culture, a theory of progress in the full meaning of the term, and other evidence, I think, shows at least indirectly that it should be taken as such.[7]

It is certain that he thought about the future as well as about the past and the present. "There never was nor will there be a man," he said, "able to decide everything on the evidence of the senses"; some things are and must remain conjectural (Fr. 34; cf. Fr. 6). As he conjectured past changes in the structure of the earth from the remains of fossils (Fr. 37), so he speculated on its impending dissolution into one of its original components (A 33 [Diels–Kranz]). It was not alien to the Greeks of his period or even of earlier periods to encompass the future in their view of life. They wished to be remembered by posterity and to live on in the memory of later generations; and to penetrate the darkness of things to come by means of oracles and prophecies was customary for them.[8] It is

[6] According to Kleingünther (*op. cit.*, p. 42) Fr. 3 and 4 indicate only that the non-Greek civilization was the older one, but this is because he interprets Xenophanes throughout as an historian of culture and neglects his concern with progress; see note 7, below.

[7] Since T. Gomperz (Griechische Denker I, 132 ff.) did so, only a "Kulturentstehungslehre," a theory of the gradual rise of mankind to higher levels of civilization, has usually been ascribed to Xenophanes; cf. e.g., Uxkull, *op. cit.*, pp. 3 ff; Kleingünther, p. 42. Only a few scholars have maintained that he was not thinking exclusively of the past, e.g., J. Delvaille, *L'Idée de progrès*, pp. 35 ff.; H. Fränkel, *Dichtung und Philosophie des fruehen Griechentums* (American Philological Association, *Philological Monographs* [New York, 1951], XIII).

[8] For this concern of the ancients to know the future, *see* J. Burckhardt, *Griechische Kulturgeschichte* ed. J. Oeri (Berlin und Stuttgart, 1898–1902), II[5], 281 ff., "Die Erkundung der Zukunft." He rightly draws a parallel between their prophecies and modern calculations of future events. (Löwith's interpretation of Burckhardt's

most likely, then, that Xenophanes, just as he surveyed the past and the present and saw progress and regress in them, did include the future in his purview, at least in terms of a vague forecast. As has rightly been said, "in achieving its ascendancy and unfolding its meaning the Idea of Progress had to overcome a psychological obstacle which may be described as 'the illusion of finality' "; it is difficult to "realize as a fact" that what lies ahead will be as different from the present as the present is from the past, or even more so.[9] The difficulty must have been especially great when men for the first time tried to visualize the future in terms of better things to come. With such a proviso one can safely maintain, I think, that the idea of progress—like so many other ideas that came to preoccupy European thought in later phases of its history—was anticipated in broad outline in Pre-Socratic philosophy with the boldness of inspired imagination.[10]

That Xenophanes' pronouncement embodied a novel truth and challenged the traditional religious beliefs he acknowledged himself by denying that the gods had revealed all things to men from the beginning, the opinion expressed by Homer, the teacher of all the Greeks (Fr. 10), and, so far as the scanty evidence goes, enshrined in the legends of the local cults. The deities of Homer, being the "givers of all things," also possess the skills and arts as their eternal prerogatives and by sharing them with mortal men enable the latter to pursue their activities on earth. According to the old cult-legends, the arts and crafts are presided over by gods, are coeval with the world, and are practised by men in the time-hallowed manner of tradition. Things are as they always were; nothing changes; nothing moves.[11] This static and as it were timeless existence Xenophanes transformed into a process in which the gods no longer have a share. He did not mean to affirm by this that what men achieve is contrary to the divine wishes, as Hesiod, the other religious teacher of the Greeks, seems to have held. (*Works*

opinion [*see* Introduction, note 35] is a slip of the pen.) The Greek desire for everlasting fame is expressed by Solon (I, 3 ff.); cf. in general, Burckhardt, *op. cit.*, IV, pp. 233 ff.

[9] Bury, *op. cit.*, p. 351.

[10] The formulation by Xenophanes is in its generality very similar to formulations of the concept of progress in later literature (cf. below, chap. IV, pp. 168 f.).

[11] For the early religious estimate of the arts and crafts see Kleingünther, *op. cit.*, pp. 5–9 (Demeter and Triptolemos cult); pp. 9–11 (Homer).

and Days, 42 ff.; *Theogony,* 103 ff.) According to Hesiod the gods, angry with Prometheus, hid fire from men so that Prometheus had to get if from them by deceit, and then Zeus in his wrath severely punished the creatures of Prometheus. Here it is implied, perhaps for the first time, that men possess and practise the arts and crafts against the divine will.[12] To Xenophanes this would have seemed to be objectionable and a confirmation of his charge that Hesiod like Homer dared to ascribe to the deity deeds and passions regarded as shameful and disgraceful even among mortals (Fr. 11).

It is not only with regard to the gods that Xenophanes differed from the early epic poets. He was at variance with their whole conception of human life and its meaning. Homer lives in the greatness of a past long gone by, when human virtue was displayed mainly in war and the heroes hoped to equal or to surpass the deeds of their ancestors, for they did not look back to a time greater than their own; but the poet, while glorifying their achievement, pays scant attention to the present and its cares. If he occasionally speaks of those who live nowadays, of men as they are now, he is satisfied to point out that they are inferior in physical prowess to the men of old.[13] On the other hand, in the *Iliad* the heroes in their actions are under the sway of a higher power. Their freedom consists

[12] Cf. Lovejoy and Boas, *Primitivism in Antiquity,* p. 196. Hesiod's main intention, however, was not to explain how fire and so the arts and crafts came into human hands but rather to emphasize the lesson that one cannot deceive Zeus as Prometheus did and go unpunished; cf. Kleingünther, *op. cit.,* p. 20. Here, as in the myth of the Golden Age, Hesiod was interested not in a theory of civilization, but in moral issues (cf. below, note 16).

[13] That the notion of a Golden Age is foreign to Homer was pointed out by E. Rohde (*Psyche* [Tübingen, 1921] I, 106, note 1). He admitted that the concept may be older than the epic but that this is not necessarily so despite the anthropological arguments on which most interpreters rely (e.g., R. von Pöhlmann, *Geschichte der Sozialen Frage und des Sozialismus in der Antiken Welt* [München, 1925], I, 304, note 3). See also below, note 17. Nor does the epic show any of the special respect for earlier generations, for "antiquity," which is "natural to mankind" (Bury, *op. cit.,* p. 8). Nestor's remarks about earlier men (I, 260 ff.) are, to be sure, those of a *laudator temporis acti;* but the phrase "as men now are" (I, 272), occurring four times in the *Iliad* and not at all in the *Odyssey* (cf. Walter Leaf (ed.), *The Iliad* (2d rev. ed.; London/New York, 1900–02), I, *ad* V, 304), does not suffice to establish the claim of a retrospective historical outlook, though it was taken to illustrate the poet's belief in the decay of the human race even by later ancient authors (e.g., Pliny, *Natural History,* VII, 16, 74; cf. Lovejoy and Boas, *op. cit.,* p. 102, note 169). Two attitudes toward the older generation are manifested in the epic: either the wish not to be inferior to one's fathers (*Iliad,* VI, 209) or the frank admission that one feels superior to them (IV, 405; VII, 479).

in accepting the advice of the deities and thus avoiding the evil that they might incur by disobedience to fate or to the decrees of gods. Even in the *Odyssey*, where man is characterized as "resourceful," as "harboring many counsels" and "thinking his own thoughts," his strength lies in bearing the whims of fortune rather than in combatting them.[14] Xenophanes can hardly have found the heroic age of human history in any bygone era. For him the virtue and power of men are manifested in the life of the city, the life of peace, the life of the intellect, of which Homer is neglectful or not yet aware;[15] and the present must be better than the past, for, even if men do decay in physical strength, they gradually master their shortcomings and improve the circumstances in which they find themselves.

As for Hesiod, he tells of four races that were created and had vanished before the present race came into being. (*Works and Days*, 106 ff.) Each was superior to its successor in happiness and ease of life and moral fiber, and men of the contemporary age are worse off than were those of any earlier age. Their mode of life having been fixed by divine ordinance, their appointed lot is to toil harder than did men of any previous age. Injustice too is greater; in fact, justice is to disappear from the world no matter how hard the individual strives for the good (213), and moral decay is in the long run inevitable. One can wish not to be "among the men of the fifth age," but to have been born "afterwards," in a future age (175).[16] Xenophanes, on the contrary, does not long for a Golden Age of the past or hope for a divinely willed and better future. He discards such "wish thoughts" of the human imagination; and his optimism defies such pessimistic complaints as Hesiod's about the hardship

[14] For the significance of the words πολύμητις and πολυμήχανος, epithets of Odysseus, cf. H. Fränkel, *op. cit.*, p. 124; for the distinction between god-given thoughts and man's own thoughts (*Odyssey*, IV, 712 f.), *ibid.*, p. 128. For the epic in general, cf. B. Snell, "Die Auffassung des Menschen bei Homer" in *Die Entdeckung des Geistes* (Hamburg, 1946), pp. 15 ff.; for the *Iliad* in particular, Fränkel, *op. cit.*, pp. 91 ff.
[15] See below, pp. 15 f.
[16] Uxkull (*op. cit.*, p. 2) emphasized the fact that Hesiod's reflections are ethical and not a "kulturgeschichtliche Betrachtung"; Kleingünther (*op. cit.*, pp. 11 ff., esp. p. 15) has given ample proof of this thesis; cf. also F. Solmsen, *Hesiod and Aeschylus* (Ithaca [N.Y.], 1949) pp. 134 ff. The story, therefore, cannot be regarded as a theory of the decline and fall of civilization; the invention of the arts is not a problem for Hesiod, whose concern is rather the moral decay of man.

of the present and makes the improvement of material conditions and moral standards man's own responsibility.[17]

Xenophanes was not alone, of course, in repudiating the tenets of archaic poetry. His philosophical predecessors, the members of the Milesian school, had proposed a natural explanation of the world and had dispensed with the interference of divine powers in accounting for the origin of the cosmos, of men, and of animals and plants.[18] In addition, the question had begun to be asked whether some of the arts were not inventions of individuals. Heroic culture-bringers came to be worshipped in some parts of Greece and were celebrated in poems attributed to Hesiod. A younger contemporary of Xenophanes, the historian Hecataeus, ventured to connect the great deeds of the past and the famous names of the old saga with the introduction of specific inventions or improvements such as the planting of the vine. His conclusions were based in part on the difference between contemporary language and that of "the ancient Greeks." (Fr. 15 Jacoby.)[19]

Although the path that Xenophanes followed had been traveled by others, he was not therefore lacking in originality. The Milesians, who had assumed that all things come into being and grow into the shape that they now have, had apparently not drawn the conclusion that civilization also comes into being and gradually assumes a more complex form; but Xenophanes did conclude that

[17] A. Doren has shown that the idea of an earthly Golden Age is merely the secularization of an earlier concept of the blessed abode of the gods and at the same time the first preformation of later utopian thought ("Wunschräume und Wunschzeiten," *Vorträge der Bibliothek Warburg*, 1924–25 [Leipzig, 1927], p. 163, and note 7, where the pertinent literature is cited).

[18] If W.A. Heidel ("Anaximander's Book, the Earliest Known Geographical Treatise," *Proceedings of the American Academy of Arts and Sciences*, LVI [1921], 256 ff.) were right, Anaximander would already have been interested in inventions. But the fragment on which Heidel bases his conclusion certainly refers to the historian Anaximander, who lived long after Xenophanes; cf. Jacoby, *Die Fragmente der griechischen Historiker*, I, p. 480 (*ad* 9 Fr. 3). I take it that the Milesian thinkers were concerned with natural philosophy and not with human affairs.

[19] Hecataeus' treatment of inventions has been analysed by F. Jacoby, *s.v.* Hekataios, *Real–Encyclopädie*, cols. 2738 ff.; cf. also Kleingünther, *op. cit.*, pp. 43 ff. For the Hesiodic catalogue and the general situation in the sixth century B.C. cf. E.J. Edelstein and L. Edelstein, *Asclepius* II, 54 ff. For the change in cult-legends, cf. Kleingünther, *op. cit.*, pp. 18 ff.; pp. 26 ff. and David M. Robinson, "Bouzyges and the First Plough on a Krater," *American Journal of Archaeology*, 2d Series, XXXV (1931), 152–160.

man, born from the elements of earth and water (Fr. 29 A 33 [Diels–Kranz]) like all that exists, at first lived in conditions different from those which were later to obtain.[20] In his evaluation of time, Xenophanes departed even further from his predecessors. Time had commonly been considered the force that keeps events from coming to a standstill. In the system of Anaximander it regulates the coming into being and passing away of all material phenomena. According to Solon, it holds sway over what happens in the sphere of human life. Xenophanes too regarded time as central to human achievement, for it is only in the course of time that the better is reached; but the creative force lies in men, and time is only the medium in which they deploy their strength and show their mettle.[21] Finally, whereas those who had brought about changes and improvements had hitherto been regarded as heroes, beings half human and half divine, according to Xenophanes the actors on the historical stage at any moment were ordinary mortals like contemporary men. Their accomplishments, however, were of increasing value, for unlike the alterations wrought by time in the realm of nature, that which is newly made by man himself is always a step toward the better. Thus "the genetic way of thinking" which thus far had led the Pre-Socratics to place only phenomena in the succession of an objective Before and After, now led to an arrangement of human events according to the relative values which they have and retain, despite the fact that the world will one day be

[20] Since according to Xenophanes the gods did not reveal any knowledge to men, Uxkull (*op. cit.*, p. 3) concludes that he must have regarded the initial stage of mankind as "primitive." I have avoided this term, for later theories of the beginning of human life define primitivism in different ways (see below, chap. II, note 7) and the evidence preserved does not give the details of Xenophanes' position.

[21] This distinction between human activity and time as contributing factors is overlooked, e.g., by P. Shorey, "Note on Xenophanes' Fr. 18 (Diels) and Isocrates, *Panegyricus 32*" (*Classical Philology*, VI [1911], 88), who takes Xenophanes' statement as an illustration of the commonplace that "time is the great discoverer." (For the latter saying, cf. below, chap. II, p. 46 and chap. III, p. 66.) In my interpretation of the early understanding of time I follow H. Fränkel, "Die Zeitauffassung in der archaischen griechischen Literatur," briefly summarized in *Dichtung und Philosophie*, p. 346. The archaic concept is well brought out in the story, genuine or invented (see below, note 28), that Thales, when asked "What is the wisest?" answered: "Time, for some of the things it has found already and some it will discover later." (Plutarch, *Septem Sapient. Convivium*, 9, 153 D; cf. Diogenes Laertius, I, 35.)

destroyed and everything resolved again into the mud from which it was produced (A 30).[22]

How did Xenophanes come to formulate this new concept of man and man's endeavor? In part, it may have been the consequence of his criticism of traditional religion, for with anthropomorphism, he must have rejected the existence of gods who possess or guide human arts and sciences. The empirical tendency of his teaching as a whole may also have influenced his attitude.[23] Although both his theory of religion and his empiricism, however, might have made him the readier to ask how civilization came to be, they do not explain his trust in man's capability of accomplishing so much. A deist and empiricist could as well think of mortals as less exalted and less powerful. Unless Xenophanes' trust in progress was merely a daydream much like the trust of believers in a Golden Age, it must have been founded on data that seemed to him to warrant a progressivist outlook; and these data are, in fact, not far to seek, for they are, no doubt, the "inventions" made in his time and earlier. Some of them he mentioned himself, and there were many more than are referred to in the fragments of his writings that are left to us. The period from the middle of the seventh century to the end of the sixth, through the greater part of which he lived, saw almost revolutionary changes take place; a new civilization arose in colonial Greece and began to spread to sections of the motherland.[24]

Not only did the Lydians, as Xenophanes observed, now first coin money; but in the time of the tyrants all economic life was reshaped by the introduction of new monetary systems and by the unification of measurements and weights. Warfare was altered to a considerable extent by the building of larger ships. The technical tasks undertaken were of a magnitude never envisaged before and

[22] The expression "the genetic way of thinking" is borrowed from A.O. Lovejoy, *Essays in the History of Ideas*, p. 12.

[23] It is in this way that Kleingünther (*op. cit.*, p. 42) and others (e.g., W. Nestle, *Griechische Geistesgeschichte* [Stuttgart, 1944], p. 67) try to account for Xenophanes' attitude.

[24] Cf. in general J.B. Bury, *A History of Greece to the Death of Alexander the Great* (New York: Modern Library, 1937), chap. II, and Helmut Berve, *Griechische Geschichte* (Freiburg, 1931–33), I, Pt. III, chap. II. In my summary I shall give specific references only to material not mentioned in these sources.

hardly surpassed even at a much later date. The daring construction of the tunnel near Miletus and of the long bridge over the Helles-pont were feats of engineering unimagined before. The pride taken in overcoming difficulties by the invention of new devices is still heard expressed in the excerpts preserved from memoranda of the architects who built the great temple of Artemis at Esphesus.[25] The arts, which the Greeks of that time considered to be only technical skills, also progressed greatly. Vase-painting evolved new styles that were rapidly perfected, and Ionian sculpture reached its highest point of development in the sixth century.

As for scientific exploits, in addition to Thales' prediction of an eclipse of the sun, which Xenophanes admired, there were maps of the earth reflecting the increased knowledge of far-distant coun-tries. In the last decade of the sixth century an envoy from Ionia addressed the Lacedaemonians, "holding in his hand a brazen tab-let, wherein was engraved the circuit of the entire earth, with the whole sea and all the rivers." (Herodotus, V, 49.)[26] In explana-tions of natural phenomena what had been the province of mythi-cal fantasy and speculation began to be scrutinized by reason in arguments which draw conclusions concerning the unseen on the basis of observed facts. And whatever details had been discovered and examined were integrated into the rational picture of the universe that was framed by the first philosophers.[27]

Finally, the old inherited values were questioned and criticized. Lyric poetry, whose novel forms of expression were developed by poets conscious of the novelty of their work, defined the aim of life as the heart's desire, the pleasure of the fleeting moment. The tale

[25] For their report (Vitruvius, On Architecture, X, 11 ff.) and for the technical accomplishments of that period generally, cf. A. Rehm, Archiv für Kulturgeschichte, XXVIII (1938), 140. The evidence for economic changes and changes in warfare has also been adduced by Kleingünther, op. cit., pp. 21 ff. to explain the interest in inventions during the seventh and sixth centuries.

[26] The event was remembered in Sparta even in Herodotus' time; cf. G. Grote, A History of Greece (New York: E.P. Dutton and Co., Everyman's Library), Pt. II, chap. 35 (V, p. 6). John Burnet (Early Greek Philosophy [4th ed.; London, 1930], p. 40, note 1) has emphasized the importance of the engineering feats of the early period for a correct estimate of Ionian science.

[27] The gradual rationalization in the explanation of natural phenomena can be traced in the works of the early lyrists; cf. J.V. Kopp, Das physikalische Weltbild der frühen griechischen Dichtung (Diss. Fribourg, 1939).

of the Seven Wise Men and of their answers to the question "What is best?" symbolizes the search for new intellectual standards.[28] For people were no longer satisfied with tradition and began the quest for the "good life"; they might be said to have discovered the truth later formulated by Aristotle that "in general all men really seek what is good, not what was customary with their forefathers." (*Politics*, 1269 A 3–4.) Bold and self-reliant in political action, they were also daring in thought and willing to set aside the traditional respect for the holy if it seemed to be to their advantage. At the beginning of the Ionian revolt against the Persian Empire, Hecataeus the historian advised using the treasures dedicated to the deity, for only in this way, he thought, would the Greeks have the means to gain mastery over the sea and their enemies be prevented from plundering the sanctuary. (Herodotus, V, 36.)[29]

In short, in such a world to trust in man and his mastery over his fate, as does Xenophanes, is to acknowledge facts, to read the signs of the time, and in accordance with them to interpret what once has happened and will happen again. The creativity of men was revealed in their very actions; they arrogated to themselves what earlier generations had reverently ascribed to deities and heroes. They were progressing. Why should what was true at present not have been true in the past or be true in the future? It is not that the idea of progress had inevitably to be conceived. The formulation of a law is always the accomplishment of an individual, a "spontaneous variation in the strictest sense of the term," and as such inexplicable;[30] but the data that called for such a law were there. And, since much is known about Xenophanes' life, his personality

[28] For the discussion of moral values in lyric poetry, cf. Fränkel, *Dichtung und Philosophie*, pp. 190 f. and 250 f.; and B. Snell, *Die Entdeckung des Geistes*, pp. 128 ff. Although the genuineness of the various sayings of the Seven Wise Men is doubtful (cf. above, note 21), the tale itself surely goes back to the sixth century; cf. Fränkel, *Dichtung und Philosophie*, p. 315.

[29] The advice was rejected; and Grote (Pt. II, chap. 35 [V, p. 5]) considers it possible that Hecataeus, who was opposed to the war against Persia, had expected this and had made his suggestion solely in order to impress upon the war-party the magnitude of the danger. Whatever Hecataeus' motives, the advice shows how far he and others had gone in freeing themselves from traditional piety.

[30] W. James, "Great Men and Their Environment," *Selected Papers on Philosophy* (New York: Everyman's Library, 1918), p. 193, continues: "[The conceiving of the law] flashes out of one brain, and no other, because the instability of that brain is such as to tip and upset itself in just that particular direction."

and his mental makeup, the hindsight of the historian can point to certain factors that may have predisposed him to grasp the meaning of the change that had taken place and to evaluate it as he did.

Living for more than ninety years (Fr. 8), he witnessed, as has been indicated, many great transformations. According to the ancient way of reckoning his experience covered the lives of three generations. He was, moreover, not a recluse but spent the greater number of his years traveling throughout the lands inhabited by the Greeks (Fr. 8). To him everything was worth knowing; he was, as Heraclitus says (Fr. 40), a polymath. He was opposed to Pythagoras' speculations about the world beyond (Fr. 7) but at home in the Here and Now. Yet he also had an eye for history, the history of the earth (A 33, p. 123, 1–5 [Diels–Kranz]) and of his city (A 1, p. 114, 5) and of science, for he saw himself in historical perspective, in relation to his predecessors (Fr. 1 *finis*). Finally, he was at heart a reformer. As a propagandizer, he was eager to correct mistakes and to bring the truth to all and sundry (Fr. 2). Being an optimist by nature and believing in the possibility of moral improvement, he wanted to make men better than in his opinion they were. Thus one might say that the first glimpse of a law of progress in past, present, and future was obtained when the reality of the existing situation was seen through the eyes of one who was of this world and who was eager to reshape it in the image of his vision of the right and good.[31]

It was more than an interpretation of facts, however, that Xenophanes gave. He advocated a new task and new values. Whether man lived under a democratic government or under a tyrant, the *kalokagathia* of the individual counted most. He contested for fame and the first place—the highest goods; and this he no longer did by deeds of war or peace so much as by striving for victory at one of the great games, Olympia or Nemea or Athens, in chariot races or

[31] I think that J. Burnet, *Greek Philosophy, Part I: Thales to Plato* (London, 1914), rightly characterizes Xenophanes as a reformer (p. 33) and is probably right too in saying that, since he was not a "scientist" himself, science was for him mainly a weapon with which to fight superstition (pp. 35 f.). Xenophanes' ability to "read the signs of his time" is, I think, in accord with the fact that his thought in many respects marks the boundary line between the archaic and the classical attitudes; cf. Fränkel, *Dichtung und Philosophie*, p. 435.

wrestling or running or boxing. Xenophanes replaced this agon by another. He considered his wisdom to be "better" and more worthy of the honor that his contemporaries bestowed upon the boxer (Fr. 2 [Diels–Kranz]). For him man the maker and man the knower ranked above the athlete; for him the contest in which human superiority shows itself was the contest in the arts and sciences where in the course of time men find "the better," the superior (Fr. 18)—a better coinage, a better explanation of an eclipse, or a better "understanding" of the divine nature. This was the true contest of life, in which the quick compete even with the dead.[32]

In maintaining this opinion, moreover, Xenophanes gave value to what hitherto had had none. In his time the exploits of the arts and crafts were enjoyed and admired; but artisans and craftsmen were held in low esteem, and philosophic and scientific inquiry was without public acclaim.[33] Although society had changed since the heroic age and civilization had been greatly refined, the ideology remained aristocratic. Of course, there were merchants as well as landowners, but they could not boast of their status; and, although wealth was sought and welcomed, what was truly cherished by the rich and by the poor was the useless rather than the useful. Existence, still relatively simple, culminated in the participation in the concerns of the city, in its festivals, its musical performances, and in the great games.[34] To be sure, philosophers predestined by birth to be citizens of renown had chosen to live for knowledge. Solon had voiced the personal, subjective feeling of those who had come to love and pursue studies when he professed his satisfaction with growing old "learning many things." (Fr. 22 [Diehl].) Xenophanes went farther. His positive assessment of the forward movement of civilization stated in objective and universal terms that the origin of

[32] Even Achilles questioned why he should continue fighting since the Greeks did not honor him (*Iliad* IX, 315 ff.).

[33] That society cared little for the new philosophy and science and that the men engaged in these pursuits were only a few I have pointed out in *J.H.I.*, XIII (1952), 597.

[34] In my description of the agonistic culture or what is now sometimes called the Homeric "shame culture" (E.R. Dodds, *The Greeks and the Irrational*, p. 17) I follow J. Burckhardt, *Griechische Kulturgeschichte* IV³, chap. II, esp. pp. 85 ff.; pp. 126 ff. Cf. also J. Hasebroek (*Staat und Handel im alten Griechenland* [Tübingen, 1928]), whose evaluation of the rôle of trade seems to me to be the most adequate.

all values lies in man's inventive power, in man's creation and promotion of the arts and sciences.[35] Thus a novel point of view, shared to some extent by a few, was extended and made fully conscious. The venture that Xenophanes himself represented in his life and work he endorsed with bold assurance as the truly human venture; and, as often when a new course is charted, he did this without lingering doubts or skepticism. His was an unquestioned belief in progress, an unqualified faith in man, derived not from philosophical premises but from a living experience. Later generations were to be more cautious and circumspect in their trust in progress; the conception of it and the arguments in its favor were to change. But it remains the merit of Xenophanes that he kindled the torch which, handed down from generation to generation, was never to be extinguished.[36]

Nor can Xenophanes have been inspired by a similar achievement in some other civilization. Those of Mesopotamia and Egypt, from which the Greeks had always been willing to learn and which originally contributed greatly to the progress of their arts and crafts, were in his time stagnant and backward-looking. The kings of Assyria were eager to return to the old wisdom, and Babylon praised the archaic inventions, while the Egyptians of the sixth century B.C.

[35] It is sometimes said that the Greek does not invent anything but finds for the first time what has preexisted conceptually (U. von Wilamowitz-Möllendorff, "Die Griechische Literatur des Altertums," *Die Kultur der Gegenwart* I, viii [Berlin and Leipzig, 1905], p. 2; see also Karl Joël, *Geschichte der Antiken Philosophie* [Tübingen, 1921] I, 78), but surely not all Greeks were born Platonists or Aristotelians. For the ancients too innovations in the arts and sciences were, generally speaking, inventions.

[36] For the metaphor of the torch, see below, chap. III, pp. 90 f. In recent literature the originality of Xenophanes' achievement has been questioned (cf. e.g., W. Jaeger, *Paideia*, trans. Gilbert Highet [New York, 1945], I, 171). It has been maintained that in opposing the agonistic ideal instead of being revolutionary he made "points which would appeal to Greek aristocrats of the sixth century." (Bowra, *A.J.P.*, LIX [1938], 277.) It may be true that his whole moral teaching is more conventional than used to be assumed, though his insistence that man should ask for divine help only in carrying out right intentions (Fr. 1, 15 ff.) certainly is unusual (cf. Fränkel, *Dichtung und Philosophie*, p. 423; also above, pp. 9 f.). Xenophanes' originality, however, is of no concern in my context. Later also men, who were steeped in the philosophy of their time but were by no means great philosophers themselves, drew the consequences of a new world-view and formulated the idea of progress most succinctly, so for example Fontenelle, the Abbé de Saint-Pierre, and even Condorcet; cf. Bury, *The Idea of Progress*, pp. 110, 143, 214.

prided themselves on their ancient culture and the glory of the remote past.[37] The Jewish prophets' eschatological vision of a Messiah evinced a belief not unlike that of Hesiod's in Zeus set forth in the story of the four ages and rejected by Xenophanes; and the tenets of Persian religion with its two gods fighting for the possession of the world are a far cry from Xenophanes' conception of a deity devoid of human passions and interests.[38] In the age of Xenophanes, only a Greek could have discovered and maintained that man is by nature self-reliant and progressive. Outside Greece the doctrine was unknown, as was the experience on which it is based.

Yet, even though Xenophanes' teaching was typically Greek and summed up the actuality of Greek life, it can scarcely have been popular with his compatriots. In the sixth century B.C. the Homeric and Hesiodic epic represented the main traditions of Ionia and of the motherland, which were still most powerful. An idealization of primitive people, something not entirely foreign to Homer, was given by Aristeas (*apud* Tzetzes, *Chiliades*, VII, 686 ff.), though his admiration was mixed with condescending pity and almost with contempt for the life of the "noble savage."[39] Hesiod's dream of an aboriginal Golden Age inspired the poet who praised "the most happy life in the time of Cronus." (*Epic. Graec. Fragm.*, p. 313 [Kinkel].) Moreover, Hesiod's pessimism was surpassed by that of later poets. It is not only Aidos and Nemesis who will leave the earth on the final day of doom (*Works*, 197 ff.); but according to Theognis "hope is the only goddess still among men, and the others (Good Faith, Moderation, and the Graces) have gone off to

[37] Concerning Assyria and Babylon cf. V. Gordon Childe, *Man Makes Himself* (The Thinker's Library, 1948, Vol. 87), p. 189; concerning Egypt cf. J.H. Breasted, *A History of Egypt* (2d ed.; New York, 1909), pp. 569 ff. and Childe, *op. cit.*, p. 226.

[38] Cf. above, Introduction, p. xii and note 3. The "progressive thought" of Jewish and Persian religion would postdate Xenophanes, if, as Baillie says in another place, it is only in the "post-exilic parts of the Old Testament, and in Zoroastrianism from the fourth century B.C. onwards," that "world history is regarded as the scene of a conflict between good and evil, which will certainly result in the final victory of good and in the inauguration by divine power of a final era of blessedness." (pp. 58 f.) This cautious restatement may indeed be more nearly correct.

[39] For this notion in Greek literature cf. Lovejoy and Boas, *op. cit.*, pp. 287 ff. Rohde (*Psyche* I, 81 ff.) showed that the picture of the happy life of distant peoples occurs for the first time in the *Odyssey*.

Olympus." (*Elegies*, I, 1135 ff.).[40] In lyric poetry from the seventh century on the sentiment prevailed that man, if not at the mercy of the deities, is the victim of fate or of circumstance, a frail being in the face of the power of events. In this sense his "helplessness" and his "lack of resources" or of "resourcefulness" came to be deplored; and finally, a new spirit of otherworldliness was inspired by the teaching of Pythagoras, the contemporary of Xenophanes, who called for the salvation of the soul and a new way of life determined by man's kinship with god, and by the Orphic movement, which proclaimed the union of man with the divine through ecstatic passion.[41]

One cannot, then, avoid the conclusion that even the Ionian contemporaries of Xenophanes were on the whole as little impressed by his trust in man's power to improve the world as, according to his own admission, they were by his teaching in general. Just so in the fifteenth and sixteenth centuries, when progress was rapid, the traditional views remained popular despite Bacon's conscious plea for progress, whose open praise of it sounded such a note that most ears remained deaf to it though it was much less novel than the thesis of Xenophanes had been. There had always been progress in human history and probably most progress in the ages identified by anthropologists as the earliest. It did not come to a stop even when almost imperceptible, and it quickened again in the seventh and sixth centuries. The two stray lines preserved from Xe-

[40] It is not certain that these verses belong to Theognis himself, but they could scarcely have been written much after the turn of the fifth to the fourth century.

[41] In my characterization of Pythagoras' phhilosophy I have followed Erich Frank, "Review of W. Jaeger, *The Theology of the Early Greek Philosophers*," *American Journal of Philology*, LXXI (1950), 191. As for the Orphics, Hirzel (*op. cit.*, pp. 79 ff.) suggested that their old doctrine favored a progressive outlook on history; W. Nestle in *Vom Mythos zum Logos* (2d ed.: Stuttgart, 1942), p. 282, note 70, parallels it with Xenophanes' theory, and R. Reitzenstein, in *Vorträge der Bibliothek Warburg*, 1924–25 (Leipzig, 1927), pp. 10 ff. ascribes to the Orphics of the sixth century a reformulation of Hesiod's doctrine of the ages of the world and their decay. Yet Fr. 292 [Kern], referred to by Hirzel and Nestle, is certainly of late origin, while Fr. 21a, of which Reitzenstein makes use, though included by Kern among the *Fragmenta Veteriora*, dates from post-classical times, and that it reflects older views is mere conjecture. Cf. in general I.M. Linforth, *The Arts of Orpheus* (Berkeley [Calif.] 1941), p. xv. The story of the realms of Phanes and Cronus also occurs only in late passages; cf. M.P. Nilsson, *Geschichte der griechischen Religion*, Handbuch der Altertumswissenschaft, V, 1 (München, 1941), 648.

nophanes' poem, however, record the first recognition of it as a characteristic of human history. Independent of the wisdom of god, man gains insight and through insight power by himself. Moreover, in fact if not in words, it is also recognized that human society is different from animal societies which, having reached a certain stage, are no longer progressive but are dominated by routine and repetition. Thus man discovered his own nature. With this self-knowledge he left the state of nonage and entered manhood. The period of enlightenment had begun.[42]

[42] J. Burnet, *Thales to Plato*, pp. 33, 109. For enlightenment as the stage of maturity of mankind see the beginning of Kant's essay "Was ist Aufklärung." A.N. Whitehead ("Foresight," in *Adventures of Ideas* [New York, 1933], chap. VI, p. 115) has emphasized "the fact of progressiveness" as the distinguishing mark of human as opposed to animal communities. The rôle of progress in prehistory is best illustrated by Childe, *op. cit., passim.*

II

mong the thinkers in the fifth century a particular aspect of the problem posed by Xenophanes came to the fore, that of mankind's rise from the original conditions of existence to the present state of civilization. Not all, to be sure, considered it to be worthy of attention. The speculations of the Eleatic philosophers, Parmenides and his followers, were centered on eternal being; and Heraclitus, though in the exposition of his philosophy he gave a prominent place to the arts and crafts, showed no concern about their origin.[1] For Anaxagoras and Democritus the subject was an important one, however; and the same holds true of the Sophists, men like Protagoras, Hippias, and others. With them it became almost fashionable to write treatises and to lecture on the prehistory of the human race.[2]

---

[1] According to Nestle (*Vom Mythos zum Logos*, pp. 103 ff.) Heraclitus greatly stimulated the study of the development of civilization; but his comparisons of natural or human activities with those of the arts and crafts and occasional remarks on inventions (e.g., Fr. 38 [Diels–Kranz]) do not amount to a theory of culture. The attitude of the Pythagoreans to the problem in the fifth century is not attested. For Socrates and Diogenes of Apollonia, cf. below, note 72.

[2] Protagoras composed a treatise περὶ τῆς ἐν ἀρχῇ καταστάσεως (Fr. 8b [Diels–Kranz]); the story that he tells in the Platonic dialogue named for him (320 C ff.) is an example of the orations given on the topic. Speeches by Hippias are mentioned in Plato's *Hippias Major* (285 D). For Prodicus, see below, note 10. Democritus treated the subject in his Μικρὸς διάκοσμος (Fr. 5 [Diels–Kranz]; and below, note 6). In treating the fifth century as an historical unit I mean to designate roughly what is usually called the classical period, that is, the time which in

Restricted in scope as these studies were, they were of great significance for a more profound understanding of progress itself, for besides making Xenophanes' general thesis more specific they changed the formulation of the problem and the principle of explanation. Instead of merely asking, as Xenophanes had done, who had made the various discoveries, one now tried to detect and fix stages of the development; and Xenophanes' emphasis on man's search for the better was replaced by the establishment of laws governing the course of events. So a true philosophy of culture arose.[3]

According to Anaxagoras, man and animals like all other things were separated out of the original mixture of the elements of the cosmos (Fr. 4 [Diels–Kranz]); and, although in many respects man is more unfortunate than other living beings, he makes them subservient to his purpose by the qualities that he alone possesses, his capacity for gaining experience, for remembering, for acquiring insight, and for developing the arts and crafts. (Fr. 21 b.) In other words civilization, arising in the course of time, is brought about by human skill and dexterity, by human endowment, which is physically predetermined, for it is because man has hands that he becomes wiser than the brutes (A 102).[4] According to Protagoras too human beings possess an instinctive ability (Plato, *Protagoras*, 321 D–E), but for some time their existence was precarious. Scattered

Aristotle's opinion marks a new phase (cf. below, note 40) and which is commonly thought to extend to the end of the Peloponnesian War; see A. Weber (*Das Tragische und die Geschichte* [Tübingen, 1943], p. 266) for a rather detailed sociological analysis of this era.

[3] As I am concerned with the *"Kulturentstehungstheorien"* only in so far as they have some bearing on the concept of progress, I do not deal here with the reconstructed details of the various doctrines. Cf. in general Uxkull, *op. cit.*, and W. Theiler, *Zur Geschichte der teleologischen Naturbetrachtung bis auf Aristotles* (Zürich, 1925), esp. pp. 38 ff.

[4] Anaxagoras' "well-known indecision between teleology and mechanism" (G. Vlastos, "On the Pre-history in Diodorus," *A.J.P.*, LXVII [1946], 57) is, of course, exactly what Plato criticized (*Phaedo* 97 B ff.; *Laws* 967 B–C). Uxkull (p. 10) calls Anaxagoras' philosophy anthropocentric; H. Fränkel ("Review of J. Zafiropulo, etc." in *Class. Philol.*, XLV [1950], 190 f.) contrasts this anthropocentrism with the physiocentrism of the other Pre-Socratics. Anaxagoras' theory is tinged by his naturalism, however, as is that of Protagoras. Anaxagoras' follower, Archelaus, from whose teaching the doctrine of the master can be supplemented (Uxkull, p. 11), also stresses the gradual distinction of the human from the animal world. In the beginning, man and beasts share the same manner of life; cf. P. Friedländer, *Hermes*, LXIX (1934), 62.

over the earth and living in isolation, they could not defend themselves against the beasts that preyed upon them. Then, when they took refuge in cities, they could at first not live together in peace, and they were dispersed again. Communities and consequently a truly civilized life became possible only when the art of politics was invented, i.e., when laws and a social and moral code were established (322 A–D).[5]

For Anaxagoras and Protagoras, the power which leads man forward depends upon his organic structure or the instinct with which he is endowed, but it is a specifically human power. In this respect their theories resembled that of Xenophanes. Democritus, on the other hand, spoke in an entirely objective and detached manner, replacing anthropocentrism by an almost consistently mechanistic explanation. According to him there was an initial period in which "Necessity separated" certain arts indispensable for human existence; there followed a later period of "superabundance," in which other arts providing a mere refinement of life, such as music, were discovered. (Fr. 144 [Diels–Kranz].) In the most important activities such as weaving, building houses, and singing, men imitated the animals and became their pupils (Fr. 154).[6]

[5] The mythical form in which Protagoras presents his doctrine in the Platonic dialogue is nothing but a stylistic device, for he gives his listeners a choice between a "myth" and a "rational account" (320 C; cf. Nestle, *Vom Mythos zum Logos*, p. 282). Hence it cannot be said, as Nestle (*ibid.*) and Kleingünther (*op. cit.*, p. 109) do say, that he seriously wished to ascribe man's progress to his share in the divine (322 A). He ascribed it instead to a power ensuring safety and preservation; "the human arts are analogous to the biological devices by which animal species survive: each species, animal or human, is endowed with its peculiar δύναμις εἰς σωτηρίαν" (320 D) (Vlastos, *A.J.P.*, LXVII [1946], 56). Concerning the question whether Protagoras' theory antedates that of Democritus, cf. F. Ueberweg, *Die Philosophie des Altertums*, ed. Karl Praechter (12. Auf.; Berlin, 1926), pp. 109 ff.

[6] Democritus' doctrine was first reconstructed by K. Reinhardt ("Hekataios von Abdera und Demokrit," *Hermes*, XLVII [1912], 492–513). From the indirect evidence it would follow that Democritus acknowledged "need" (χρεία) in addition to necessity (ἀνάγκη) as a motive-power. (Reinhardt, pp. 499 and 503 [Fr. 5, par. 1 (Diels–Kranz)]). For the later debate on Democritus' theory, cf. Vlastos, *A.J.P.*, LXVII (1946), 51 ff.; for details of his views, Vlastos, "Ethics and Physics in Democritus," *The Philosophical Review*, LV (1946), 53 ff. Recognition of Democritus' mechanistic outlook should not, however, make one forget such features of his doctrine as the "psychological" explanation of religion (Fr. 30); cf. Reinhardt, p. 511; E. Norden (*Agnostos Theos* [Leipzig, 1913], pp. 397 ff.), who has shown its relation to Critias' famous aetiology of religious beliefs (Fr. 25, 12 [Diels–Kranz]); also Kleingünther, *op. cit.*, pp. 111 ff.

Although these theories differ in detail, according to all of them the history of the past is the history of "progress"; its content is the progressive humanization of the animal, man, even though there may have been interruptions in this forward movement. Moreover, since human existence was initially "brutish" or animal-like or at least "savage," the advance achieved was not merely an improvement or "betterment" of human conditions but was primarily an advance from a "prehuman" stage to a truly human stage.[7] For Anaxagoras, Protagoras, and Democritus progress up to a certain point was also the necessary condition for the survival and preservation of the human race, which otherwise could not have perpetuated itself. So far, it was not simply man's striving for the better, an agon in which he is engaged, but as the very presupposition of his life was what might be called a biological value; and so both man and nature are agents of progress.[8] Moreover, material and spiritual values together constitute the prerogative of human life. Mastery over the physical environment is inseparable from intellectual, moral, and aesthetic accomplishments. No distinction is made between the rise of a technical civilization in the strict sense of the word and the rise of cultural values.[9]

It goes without saying that for Anaxagoras, Democritus, and Protagoras any belief in a Golden Age was anathema; and the same holds true of the Sophists who, in general, accepted the progressive

[7] The designation of early human life as "brutish" ($\theta\eta\rho\iota\tilde{\omega}\delta\epsilon\varsigma$) is attested for Democritus (Fr. 5, p. 135, 33 [Diels–Kranz]-Diodorus I, 8, 1). For Anaxagoras' identification of man's first form of life with that of animals cf. above, note 4. (For the use of the term by other authors see below, note 73.) From Protagoras' condemnation of the life of the savages, i.e., of men without civilization (*Protagoras* 327 C; cf. below, p. 25), I conclude that for him the beginnings of mankind were savage rather than brutish. It is this kind of difference in the views of primitivism which prevents a specification of Xenophanes' opinion on the matter (cf. chap. I, note 20).

[8] Cf. above, p. 14. As will be seen later, the way in which the ancients formulated the second proposition included in the definition of progress varies in its emphasis.

[9] Kleingünther uses only the term 'civilization' (in the German sense) in his analysis of the Pre-Socratic doctrines (*op. cit.*, pp. 66, 120) and finds the first appreciation of "culture" (*Kultur*) in Isocrates; but surely Protagoras did not think of the development of technological devices alone (cf. Nestle, *Vom Mythos zum Logos*, p. 286), and Anaxagoras and Democritus would have been the last to deny the positive value of scientific insight and aesthetic experience; cf. below, pp. 54 f. Concerning the general use of the terms 'civilization' and 'culture,' see Introduction, note 37.

doctrines, men like Polos, Critias, and Prodicus, and produced variations on the theme.[10] All of them were progressivists pure and simple and could have looked only with contempt on the one philosopher who, his evolutionism and Darwinian belief in the survival of the fittest notwithstanding, spoke of the existence of a state of perfect bliss and happiness at the height of the world-cycle, when Cypris reigned supreme and men worshipped her with truly holy gifts, when no blood stained the altar (Empedocles, Fr. 128 [Diels–Kranz]), when "all things were tame and gentle to man, both beasts and birds, and friendly feelings were kindled everywhere" (Fr. 130). The adherents of progressivism scorned even the enthusiasts for the happiness of the Noble Savage. If these "Rousseauans before Rousseau" were forced to live among the primitives whom they admire so much, said Protagoras, they would "sorrowfully long to revisit the rascality of this part of the world," for compared with the savage as he exists in reality the most unjust man alive here and today would seem to them to be "a just man and a master of justice" (Plato, *Protagoras*, 327 C–D).[11]

Those who studied and described the progress made in the past themselves made great strides in the advance of knowledge. Anaxagoras and Democritus, not to speak of the originality of their philosophical systems of which they were not unaware (Anaxago-

[10] Polos, the pupil of Gorgias, traced the discovery of the arts and crafts to experience (Plato, *Gorgias* 448 C), thus assuming their gradual improvement (Nestle, *Vom Mythos zum Logos*, p. 331). The same should have been true of Gorgias, though in one of his declamations, the *Palamedes*, he ascribed the invention of practically all the arts to this one hero (but a rhetorical encomium cannot be taken literally [contrary to Nestle, *ibid.*]). Cf. also below, p. 43 on Aeschylus' *Prometheus Bound*. For Critias, cf. Frs. 2 and 25 (Diels–Kranz). Prodicus explained the belief in gods as the deification of that which is useful to men (Fr. 5 [Diels–Kranz]). His book on the *Horae* was perhaps a treatise on the rise of civilization comparable to Protagoras' work; cf. Nestle, *Vom Mythos zum Logos*, pp. 351 ff. The Anonymus Iamblichi (89, par. 6 [Diels–Kranz]) refers to necessity as the all-powerful agent; the Anonymus Περὶ νόμων (M. Pohlenz, *Göttingische gelehrte Nachrichten* [1924], pp. 19 ff.) speaks of human inventions which are at the same time gifts of the gods, and so does the Hippocratic treatise *On Ancient Medicine*, chap. 14 (cf. Nestle, *Vom Mythos zum Logos*, p. 433, note 31). This, I think, is a variation of Prodicus' notion that the useful is identical with the divine.

[11] Nestle (*Vom Mythos zum Logos*, p. 286) has emphasized Protagoras' opposition to the idealization of primitive people (cf. below, p. 50), but the statement may well be taken as characteristic of all who saw in civilization the force that had ameliorated the originally primitive conditions of life, for it is the logical consequence of such a view.

ras, Fr. 17 [Diels–Kranz]), were productive scientists. Their solution of the problem of mathematical perspective, their exploration of the concept of infinity, Anaxagoras' explanation of the eclipse of the sun, Democritus' investigation of specific natural phenomena in his "Aetiologies," are merely samples of their achievements. The Sophists laid the foundations for a study of language and rhetoric and refined the analysis of political and social phenomena. The establishment of the moral sciences was to a large measure their merit.[12] One can hardly expect men of such stature to have believed that progress had reached its end before their time. Hippias, who was always eager to say something new (Xenophon, *Mem.*, IV, 4, 6; cf. B 6 [Diels–Kranz]), expressed his admiration for the contemporary advance in rhetoric and sculpture and approved the assertion that all skills and all knowledge have "now" progressed greatly. (Plato, *Hippias Major* 281 D; 282A.) Surely he could not have been the only one to feel this way; and his opinion is not surprising if besides the progress in the sciences and technology the contemporary achievements in the arts are remembered—in sculpture, painting, architecture, tragic poetry, and music, which was revolutionized by Philoxenus, Agathon, and Timotheus.[13]

Whether it was expected that this progress would continue, however, is a question unanswered by the fragments that remain from the writings of the Pre-Socratics. Aristotle taunts "the philosophers of old" for their assurance that they had "perfected" philosophy—an assurance which he attributes to their naïveté or their vainglory (Cicero, *Tuscul. Disp.*, III, 28, 69 = Fr. 53 [Rose]). His accusation, if not his explanation, may contain a grain of truth. It is

[12] For the scientific studies of Anaxagoras and Democritus, cf. E. Frank, *Plato und die sogenannten Pythagoreer* (Halle, 1923), pp. 19 ff. and 46 ff. Even if tradition errs in attributing certain discoveries to them (*cf.* Ueberweg–Praechter, *op. cit.*, pp. 101 ff.), their active participation in research is unquestionable. The contributions of the Sophists to the development of the humanities has been most adequately illustrated by Nestle (*Vom Mythos zum Logos, passim*).
[13] For the *nuove musiche* of the fifth century, perhaps less well known than the other artistic achievements of the time, cf. *Republic* III, 396 B and Frank, *Plato und die sogenannten Pythagoreer*, pp. 8 ff. For Timotheus, cf. below, pp. 35 f. Of the technologists of the period I mention e.g., Meton, who was famous for his many inventions (Phrynichus, *The Hermit*, Frs. 18 and 21 f.), and Hippodamus, who planned the layout of cities; cf. below, p. 30.

limited, however, to a single field of intellectual activity, and philosophers of all ages have been prone to claim that their teaching was the last word. A statement of Plato's (*Laws*, X, 889 C–890 A) is, I think, more revealing, for it points to certain assumptions of Pre-Socratic philosophy which seem, on principle, to narrow down the possibility of the further advancement of all human knowledge.[14]

As Plato says, the early philosophers distinguished two kinds of art, "the subsequent late-born product" of natural causes. The first of these brings forth "toys with little real substance in them, *simulacra* as shadowy as the arts themselves, such as those which spring from painting, music, and the other fellow crafts." The second, by which things of genuine worth are produced, embraces "those [arts] which lend their aid to nature, like medicine, husbandry, gymnastics." In other words, man succeeds in his "serious" activities by developing the power of nature. This being the case, he cannot go farther than nature will permit. Pre-Socratic thought makes the possible dependent upon the given and regards what may come to pass as determined by what is.[15] It is in this spirit that a philosophically trained medical writer of the period, faced with complaints about the imperfection of the medical art, retorts that the physician cannot be expected to go beyond the possibilities of his art and

[14] That Plato's criticism is directed against Pre-Socratic philosophy and the Sophistic movement in general was pointed out by Otto Apelt, *Platons Gesetze* (Leipzig, 1916), II, 536, *ad* 402. Cf. also Paul Friedlander, *Platon* III, 405 ff. (For the recent literature on the passage see H. Cherniss, "Plato (1950–1957)," *Lustrum*, IV [1959] and V [1960], pp. 112 ff.) Anaxagoras is surely meant to be included, since for Plato his philosophy was not fundamentally different from that of the other naturalists; cf. above, note 4. For Aristotle's criticism see below, chap. III, note 78.

[15] Cf. A. Faust, *Der Möglichkeitsgedanke* (Heidelberg, 1931–32) I, 24. In my paraphrase of the Platonic passage I make use of A.E. Taylor's translation, *The Laws of Plato* (London, 1934). Vlastos, who also characterizes Democritus' general concept of nature as that of "an order of what is 'possible' and 'impossible'" (*Philosophical Review*, LV [1946], 60, with reference to Frs. 58 f. and 191 [Diels–Kranz]), adds that "man's nature is not fixed" and attributes to Democritus a "dynamic view of human nature" (*ibid.*); but, although teaching does create in man a kind of second nature, this development, as Vlastos himself points out, "can proceed only within the limits of the 'possible.'" (*Ibid.*) Such an acknowledgment leads to a limitation of further advance and differs from the later belief in man's "perfectibility," which becomes an incentive to progress; see below, chap. IV, pp. 167 f.

of all human art. To aim at more, to aspire "to do everything," to undertake what nature and art do not permit one to undertake, would be utter folly. (Ps. Hippocrates, *De Arte*, chap. 8.)[16]

Such an attitude Bacon was to denounce as an "unfair circumscription of human power," disturbing "the auguries of hope," cutting "the sinews and spur of industry," and throwing away "the chances of experience itself, and all for the sake of having their art thought perfect, and for the miserable vainglory of making it believed that whatever has not yet been discovered and comprehended can never be discovered or comprehended hereafter." (*Novum Organum*, I, 88.) Bacon did not, of course, deny that even men of this persuasion would hope for some progress; and it would be unfair to judge the philosophers of the fifth century otherwise. As a matter of fact, the physician just quoted expressly states that one can still discover more than has been discovered already (chap. 1). Nevertheless, it remains true that a realism and naturalism like that embraced by the Pre-Socratics severely limits the expectations of progress to come.

As an especially important example of the type of shadowy fellow crafts "which have little in common with nature" and are "mainly a business of art" Plato mentions besides the fine arts statesmanship and legislation, whose "positions are unreal." For men in consequence of their philosophical opinions "are eternally disputing about rights and altering them; and every change thus made, once made, is from that moment valid, though it owes its being to artifice and legislation, not to anything you could call nature." He has in mind the moral and epistemological skepticism which in the second half of the fifth century accompanied natural philosophy or took its departure from it.[17] There is hardly any doubt that this skepticism also impaired the belief in future progress and especially in social progress, for, if nothing is really right or wrong, how can one decide what is better or worse? The new, to be sure, will appear to be desirable to some and unacceptable to

---

[16] Even though the book *On the Art* can certainly not be ascribed to Protagoras, as was once suggested by T. Gomperz (*Die Apologie der Heilkunst* [Leipzig, 1910], pp. 22–29), it can hardly have been composed later than the end of the fifth century.

[17] For the skepticism of Democritus and Protagoras, cf. H. Cherniss, *J.H.I.*, XII (1951), 343 ff.

others. A progressive development in which each step is considered to lead further forward cannot be in store, and the incentive to further advance is blunted.

It is therefore justifiable to say that the Pre-Socratics as well as the Sophists were progressivists and antiprogressivists at the same time. They thought highly of the advances made in the past and in the present; they emphasized the importance of civilization for the survival of mankind; they championed the superiority of civilized life to that of primitive peoples. Once security and stability had been established, however, and once the refinement of the arts and of knowledge had reached its present level, they did not look forward to things that would be much better than they were. They credited man with as much as they denied him. This ambivalent verdict or this inconsistency, if so one prefers to call it, constitutes the true limitation of their concept of progress. It matters little that at least the philosophers among them, Anaxagoras and Democritus, assumed that the world built up by men is destined one day, sooner or later, to be destroyed together with the earth on which men live.[18] As has already been said, it is not an intrinsic property of the law of progress that the advance to be made must be infinite; and those who foresee an end of humanity are not by this very fact disbelievers in progress. Did not Xenophanes "invent" the idea of progress and yet assume the dissolution of the cosmos? Nor can it be decided on a priori grounds how far into the future time must be thought to extend if men are to feel optimistic and confident about what is to be. In periods of Greek and Roman history subsequent to the classical age the idea of continuous progress was accepted and glorified, and men were eager to work for the future despite their conviction that the total destruction and ruin of all things by cosmic catastrophe might be imminent. Why should the Pre-Socratics have felt differently on that score, no matter how distant or how near the final day in their opinion was? If they were

[18] That Democritus believed in periodic destruction of the various world-systems is certain (A 40 [Diels–Kranz]). (They take place through collision, that is suddenly, or through the gradual diminution of the body of the world.) For the opinion of Anaxagoras the evidence is ambiguous, but the "best" evidence seems to show that the various worlds were to be resolved into the original mixture of all things; cf. F.M. Cleve, *The Philosophy of Anaxagoras* (New York, 1949), pp. 131 ff.

somewhat pessimistic rather than over-optimistic about the future, they had other reasons for being so.[19]

It must not be forgotten, however, that in the debate about the future carried on outside the circle of these philosophers a very different note was sounded. The schemes for political reform that began to be devised by statesmen and others not engaged in practical politics are themselves evidence of an interest and a belief in the possibility of improving conditions. The constitution outlined by Phaleas of Chalcedon (Aristotle, *Politics*, II, 7, 1266 a 39) was a blueprint for the best or perfect state;[20] and such programs, proposed in the conviction that things could be improved, were ideals to be realized by men and not, as were the chiliastic dreams of later ages, visions of what divine providence would one day accomplish. One of them even made trust in future advance a basic political principle. Hippodamus of Miletus, who wrote a few decades after Xenophanes' death, did not merely put down what seemed best to him but in addition "proposed a law that those who discovered something of advantage to the state should receive honor." (Aristotle, *Politics*, II, 8, 1268 a 6–8.) In other words, he intended to legalize progress in constitutional and political affairs, and by so doing to encourage and secure it for the future.[21]

One might at first be inclined to take this proposal as the fancy of an eccentric; and Aristotle does, in fact, characterize Hippodamus, the architect and city planner who "invented the division of cities into blocks and who cut up Piraeus," as slightly eccentric at least "in his general mode of life, owing to a desire for distinction." (1267 b 22 ff.) Yet Aristotle also takes him seriously when he later discusses the value of his proposal (1268 b 22 ff.). Moreover, Thucydides, almost as if stating a truism, expresses the conviction that

[19] See above, Introduction, note 41.

[20] Phaleas seems to belong to the end of the fifth century, and his work certainly antedates the *Republic* of Plato; cf. E. Barker, *Greek Political Theory* (London, 1951), p. 80.

[21] Hippodamus is sometimes called a Pythagorean (cf. e.g., Wilhelm Schmid and Otto Stählin, *Geschichte der griechischen Literatur* I, 2, p. 589), but this epithet is hardly warranted by the few passages in which Aristotle speaks of him (39, 1 and 2 [Diels–Kranz]), even though Aristotle does appear to classify him as a philosopher or at least as one trained in philosophy. According to Barker (*Greek Political Theory*, p. 80), Hippodamus, though he was a contemporary of Phaleas, was already active in 450 B.C.; cf. Schmid–Stählin, *op. cit.*, p. 550.

30

in the sphere of political activity it is useful to be constantly on the lookout for new things. In a speech, which he puts into the mouth of the Corinthian ambassadors sent to Sparta in 430 B.C., the clinching argument against the conservatism of the Lacedaemonians is that in times of war or, at any rate, of great political turmoil changes of the established principles are needed. "For as in every other technical skill, so in the art of politics the new must always prevail over the old." (I, 71, 2.)[22] The very novelty of the changes possible is supposed to guarantee their greater effectiveness. Though the new is perhaps not morally superior, it is apt at least to preserve the safety of the state better than do the outworn methods of the past.

How such an inexorable and morally indifferent political "futurism" originated Thucydides indicates by the analogy assumed to exist between what is true of the arts and crafts generally and what holds true of politics. To the ancients politics was also an art or skill. It had been discovered that in the other arts and crafts the new was superior to the old, and it was expected that what was invented in the future would be superior even to what was now known. Therefore, if politics is to be successful, it requires continually new inventions in techniques, plans, and views. As follows from Aristotle's criticism of Hippodamus' theory, the latter's more benign trust in the "usefulness" of further inventions was also based on the analogy of the ever-increasing efficacy of the arts and crafts and sciences. (II, 8, 1268 b 32 ff.)[23]

It should now be clear that in the second half of the fifth century the bold thesis of Xenophanes had been considerably elaborated in political theory and in historiography, even in regard to that aspect which is most essential for the concept of progress, "its bearing on

[22] This is the passage to which Gomme in his commentary (cf. above, Introduction, note 13) has recently drawn attention. Cf. also Thucydides I, 70, 2, where the Athenians are characterized as "given to innovations and quick to contrive plans," in other words, progressive. The importance of the Thucydidean testimony lies in the very fact that belief in progress is represented not as a thesis to be defended but as a commonplace; and such it must have been, at least outside of Sparta—even though the Corinthians were surely more "modern" than the people in some of the backward regions of Greece; cf. below, pp. 41 f.

[23] For Aristotle's refutation of the analogy between politics and the arts and for his recognition of the different values of progress in the several fields of human activity, see below, chap. III, pp. 119 f.

the future." Whether the expectations were humble or exaggerated, the evaluation of what time may have in store was becoming more precise and definite.[24] One is almost tempted to see in the Corinthians' insistence that the new will "always" win out the recognition of an infinite progress. Yet this would probably be giving too much weight to a single word. People often say "it will always be so" when all they wish to stress is the absoluteness of their favorite convictions; they would find it difficult to answer the question what this "always" stands for.[25]

It should be said that *a parte anteriore* too the idea of progress had been made more specific by historians. While philosophers and sophists had drawn the general outlines of the past, historians had turned to the investigation of more concrete problems. Herodotus ventured to analyze the affiliation of cultures. His scheme—on the whole, a diffusion theory—was undoubtedly crude. He found the original source of everything in the Orient and especially in Egypt, and the category of borrowing became for him a magic formula. He seldom suggests the possibility of independent "invention" in cases where customs, techniques, or religious tenets are identical in different places. Nevertheless his method of connecting national cultures and explaining in some way their common characteristics is vastly superior to the mere cataloguing of material done in the books written since the end of the fifth century under the title, "On Inventions." In breadth of view also he surpasses those historians who like his older contemporary, Hecataeus, mentioned individual inventions in the course of their narratives, even though they dated them exactly and thus gave them the fixed place in history which they lack in the Herodotean tale.[26] Thucydides (I, 2–19), on the

---

[24] Concerning progress and the future see above, p. xi. Concerning Xenophanes' conception of the future see above, chap. I, pp. 5 f.

[25] It should, however, be pointed out again that Thucydides' formulation does not differ greatly from formulations made in the first century after Christ; see below, chap. IV, pp. 168 f.

[26] For Hecateus, see above, chap. I, p. 9. Herodotus' theory of the affiliation of cultures, if strictly speaking it does not imply progress, certainly implies the ascent of the human race; see below, note 28. On his treatment of inventions see esp. Kleingünther, *op. cit.*, pp. 46–65. The independent invention of the same thing in my opinion suggested at least as a possibility in II, 16, 7; II, 4, 1 (but cf. Kleingünther, pp. 53 and 57 ff.); IV, 180, 4 assumes the priority of the Greek invention of arms. For the books "On Inventions," cf. Kleingünther, pp. 136 ff.; for

other hand, described the changes by which the simple Greek life of Homer's time had been transformed into the highly intricate social fabric of his own age and showed how the economic forces which make history had come to be identified. The means of communication, technological devices, types of weapons, and financial resources, all these in their bearing on political decisions he evaluated; and, putting together the details with mastery unsurpassed in antiquity, he proved his thesis that the states involved in the war which was his subject had reached the highest point in their development and that consequently this war itself had to be regarded as the greatest ever fought. At the same time, his "archaeology" illustrated the principle that he made the Corinthians enunciate to the Lacedaemonians, that superiority follows from "inventions." (I, 4; 13, 1, 2.)[27]

Despite this better understanding of the scope and importance of progress and this elaboration of principles and criteria which set the pattern for all later studies of the topic, the terminology of the fifth century remained essentially that of Xenophanes. "Invention" remained the key word; and there was as yet, it seems, no single term to unify the various phases of the continuous process of advance or by making them interdependent to indicate the superiority of the new to the old. Thucydides speaks of "that which comes to be born afterward" (τὰ ἐπιγιγνόμενα) and adds that it "gains the upper hand (κρατεῖ)" over the old-fashioned (ἀρχαιότροπα [I, 71, 2]). Medical writers speak of "finding something not yet found which, if found, would prove to be stronger than if it were left undiscovered," and also of "working out the half-completed to its end" (Ps. Hippocrates, De Arte, chap. 1), or of "discovering what is left," or

Hellanikos, ibid., pp. 125 ff. Such lists also occur in poetry and in the sophistic literature (Critias, Fr. 2 [Diels–Kranz]).

[27] Thucydides also touches upon the change in moral values connected with the change in modes of life (I, 5 [the attitude to piracy]) or in customs (I, 6 [Greek dress]). Using such observations as the starting-point for his conclusions, he anticipated a method perfected in the Peripatos; cf. J. Bernays, Theophrastos' Schrift über Frömmigkeit (Berlin, 1866), p. 51, and below, chap. III, pp. 94 f. As has been shown, the conception of progressive development, on which Thucydides' survey is based, was not so unusual as most commentators assume. A similar procedure may have been followed in some of the sophistic writings now lost (e.g., Hippias' Archaeology, or Prodicus' Horae). (Hecataeus had already made use of linguistic data; cf. above, chap. I, p. 9.)

"discovering the whole art." (Ps. Hippocrates, *On Ancient Medicine*, chaps. 2 and 8.) Herodotus says that Melampus did not show the Greeks "the whole doctrine" of the worship of Dionysus, that later sages "brought it to light to a greater extent." (II, 49, 1.) Where the subject matter had obviously remained constant and had simply been transformed, the process of improvement was expressed in a circumlocutional and cumbersome manner: the alphabet introduced from abroad was first used by the Phoenicians as they had received it, and then "in the course of time, the characters changed together with the change of language"; the Greeks adopted from the Phoenicians the letters of the alphabet "with some few variations in the characters." (Herodotus, V, 58, 1–2.)[28] Thus progress was still understood in merely additive terms. The various periods were thought of as knowing more or less, and the inventor was assumed to have added to the fund of knowledge at his disposal by his own creativity without recognizing any debt that he might owe to his predecessors or admitting what one may properly call "influences." The change is treated not as qualitative but as quantitative, and the various inventions and additions taken together are like stones in a mosaic, individual and distinct entities. The formula of *heuremata*, it has been rightly said, is an example of a "crude externalization of the history of ideas."[29]

In one respect only did the fifth century create a new terminology that points to a new perspective. Xenophanes, castigating the errors of Homer and Hesiod, had spoken simply of "men of former times." (Fr. 1, 22 [Diels–Kranz].) Hecataeus had already referred

---

[28] W. A. Heidel, *The Heroic Age of Science* (Baltimore [Md.], 1933), p. 46, emphasized the importance of this passage for the development of a truly historical understanding of the past. Any generalization concerning the terminology of fifth-century writers is hazardous, since so very little of the large body of literature then current is extant; but the evidence, so far as it goes, appears to justify the statement made in the text. When Socrates in his conversation with Hippias (Plato, *Hippias Major* 281 D; cf. 282 B) talks of "the growing arts and crafts (ἐπιδεδωκέναι)" he speaks, I presume, in the language of the fourth century (cf. below, chap. III, pp. 92 f.). I should note, however, that once Thucydides uses the term αὐξηθῆναι (I, 12, 1; 16); cf. Heraclitus, Fr. 115. How difficult it still was to express the idea of progress is shown by the trouble that Timotheus had in expressing his superiority to earlier poets (vv. 234 ff., and U. von Wilamowitz–Möllendorff, *Timotheus*, *Die Perser* [Leipzig, 1903], pp. 47 ff.).

[29] H. Cherniss, "The History of Ideas . . . ," p. 33.

to "the ancient Greeks" (Fr. 15 [Jacoby]), though surely the word for him had had a purely chronological connotation.[30] With Prodicus, who tried to explain the origin of the religious beliefs of "the ancients" (Fr. 5 [Diels–Kranz] = Sextus Empiricus, *Adv. Math.,* IX, 18), the term in question may have had the same implication. Hippias coined the term "archaeology," that is, "ancient lore," as a title for his account of "the races of heroes and men, of the settlement of cities in olden times." (Plato, *Hippias Major,* 285 D.) Since he was so proud of the advance of his own time over previous centuries, he can hardly have used the word "ancient" in a eulogistic sense.[31]

The new terminology shows that one had come to feel and accentuate the superiority of the moderns to the ancients, and there is much other testimony to the fact that the fifth century was engaged in the first *Querelle des anciens et des modernes.* Naturally, not everyone was of the opinion that the present outshone the past; and the ancient tradition, now considered by some to be antiquated, could be upheld by others as hallowed and above all criticism or reproach. Examples of this rivalry between progressivism and antiprogressivism are to be found in song and poetry, as well as in scientific literature.

To begin with the former, Timotheus, one of the musical revolutionaries of his time, proudly announces in verses preserved from an unknown work of his: "I do not sing ancient melodies, my own are better by far; young Zeus now is king, Cronus of old was the ruler; ancient muse, begone." (Fr. 21 = Athenaeus, III, 122 C–D.) As he himself admits in another poem, he is accused of having dishonored the "ancient" kind of music by his innovations (*Persae,*

[30] Cf. above, chap. I, p. 9. It is interesting to observe that Xenophanes follows the Homeric usage (cf. *Iliad* IV, 308; V, 637; XXI, 405; XIII, 332), which still survives in Aeschylus' *Agamemnon* (1338); cf. E. Fraenkel (ed.), *Aeschylus, Agamemnon* III (Oxford, 1950), *ad loc.*

[31] For Hippias' judgment of his time, cf. above, p. 26. That he coined the term ἀρχαιολογία was shown by E. Norden, *Agnostos Theos* (Leipzig, 1913), pp. 373 ff. (The translation "*Altertumskunde*" [Nestle, *Vom Mythos zum Logos,* p. 364], though correct, does perhaps have overtones alien to the meaning that Hippias intended.) The word ἀρχαῖος seems not to occur before the fifth century (Homer uses only παλαιός, and so does Hecataeus). It may have been chosen to denote "what is at the beginning [of time]," with a play on ἀρχή (cf. "*anfänglich*"). As early as Aeschylus' *Prometheus Bound* (317), however, it means "antiquated."

219–25); but he does not care. Surely, it is not his intent to prevent anyone, young or old, from listening to the antiquated music, but he would drive out the poets who are "bad imitators of the ancient art." (vv. 226–33.) As for himself, he has left behind the beginnings made by Orpheus, by Terpander, and by others and "now leads into the light of day the song that suits in metre and rhythm the cithara of eleven strings" (vv. 234–43), the new instrument that he has invented for "a new type of music."[32]

Aristophanes, on the other hand, pleads the cause of the reactionaries. In his *Clouds*, he tries—half jokingly, half seriously, and perhaps all too irresponsibly—to pillory those who in his opinion are the enemies of society; and he caricatures in the person of Socrates all philosophy as well as the sophistic movement of his day, the new learning which to him is merely "traversing the air." (225 and 1503.) The evil consequences for morality, which he attributes to the novel views, are emphasized in the contest between "Just Discourse" and "Unjust Discourse" over the "old" education and the "new"; and the ancient ethical code is glorified. (889 ff.) The most deadly, because most clear-sighted and objective, criticism is that which is expressed by the example of wisdom acquired by the freshly initiated pupil of Socrates. Contending that children have the right to punish their parents (1420 ff.), he supports his thesis with the argument that the legislator who "first" passed the law permitting fathers to chastise their children was himself a human being like all others and gained approval for his proposal by persuasion, so that it should be permissible for still others to seek to establish different laws. This persiflage strikes at

[32] Timotheus lived *ca.* 450–360 B.C. Wilamowitz (*Timotheus, Die Perser*, p. 63) dates the work between 398–396; but it is now dated 419–416 B.C.; cf. C.M. Bowra, *s.v.* Timotheus, *Oxford Classical Dictionary*; A.W. Pickard-Cambridge, *Dithyramb, Tragedy, and Comedy* (Oxford, 1927), p. 55. The lines from the unknown work of Timotheus cannot be dated at all (cf. Wilamowitz, *Timotheus, Die Perser*, p. 65). Plato (*Republic* IV, 424 C) carefully distinguishes an innovation in the modes of music such as Timotheus' from the natural and philosophically unobjectionable desire of the poet to compose a new song in the old genre; *Odyssey* I, 351; also Pindar, *Olymp.* III, 4; cf. P. Shorey (ed.), *Plato, The Republic* I (Loeb Classical Library, 1930), *ad loc.* as against J. Adam (ed.), *The Republic of Plato* I (Cambridge, 1902), *ad loc.* On the other hand, the feeling expressed by Timotheus can be found in other poets and musicians, such as Ion or Cinesias. It is characteristic that Glaucus of Rhegium wrote a book on the ancient poets and musicians.

the very foundation of the new-fashioned attitude and its proud conceit that what is new must also be better.[33]

In the poetical evidence the dissension is seen through the eyes of great personalities, and the argument is colored by their temperaments. The authors of the medical treatises in which the same debate occurs are lesser figures; and in their books, parts of the so-called *Corpus Hippocraticum*, which is the only scientific material remaining intact from the fifth century, the argument goes on within the framework of daily reality. Concern with the question must have been general, for otherwise it would be hard to understand why physicians writing for their colleagues as well as for laymen on problems of a technical nature should have felt obliged to take a stand in the matter and, moreover, to state their position with the kind of passion aroused only by an issue felt to be of vital importance.[34]

[33] The Aristophanic play was first produced in 423; the dialogue between "Just Discourse" and "Unjust Discourse" seems to belong to the second version, which was between 421–418 B.C.; cf. Schmid–Stählin, *Geschichte der griechischen Literatur* I, 4, p. 247. According to Kleingünther (*op. cit.*, p. 97) Aristophanes' words about the first lawgiver are censorious and point to the later curses heaped upon the inventors of things, but I see no reason to think that the speaker means more than that laws have a human origin. The passage quoted in the text is only one example of many. For Aristophanes himself, compare e.g., *Birds* 1371 and *Eccl.* 197 and 564; for Pherecrates cf. *Chiron*, Fr. I (the complaint of Music herself about the innovators).

[34] Of the four Hippocratic writings to be mentioned, two are commonly agreed to belong to the last decades of the fifth century, *On Hebdomads* (cf. J. Ilberg, "Die Ärzteschule von Knidos," *Berichte über die Verhandlungen der Sächsischen Akademie der Wissenschaften zu Leipzig*, Phil.–Hist. Klasse, LXXVI [1924], Heft 3, p. 5; also J. Mewaldt, "Review of J. Ilberg, 'Die Ärzteschule von Knidos,'" *Gnomon*, III [1927], 140, note 2), and *On Muscles* (cf. K. Deichgräber, *Hippokrates, Über Entstehung und Aufbau des Körpers* [Leipzig, 1935], p. 27, note 4). Of the other two, *On Ancient Medicine* is usually given the same date (440–410 B.C.), H. Wanner, *Studien zu Περὶ ἀρχαίης ἰητρικῆς* (Zurich, 1939), p. 101; before 400, W. Jaeger, *Diokles von Karystos* (Berlin, 1938), p. 170, and *Paideia* II, 33. The recent attempt by H. Diller, in "Hippokratische Medizin und Attische Philosophie," *Hermes*, LXXX (1952), 385 ff. to prove that the book is contemporaneous with Plato or even Aristotle seems to me to be unconvincing (cf. F. Heinimann, *Museum Helveticum*, XVIII [1961], 112, note 32). The treatise *On Regimen*, likewise, has generally been dated at the end of the fifth century; cf. A. Palm, *Studien zur Hippokratischen Schrift Περὶ Διαίτης* (Diss. Tübingen, 1933), p. 99. Jaeger (*Diokles von Karystos*, p. 171 and *Paideia* II, 33) considers it to be more likely that the work was composed after 400 B.C. (G.S. Kirk in *Heraclitus The Cosmic Fragments* [Cambridge, 1954], p. 27, thinks of the middle of the fourth century.) I agree with Diller (*Das neue Bild der Antike*, I [1942], 303 and 309), who sees in the author a follower of the Heraclitean sect formed at the end of the fifth century.

In an essay, the very purpose of which it is to defend the ancients, the author bitterly opposes medicine based on hypotheses that have been newly erected (*On Ancient Medicine*, chap. 1), "the warm," "the cold," or whatever, and especially doctrines influenced by the philosophy of Empedocles (chap. 20). Such a "new approach" to the medical art (chap. 13) is, in his opinion, a complete failure. The right method of investigation, he holds, was developed long ago; and those who search for another attempt the impossible and are "deceived deceivers" (chap. 2). Only by following the example that was set of old can further discoveries be made (*ibid.*). It would be folly to abandon "ancient" medicine merely because it has not yet attained perfect accuracy; one should admire it instead for what it did accomplish and accomplished by reasoning rather than by chance (chap. 12). Other partisans of the ancients are briefer but hardly less vigorous in their rejection of what is new. Thus one author states emphatically that it is not his intention to oppose theories correctly framed by "the ancients" (*On Hebdomads*, chap. 53), for it is better to make an attempt to understand what was said rightly "of old" than to pronounce "new" but erroneous ideas (*ibid.*) The charge implied is undoubtedly that the novel gets preference solely by virtue of its novelty.

Then, on the other hand, the superiority of the present to the past is stated boastfully. Taking up one of those new theories that the author of *On Ancient Medicine* calls empty hypotheses, one writer declares that "what we denote by the term 'the warm' appears to be immortal; and it apprehends, sees, hears, and knows everything, that which is as well as that which will be" (*On Muscles*, chap. 2). He adds that the ancients, in his opinion, had this quality in mind when speaking of the ether. Just as Timotheus was proud of the new melodies that he had invented and of the new instrument that he had devised, so the physician glories in the new philosophy, which allows him to replace concrete words of ancient usage by abstract terms, a novel invention.

The relation of current science to that of yesterday is discussed more generally at the beginning of a treatise intended to familiarize the public with a doctrine which, in the eyes of its originator, provided insight that physicians before him had not even envisaged. (*On Regimen*, I, 1, 2; cf. III, 68.) His predecessors, "men of former times," he says, treated the subject of dietetics in a most unsatisfactory manner. While some of their specific observations were sound, he admits, and not to adopt them would be unwise, he holds that for the rest it hardly pays to refute the earlier views but is better to proceed with the exposé that will show what he finds wrong with them. This preamble to his work he justifies on the ground that many people are unwilling to listen to the account of a "late-comer," because they do not understand that the same intelligence is required to recognize what has already been correctly said and to discover what has not yet been said at all. In other words, nothing can be taken on authority; but the correctness of theories formerly held must be confirmed by one's own judgment; and, if the work hitherto done is carefully weighed and sifted, not much of it remains that is of worth. "I do not sing ancient melodies, my own are better by far," to quote Timotheus again.

From this evidence, the poetic as well as the scientific, two conclusions can safely be drawn. First, in the fifth century the progressivists were self-consciously "modern"; and it is useless to deny that the Greeks had such awareness,[35] which is characteristic of the attitude to progress in recent times. Second, while the progressivism of the classical age gave rise to a depreciation of the ancient as archaic, it also provoked the first worship of "antiquity." Adoration of the past, within Greek history at any rate, appears to be the counterpart and shadow, as it were, of the insistence on the superiority of the present generation. Those who rejected the new completely or even in its exaggerated form turned self-consciously traditional when they used the term, "the ancients," eulogistically.[36]

It also follows that this first *Querelle des anciens et des modernes*

[35] As does Bury (cf. above, Introduction, p. xvii). K. Joël too maintains that in antiquity there was *"keine Fortschrittspartei"* (*Geschichte der Antiken Philosophie* [Tübingen, 1921], I, 77).

[36] It is commonly thought that it is natural for mankind to venerate antiquity; and few agree with U. von Wilamowitz–Möllendorff (*Aristoteles und Athen* [Berlin, 1893] I, 119, note 31) in his verdict, *"ursprünglicher ist die verächtliche beurteilung des 'grauen altertums' der zeit vor der civilisation."* Whatever the truth of this may be, in the literature of the fifth century B.C. modernism seems to have preceded the defense of antiquity as in Russia in the nineteenth century Pan-Slavism was provoked by western intellectualism. That the Homeric Epic does not reveal a specific reverence for the past and that the term "the ancients" appears first in sophistic writings, I have shown above, p. 35 and chap. I, p. 7 and note 13.

had the result that is often attributed to the battle between the ancients and the moderns in the seventeenth and eighteenth centuries. Being self-consciously modern, the progressivists of the classical age drew a line between today and yesterday and established the right of the new generation to be itself. The past became irrevocably past. It is the ancient and not the modern *Querelle des anciens et des modernes* that was "a ripe event in the history of the human spirit." That first announcement of "an irreversible advance," which according to Comte was made in modern times, was actually made in the classical age;[37] and the declaration of independence was inspired by a feeling not unlike that which inspired many a champion of the moderns in the later battle. The moderns of antiquity too showed little inclination at first to condemn the old as totally inferior or obsolete but wished only to say, in the words of Molière, "the ancients are the ancients, and we are the people of today";[38] and, aware as they were of the gulf separating the ways of life of the earlier and later generations, they would have subscribed to the verdict of Pascal: "What can be more unjust than to treat our ancients with greater consideration than they showed their own predecessors and to have for them this incredible respect which they deserve from us only because they entertained no such regard for those who had the same advantage (of antiquity) over them?"[39]

That a progressive philosophy such as has been pieced together from the evidence was of concern beyond a small circle of initiates can be asserted without elaborate proof. The evidence for it comes not only from recondite philosophical writings but also from technical books and to a large extent from poetry. Moreover, the Sophists, the heralds of the idea of progress, carried the new creed throughout Greece; and almost everywhere there existed an interest

[37] Cf. above, Introduction, pp. xvi f.
[38] Bury, *The Idea of Progress*, p. 83.
[39] B. Pascal, *Fragment de Préface sur le Traité du Vide*, pp. 135–36; cf. Bury, *The Idea of Progress*, p. 68. Pascal's statement recalls that of Horace: "*quod si tam Graecis novitas invisa fuisse quam nobis, quid nunc esset vetus . . .*" (*Epistulae* II, 1, 90 ff.) Timotheus said substantially the same thing when comparing himself with Terpander (237 f. and Wilamowitz's interpretation of the lines [*Timotheus, Die Perser*, p. 68]).

in novel teachings that was unknown in the time of Xenophanes. Herodotus rightly rejected as a tale "vainly made up by the Greeks themselves" the story told him by the Peloponnesians, according to which in the time of Anacharsis "all Greeks were zealous for every kind of learning, save only the Lacedaemonians." (IV, 77.) This was indeed a fabrication that projected back into the sixth century the situation prevailing in his time. It was in fact only from the beginning of the fifth century that all Greece showed an unprecedented concern with knowledge of every kind. As Aristotle puts it, during the years after the Persian wars and even earlier the Greeks, proud of their successes in war and politics, were "anxious to explore fresh fields" and "adopted all studies indiscriminately as their province." (*Politics*, VIII, 6, 1341 a 28–32.) The substance of this famous characterization of the classical age, echoed by later Greek historians and by the Roman admirers of Greek culture, has aptly been compared by modern commentators to "what we read of the intellectual and artistic progress of the United Provinces after the War of Independence."[40] Where such a spirit was abroad, the doctrine of progress cannot have failed to find a hearing.

Yet, was it a sympathetic hearing? Was the new idea accepted by many, and did it have "the public regard" that Comte, in his appraisal of its history, said it had had only in the eighteenth century? Compared to the one piece of testimony preserved from the sixth century, the evidence extant from the classical age is impressive; but in such matters numbers—and numbers which reflect the arbitrary selection of tradition—are deceptive. The decision, therefore, must in the end depend upon an assessment of the force of the countermovements. And here too the situation is precarious, for most of the material on which judgment has to be based comes from sources that echo the temper of Athens, where approval of the novel trend was surely strongest.[41] Nevertheless,

---

[40] W.L. Newman (ed.), *The Politics of Aristotle* (Oxford, 1887–1902), III, *ad* 1341 a 28. Newman also shows the connection between Aristotle's assertion and the story related by Herodotus. Compare Aristotle's verdict with Diodorus XII, 1, 4 and Horace, *Ep.* II, 1, 93 ff.

[41] The general belief in progress current in Athens around the middle of the fifth century has been observed by J.H. Finley, *Thucydides* (Cambridge [Mass.], 1947), pp. 82 ff.; see also above, note 22.

what is true of Athens should be more or less true of the rest of Greece, for Athens had already come to be considered the center of culture (Thucydides II, 41). Its influence varied, no doubt; and, furthermore, Megara was not Corinth, and Thebes was not Syracuse. Sparta probably was a case apart. Thucydides makes the Spartan king condemn the Athenian civilization as useless (I, 84), and Timotheus was driven out of Lacedaemon (*Persae*, 219 ff.); but the Platonic Hippias reports that even in Sparta, where people did not want to hear about his other accomplishments, they were eager to listen to his "archaeology," his story about the beginnings of history (*Hippias Major*, 285 D–E), and Aristotle testifies to a common intellectual attitude. One may, then, venture with some confidence to attempt a description of the general situation, even though one must rely primarily on witnesses who were most susceptible to novelty.[42]

It seems to be certain that the dream of a Golden Age in the past and the hope for its return in the future, that view of history which is the extreme opposite of a philosophy of progress and which is said to have been prevalent in antiquity, was not widely current in the fifth century. Undoubtedly, there were people who took the side of Hesiod, and even Attic comedy refers to the Golden Age of Cronus and speaks of a life of peace and bliss once enjoyed by men under the aegis of mythical kings.[43] Praise of a happy past competes, however, with hymns to Need and Poverty, to whom mankind owes everything and who, as if assuming the place of Prometheus, are honored because they have led men onward, for whatever

[42] This is not due merely to the accident of tradition. In the fifth century Attic literature began to supersede Ionian literature, a fact that of itself indicates the preponderance of Athens at that time. Moreover, in Sparta itself the old attitude was changing (see Herodotus I, 82 and Grote, A *History of Greece* III, 8 [p. 21]), and even the Spartans who opposed Athens politically were influenced by her culture (cf. Wilamowitz, *Timotheus, Die Perser*, p. 64).

[43] E.g., Cratinus' *Ploutos* (Athenaeus VI, 267 e) and Teleclides' *Amphictyons* (Athenaeus VI, 268 a–d). The comic descriptions of a Golden Age may be due in part to the wish to simulate the visions characteristic of worshippers of Dionysus, the god at whose festivals the plays were produced; cf. Pöhlmann *op. cit.*, I, 308 ff. The caricatures of the blessed life of the dead are entirely different, of course, e.g., Pherecrates, *Metalles* (Athenaeus VI, 268 e); cf. Rohde, *Psyche* I, 314 ff. See in general Wilhelm von Christ and Wilhelm Schmid, *Geschichte der griechischen Literatur* (Handbuch der klassischen Altertumswissenschaft, VII [München, 1929] 1, 1, p. 275, note 2).

makes life worth living is their gift.[44] It is still more striking that in the language of comedy an adjective derived from the name of Cronus came to mean "old-fashioned" or "outmoded" and to imply ridicule and contempt. Even earlier than this the phrase, "the Golden Age," had become a figure of speech and was used not of the beginning of human history but of any age that seemed to be preferable to the present. Thus, according to Aristotle, it was a common saying in Athens after the reign of Pisistratus that his tyranny had been the Golden Age (*Constitution of Athens*, 17, 6); and to the allies of Athens the time of Aristides was the Golden Age. (Plutarch, *Aristides*, 24.)[45]

Tragedy, when dealing with the early history of the human race, could not dispense with mythology, and yet it too had evidently fallen prey to progressive thought. According to Aeschylus, Prometheus out of "love of mankind" (*Prometheus Bound*, 10–11 and 28) provided men, who at first were "like shapes in a dream" (449 ff.) and destitute of all the goods of life, with the blessings that attend the possession of the arts and crafts. (450 ff.)[46] Another culture-hero presented by the three great tragedians is Palamedes; and this participant in the Trojan War was credited not

[44] Cf. W. Meyer, *Laudes Inopiae* (Göttingen, 1915), esp. pp. 7, 28, who also discusses the connection of the views expressed by Aristophanes with those of Democritus.

[45] Wilamowitz (*Aristoteles und Athen* I, p. 119) suggests that the comparison with the Golden Age is an addition of Plutarch's; but this is improbable in view of the fact that Aristotle in the passage quoted (for the restoration of the text cf. K. von Fritz and E. Kapp, *Aristotle's Constitution of Athens* [New York, 1950], p. 184) attests the use of the phrase in the fifth century. So also at the end of that century the term "ancestral constitution" was understood to mean not one that had existed at the beginning of time but rather the constitution of Cleisthenes, Solon, or Aristides (cf. G. Murray, *Aristophanes* [New York, 1933], p. 56). The evidence for Cronus as a symbol of dotage was collected by Lovejoy and Boas, *op. cit.*, pp. 78 ff.

[46] The origin of the Aeschylean passage is much debated; Xenophanes, the Pythagoreans, and the religious tradition concerning the "first inventor" have all been suggested as the poet's source; cf. F. Solmsen, *Hesiod and Aeschylus*, p. 143, note 92. I think it most likely that he was influenced by Pre-Socratic theories; cf. Jaeger, *Paideia* I, p. 263. If the account given is boldly materialistic (G.D. Thomson, *Aeschylus and Athens* [London, 1941], p. 327), it is no more so than that of Xenophanes or Anaxagoras; cf. above, p. 22. Whether or not there was a sequel to *Prometheus Bound* (cf. Solmsen, *op. cit.*, p. 147), the speech of Prometheus is not an exhaustive list of inventions; he foresees that men will add many more to those that he enumerates. See also L. Golden, "Zeus the Protector and Zeus the Destroyer," *Classical Philology*, LVII (1962), 20 ff.

43

only with the invention of the letters of the alphabet and of dice but also with that of weights and measures, of numbers, and of the division of the day into hours.[47] Even the share of mere mortals in the progress of human life was acknowledged. The Aeschylean Prometheus does not forget to say that men, since they are in possession of fire, will learn many arts in the future (253 ff.). Sophocles celebrated the inventive genius of man who, by himself, overcame the primitive conditions in which he originally lived, and built up the world of civilization: "with plans for all things, planless in nothing, meets he the future!" (*Antigone*, 394.)[48] Tragedy, being Attic, had special praise for the contribution of Athens to the rise of civilization; and ample evidence of the popularity of this topic is provided by its employment in the funeral orations honoring those who died in war. Pericles' memorable speech in 431 B.C., in which according to Thucydides (II, 41) he described the growth of Athens in political power no less than in all that makes life worth living, is but one example of such encomiums.[49]

Religious sentiment too endorsed the belief that the beginnings of mankind had been savage rather than idyllic. Athena and Hephaestus bestowed their gifts upon beings whose existence was at first like that of the animals (Homeric *Hymn to Hephaestus*, XX, 3), and Orpheus had contributed to the rise of civilization (Aristophanes, *Frogs*, 1032); and, when in 418 B.C. the Athenians invited all Greeks to send sacrifices to Demeter, their plea was most probably based on the claim that Eleusis was the cradle of agriculture and therefore of all civilized life.[50] Greek religion even in its

[47] Cf. *s.n.* Palamedes, R.–E., 18, 2, cols. 2505 ff. He was a favorite subject of poetry, as may be inferred from Plato, *Republic* VII, 522 D.

[48] For an interpretation of this Sophoclean chorus see Friedländer's essay, *Hermes* LXIX (1934), 56–63.

[49] In general cf. O. Schröder, *De laudibus Athenarum* (Diss. Göttingen, 1914), pp. 20 ff. Parochialism was not to be found among the Athenians alone. Arcadia too was celebrated as the home of inventions (Pausanias, VIII, I, 4 ff.; see Nestle, *Vom Mythos zum Logos*, pp. 145 ff. [from Hellanicos?]). Remnants of other catalogues of inventions survive from the fifth century; cf. Lovejoy and Boas, *op. cit.*, p. 383; see also Simonides of Ceos, 8 T 1 (Jacoby, *Fr. gr. Hist.*).

[50] For the cult of Demeter and the festival of the year 418 cf. M.P. Nilsson, *Greek Popular Religion* (New York, 1940), p. 56; for Orpheus cf. Linforth, *op. cit.*, pp. 67 ff. The hymn to Hephaestus cannot be dated exactly. According to Jaeger (*Paideia* I, 472, note 73) it may have been "already a reflection of Aeschylus' Prometheus." At any rate, there is no reason to put the poem later than the fifth century. For its

earliest stage was not antagonistic to the achievement of the arts and crafts (were they not god-given?) but opposed only the attempt to equal or surpass divine mastery, for it was feared that such *hubris* would evoke the wrath of the deity. The subsequent worship of "culture-heroes" sanctioned the belief that the arts and crafts had been inventions of especially gifted individuals; and by the fifth century this cultural optimism, rare in the preceding century, had permeated the popular religion.[51]

Wherever people looked back, then, progressivism seems to have made inroads. It cannot have been the opinion of the majority that the gods revealed everything to men at the beginning and that the happiest times were behind them, nor can there have been many dreamers who, with Hesiod, hoped for a new and better world to be created by Zeus. The political planners of the fifth century were quite determined not to leave the future welfare of mankind to a benign deity or in the hands of any god, for that matter. The vogue of their schemes is amply attested in comedy, which caricatures them and makes utopians of them.[52] More immediate and less extreme means of repairing the current situation were found in democratic procedure and legislative changes. The advocates of the written law as against the unwritten law saw in the codification of the laws a special instrument for the improvement of prevailing con-

---

possible Athenian origin cf. T.W. Allen, W.R. Halliday, and E.E. Sikes (eds.), *The Homeric Hymns* (2d. ed.; Oxford, 1936), pp. 410 f.; and for the date of the minor hymns in general, *ibid.*, p. cix.

[51] For the *Kulturoptimismus* of the religion of Demeter cf. Nilsson, *Geschichte der griechischen Religion* I, 631; for that of the cults of the culture-heroes cf. Kleingünther, op. cit., p. 39. For the Homeric conception of the envy of the gods, cf. K. Lehrs, "Vorstellungen der Griechen über den Neid der Götter und die Überhebung," *Populäre Aufsätze aus dem Alterthum* (2d. Auf.; Leipzig, 1875), pp. 33 ff.; F. G. Welcker, *Griechische Götterlehre* (Göttingen, 1857–62), II, 738. Lovejoy and Boas (*op. cit.*, p. 192) hold that the Greek concept of "the gods' jealousy" conflicts with anti-primitivistic thought, but so far as I can see the old saga never considers knowledge as such to be an object of divine jealousy. The belief in the fifth century that Zeus harbors a grudge against men and destroys their happiness (cf. Lehrs, *op. cit.*, pp. 40 ff.) is merely an indication of the pessimism current at that time; cf. below, p. 53.

[52] Cf. Pöhlmann, *op. cit.*, I, 313 ff. and 322 ff. As has been pointed out by A. Doren (*Vorträge der Bibliothek Warburg*, 1924/25, p. 164, note 9), Pöhlmann sometimes goes too far in his interpretation of the evidence outside of the two Aristophanic plays (pp. 307 ff.); but on the whole he is quite justified in emphasizing the importance of "utopianism" in Aristophanes' time and in holding that it is in general a sign of progress (II, 120).

ditions. "And that [cry] too is of liberty, 'Who having some good counsel for the city is willing to bring it in the middle of all?' " says Euripides in his defense of "the laws written down." (*The Suppliants*, 438 ff.; cf. 433.) It is perhaps a sign of the same assurance that at the end of the fifth century there was greater trust in the goddess Hope and a firmer belief in man's ability to work things out for himself.[53]

The possibilities could not have appeared to be seriously limited by theories about the meaning of time either. It is true that the Pythagoreans of the fifth century probably taught the eternal recurrence of identical events, and Empedocles believed in a continually recurring cycle of events. There is no evidence that the other Pre-Socratics believed in world-periods that would be identical in number rather than in kind.[54] Apart from such speculations, time as ordinarily experienced by men was thought to be the realm of new happenings. For men like Polos and Gorgias "experience makes our life proceed in accordance with art, and lack of experience in accordance with chance" (Plato, *Gorgias*, 448 C); and the discussions beginning with those among the Seven Sages about the nature of time—whether or not it is the wisest—reveal this same tendency. Time either refutes or confirms opinions.[55] The outstanding contemporary historical writings reveal a similar attitude. Herodotus,

[53] Cf. L. Schmidt, *Die Ethik der alten Griechen* II, 74. (Concerning the connection between hope and progress see below, chap. III, p. 115.) For the debate on the written and the unwritten law and its political significance, cf. Hirzel, *op. cit.*, pp. 63 ff. Euripides consistently defends the written law, while Sophocles speaks equally consistently in favor of the unwritten law (Hirzel, pp. 69 ff.); for further material see F. Leo, *Plautinische Forschungen* (2. Auf.; Berlin, 1912), pp. 141 ff.; Euripides, Fr. 388, 2 is characteristic.

[54] According to Bury (*The Ancient Greek Historians*, p. 205 [cf. *The Idea of Progress*, p. 9]) a cyclical theory of the world-process was implied by Anaximander and Heraclitus; but it is now generally recognized that such a concept was foreign to the latter (cf. G.S. Kirk, *Heraclitus*, pp. 318 ff.), and to Anaximander the notion of recurrent periods is ascribed only by later Peripatetic sources. The Pythagorean belief in cycles is attested for the first time by Eudemus (Fr. 88 [Wehrli]), and so it is not certain that this view was held even by the Pythagoreans of the fifth century.

[55] For the archaic concept of time cf. above, chap. I, p. 10. For the debate among the Sages cf. above, chap. I, p. 13 and note 28; for the sophists cf. Nestle, *Vom Mythos zum Logos*, pp. 155, 331, and 373. Material from poets and medical writers has been collected by W.A. Heidel, *The Heroic Age of Science*, pp. 45 ff. On the Greek commonplace that "time discloses and teaches all things" (*ibid.*), see also below, chap. III, p. 66.

46

whose description of the conflict between the Greeks and the barbarians is a history of the world, looked upon historical development as leading up to the victory of Athens, the spiritually superior power. He assumed that enlightenment was waxing. The cycle of events of which he spoke refers to the instability of human happiness, which never remains the same (I, 5; cf. 86); but this pessimistic belief that the "wheel on which the affairs of men revolve" (I, 207) raises one and brings another low he shared with other ancient progressivists.[56] As for Thucydides, although he did hold that history repeats itself, he hardly meant to assert that there will be nothing new under the sun or that "all things are forever as they were." By writing of the events that he had himself witnessed, he hoped to help others acquire a better understanding of events that will occur in their own time. Their experience, however different in detail, will, he believed, resemble his own, for they are men too. His book is not "a sort of horoscope" of things that are bound to come, but was intended to be a guide for future generations and for future action.[57]

Thus, on the whole, the climate of opinion was more favorable to the idea of progress than it had been when Xenophanes first announced his confidence in the advance of mankind. Then "the cake of custom had been broken," and a few were capable of sharing in the new vision; but now enlightenment had spread. Perhaps nothing better characterizes the change of temper than the way in which Herodotus criticizes the Athenians, who at the end of

[56] Cf. below, p. 53. For the political point of view of Herodotus see A. Täubler, *Tyche: Historische Studien* (Leipzig, 1926), pp. 66 f., and F. Jacoby, *Atthis* (Oxford, 1949), p. 129, note 5. The explanation of his conception of the cycles of events I owe to K. Reinhardt ("Herodots Persergeschichten," *Von Werken und Formen* [Godesberg, 1948], pp. 167 ff.), but the conception ought not to be classified as religious or metaphysical. Reinhardt himself underestimates the historical consciousness of the Greeks; but his interpretation is an effective refutation of the common view that Herodotus taught identical recurrence, e.g., Löwith, *op. cit.*, pp. 66 ff. and C.N. Cochrane, *Christianity and Classical Culture* (Oxford, 1940), p. 468, and does not require even the support of a reference to Herodotus' interest in inventions, which itself also argues against a pattern of events.

[57] Cf. Gomme, *op. cit.*, I, 149. K. Weidauer's attempt in *Thukydides und die Hippokratischen Schriften* (Heidelberg, 1954), to show that Thucydides considered his work to be useful because of the repetitiousness of history was refuted by H. Diller (*Gnomon*, XXVII [1955], 13). As in the case of Herodotus, I disregard the progressivism of Thucydides, the historian of culture.

the sixth century had allowed themselves to be tricked by a religious ruse. Pisistratus after his expulsion from Athens had had a woman, clad like the goddess Athena and riding in a chariot, enter the city preceded by heralds who proclaimed that Athena herself was conducting the tyrant back. The historian is at a loss to understand the success of this device, "the silliest to be found in history" (I, 60), "considering that the Greeks from very ancient times have been distinguished from the barbarians by superior sagacity and freedom from simpleness, and remembering that the persons on whom the trick was played were not only Greeks but Athenians, who are credited with surpassing all other Greeks in cleverness." (*Ibid.*) Such "foolish simpleness" had vanished by the fifth century. The sagacity which according to Herodotus naturally distinguished the Greeks from the barbarians, their wisdom, as he calls it elsewhere (VII, 102), was becoming the ideal of life for those who had united Greece and had set themselves apart from the barbarians.[58]

This change brought new values with it. People were primarily citizens and still honored the athletic victor and rejoiced in his success; but unlike their forefathers, who had failed to honor Xenophanes, they admired and honored Herodotus and Gorgias too. When Aristotle speaks of the new learning which all of Greece embraced, he cites by way of example the fact that the Spartans learned to play the flute. (1341 a 32 f.) The new music that they welcomed was realistic rather than hieratic, imitating sounds of nature and scenes of daily life. The new art-forms in poetry—comedy and tragedy—reflected the currents of the intellectual movement either in interpreting the old stories or in subjecting the modern ideas to ridicule and criticism. The power to analyze and account for what one is and does—a Greek gift if any gift is peculiarly Greek—expressed itself in novel techniques and in novel concepts. The sublimity and monumentality of the new sculpture which was extolled conjured up before the very eyes of man the

[58] On the Herodotus passage cf. G. Murray, *Five Stages of Greek Religion*, (New York: Anchor Books, 1955), chap. II, *init.*; also Grote, *A History of Greece* IV, 30 (p. 281, note 1). A similar opinion is expressed by Euripides, *Medea* 190 ff. For the contrast between Greeks and barbarians see H. Diller, *Fondation Hardt*, Entretiens, VIII (Genève, 1962), 39 ff. and esp. 67 f.

ideal of a human being sure of himself and master of his fate. Progress meant enlightenment more than material progress. In fact, the conditions of daily life did not alter considerably as compared with those of the sixth century. It was as if people felt that in this respect what had been done in the past was sufficient, whether it had been done by Greeks or Orientals; and, although the rôle of economic power and of technological advance in politics and warfare was better appreciated, control of the environment was not of primary concern. Advance was not measured by statistics of export and import or industrial production in general. The new culture that arose was above all an intellectual and aesthetic culture.[59]

In these circumstances it is no wonder that mythology receded into the background. The disenchantment of the world was not complete. The gods were still powerful and were still recognized and revered, and their advice was still asked through oracles and prophets. Natural phenomena such as the eclipse of the sun, although they had been explained by science as regular occurrences, were still taken as omens especially in times of trouble or of war. The hand of the deity was visible in human affairs even to rationalists like Herodotus, and even the Athenians could expel philosophers for impiety. The rationalization of myth as such had become common, however; and the old inherited stories were openly and violently attacked. Allegorical exegesis had sought to make the tales of Homer and Hesiod acceptable by finding the wisdom of the day hidden in statements quite innocent of such advanced knowledge. "The fictions of earlier men" against which Xenophanes had turned were no longer a serious threat.[60]

If there was a general feeling that ran counter to progressivism, it

[59] For this brief sketch I am indebted mainly to Burckhardt's analysis of "Der Mensch des V. Jahrhundert." The emphasis placed on the progress of culture and of culture as represented by music and poetry will be understood if it is remembered that in the Greece of the fifth century these arts were the concern not merely of private individuals, but of the state, which organized performances, and that they also formed the basis of all education. Cf. in general B. Snell, *Poetry and Society* (Bloomington [Ind.], 1961).

[60] For the beginnings of the allegorical interpretation in the fifth century, cf. F. Wehrli, *Zur Geschichte der allegorischen Deutung Homers im Altertum* (Zürich, 1928). At the same time a rationalization of all mythology was undertaken by writers like Herodorus and Palaephatus (cf. Nestle, *Vom Mythos zum Logos*, pp. 148 ff.).

was the idealization of the "Noble Savage," to which Protagoras took such vigorous exception. It became more common than it had been in earlier literature to paint in glowing colors the easy affluence of races in distant lands. There can be discerned also the beginnings of what has been called animalitarianism, praise of the life of the brutes, so much more carefree and self-sufficient than man.[61] This disparagement of civilized life indicates the first awareness of the burden that progress puts upon society. Economic competition increased, and social unrest was intensified. Technological advances made fighting more deadly; and imperialistic policies, dependent to a large extent upon the new technology, made war more frequent and more devastating, as the fifth century learned not from books but from bitter experience.[62] Besides, among the population of the city-states political interest preponderated and bred for manual work a contempt hitherto unknown or, at any rate, less extreme and emphatic. Having no professional ambitions, men were more eager to enjoy the advances in the arts and crafts than they were willing to labor in their service. Consequently, they loved to indulge in fantasies and tales of a fairyland where everything was different and therefore better.[63] It is daydreaming of

[61] For animalitarianism see Lovejoy and Boas, *op. cit.*, p. 19 and pp. 389 ff. I take it that this movement began in the fifth century—Aesop's fables are well known in Aristophanes' time (*Birds* 471)—; but I am not convinced that Democritus, Fr. 198 is an anticipation of animalitarianism (contrary to Lovejoy and Boas, *op. cit.*, p. 391), for the statement in question is not meant to show how much wiser than man the animals are but implies instead that man's senses are wiser than his reason. (Cf. Frs. 125, 159; also Zeller, *Die Philosophie der Griechen in ihrer geschichtlichen Entwicklung* I, 2, 928.) For the Noble Savage see Lovejoy and Boas, pp. 287 ff. The increasing frequency of idealized pictures of the savage is observed by Nestle (*Vom Mythos zum Logos*, p. 286).

[62] As Herodotus (VI, 98) says, between 522 and 424 "more ills befell Hellas than in twenty generations before Darius, ills which came in part from the Persians and in part from the wars fought for preëminence among the chief states of Greece themselves." The significance of this statement and of one by Thucydides (I, 17), which may have the same meaning, is emphasized by A.J. Toynbee, *A Study of History*, p. 190.

[63] Rohde (*Der griechische Roman*, p. 214) was perhaps the first to observe that the exclusion of all manual work from the representation of a perfect life is connected with the fact that the concept of "the nobility of toil" was foreign to Greek thought. Cf. H. Michell, *The Economics of Ancient Greece* (New York, 1940), p. 14, who has also shown that democracies and oligarchies alike in the fifth century were more contemptuous of the workman than in the pre-classical centuries (*ibid.*, pp. 11 ff.).

a kind not uncommon among those who live in a period when civilization is making great strides, but it is also the vehicle for criticism of certain aspects of civilization (e.g., Herodotus, IV, 79); and both romantic escapism and critical reflection were bound to increase with the awareness that culture is the work of man and is both his deed and his responsibility. In this sense both are a symptom of the acceptance of progressivism rather than its refutation.

In sum, it is hardly hazardous to assume that in the classical age the modes of thought that had once opposed Xenophanes' contention had grown weaker, that the appeal of the idea expressed by him was growing much stronger, that instead of having few adherents his thesis had acquired a zealous faction consisting of people from all walks of life and of all political persuasions, democratic and aristocratic alike, and that progressivism and anti-progressivism at least held each other in balance.[64] Even many of those who chose to champion what was old, men like Aristophanes or the author of *On Ancient Medicine*, were not altogether unaffected by the new that they denounced. Aristophanes like other comic poets was proud of having "new ideas," as he says in the same play in which he inveighs against the new (*Clouds*, 547), and "of doing things that nobody has done before" (*Wasps*, 1536); and the Hippocratic author defended what was old with all the sophistication and learning of his day. It is safe to believe also that just as according to Protagoras the partisans of the Noble Savage, had they had to live with him, would have longed "to revisit the rascality of this world," so the defenders of what was old, had they been transported into the past, would have longed for the present. The assertion is, of course, beyond proof; but, as it would probably be plausible in any age, it was especially so in the fifth century. Uncivilized life could still be observed—in the neighborhood, as it were. Even in Greece itself rather old-fashioned conditions prevailed to a large extent, and there was outspoken contempt for the people of Megara and

---

[64] Lovejoy and Boas in writing the history of primitivism came to the conclusion that anti-primitivism in the fifth century was "increasingly conspicuous" and "aggressively manifest" (p. 194) and also observed that anti-primitivism ignored political distinctions.

Boeotia as simple-minded country folk. In such circumstances it must have been obvious that, while one might dream about the ways of life at the end of the earth and glorify a past when values now missing were cherished, the distant and the past lacked much of the present that one would not willingly abjure.[65]

Moreover, the progressive trend of the fifth century must have been difficult to resist just because its sanity and its toughness reflect the tragic sense of life that characterizes the age. It cannot be denied that the enthusiasm for progress sometimes has a tone of playfulness, that the new is considered pleasing simply because it is new, and there were modernists especially among the artists, who were "lovers of the new," as they were called later (Ps. Plutarch, *On Music*, 12, 1135 c) [66]; but, whenever reasons are given, the tenor of the language is sober and quite different from Xenophanes' passionate and unequivocal endorsement of the new as the better. The rise of civilization is now held to be a biologically or mechanistically determined *conditio sine qua non* of human life and its survival. The new is thought to win out over the old because it is stronger. What is and can be improved within the limits of the possible is taken to be the general situation, the structure of institutions, the state, the city.[67]

Improvement of the individual, of his moral character and his happiness, was hardly envisaged. The subject of much of Thucydides' history is the corruption inevitably linked with the rise of political power, itself largely the outcome of material welfare (e.g., V, 85–113). The relativism of the Sophists, the acknowledgment by a Callicles, for example, that might is right, eliminates any

---

[65] The difference between the levels of civilization within Greece and in the neighboring "barbaric" countries hardly needs comment. The funeral speech of Pericles in its praise of Athens as the center where all the products of the earth come together (Thucydides II, 38) indicates clearly that such riches were not yet taken for granted.

[66] In calling the theory of progress in the fifth century modernistic I mean to say that change itself was understood as good, just as sometimes it has been regarded as evil. The theoretical possibility of such a theory of progress is discussed by Simmel, *Die Probleme der Geschichtsphilosophie*, pp. 200 f.; see also above, Introduction, pp. xxix f.

[67] Cf. above, pp. 31 f., 33, 35. I need not comment on the fact that some of the formulations of the concept of progress in the fifth century retain the agonistic overtones of Xenophanes' statement.

thought of moral progress. Even those who avoided such extremes viewed the situation with grave realism. Sophocles, though far from belittling the greatness of human achievement and even marvelling at the daring of man the inventor (*Antigone*, 322 ff.), still renders a final verdict that is deeply skeptical: "passing the wildest flight of thought are the cunning and skill that guide man now to the light, now to the counsels of ill" (367 f.). It was not imagined that the individual can hope for a life free from unhappiness. Democritus declared that human existence is feeble and short, immersed in pain and difficulty, and its hardship can be diminished only by using as a standard for one's needs and wishes the absolutely necessary and indispensable. (Fr. 285 [Diels–Kranz].) The system of Prodicus was probably the first consistent formulation of pessimism. Antiphon emphasized over and over the dark aspects of life, endeavored to teach an "art assuring freedom from pain" (80 A 6 [Diels–Kranz]), and wrote the first *consolation of philosophy*.[68] Obviously, the progressivists shared the pessimistic outlook of classical poets and historians and took a somber view of the possibility of human happiness, as did the intellectual elite generally. "Man is altogether a thing of chance," says Herodotus (I, 32); and "learning comes from suffering." (I, 207.) Like some later believers in the reality of progress past, present, and future, those of the fifth century could not convince themselves of the validity of a hedonistic calculus. Their creed might rather be expressed in the words of a philosopher and statesman of the eighteenth century: "Although I do not with enthusiasts believe that the human condition will ever advance to such a state of perfection as that there shall no longer be pain or vice in the world, yet I believe it susceptible of much improvement, and most of all in matters of government and religion; and that the diffusion of knowledge among the people is to be the instrument by which it is to be effected."[69]

[68] H. Diels, *Der antike Pessimismus* (Berlin, 1921), p. 21.

[69] I quote Jefferson's credo from H.J. Muller, *The Uses of the Past* (New York, 1952), p. 278. James in a similar vein said that despite all progress "the solid meaning of life is always the same eternal thing," that no matter how great the number of improvements they will not "make any genuine vital difference on a large scale." (*Talks to Teachers* [New York, 1900], p. 299.) The pertinent material on pessimism is collected by Diels, *op. cit.*; cf. also W. Nestle, *Neue Jahrbücher für das Klassische Altertum*, XLVII (1920), 81 ff.

In one respect only can appreciation of the rise of civilization have ameliorated skepticism and pessimism. Anaxagoras and Democritus celebrated the power of the mind to overcome the blows of fortune (A 33 [Diels–Kranz]) and its capacity to provide happiness greater than the happiness that riches bring. (Fr. 118 [Diels–Kranz].) As Euripides puts it: "Blessed is he who has gained the knowledge of science. He has no impulses to harm his fellow men or to do unjust deeds; he contemplates the ageless order of deathless nature, how it came to be formed, its manner, its ways. Such men have no care for deeds of shame." (Fr. 910 [Nauck].) Like the poet of old (*Odyssey*, III, 267 ff. and Athenaeus I, 14 a–d) those to whom knowledge is given are prudent and temperate. This belief in the blessedness of the contemplative life as the highest accomplishment of civilized man, this intellectualism, checked to some extent the native Greek pessimism inspired by the vicissitudes and misfortunes of active life, and thus indirectly gave to civilization itself a moral and eudaemonistic value.[70]

At the end of the fifth century, it is true, a much more extreme optimism made its appearance. There are those, Euripides says, who claim "that amongst men the worse things are more than the better." He espoused the contrary opinion, however. "There are more good things for mortals than bad, for, if this were not so, we should not exist in the light." (*The Suppliants*, 196–200.) By means of reason, speech, the invention of the arts and crafts, and agriculture the confused and brutish state of human life "was regulated." (201–13.) It is a god, however, who accomplished this feat (201 ff.); and it is he who must be praised, whose wisdom we must admire, content with what he has given us. (214 ff.)[71] Xeno-

[70] See in general F. Boll, "Vita Contemplativa," p. 15. Euripides, Fr. 910 goes with Gorgias, *Palamedes* 31; cf. Nestle, *Vom Mythos zum Logos*, p. 330. The debate about the value of the practical and the theoretical life in Euripides' *Antiope*, fragments of which are preserved, must have been especially famous.

[71] The Euripidean verses are the echo of a philosophical disputation, and the question "is there more of the good for man than there is of the bad?" must have been asked frequently; cf. H. Diels, *Der antike Pessimismus*, pp. 20 f. There is no need to assume a contamination of sources on the part of Euripides because he speaks alternately of man and of god as inventors (contrary to W. Theiler, *op. cit.*, p. 38), for the author of the Hippocratic treatise *On Ancient Medicine* does the same thing (cf. chap. 3 with chap. 14).

phon ascribes a similar opinion to Socrates. Civilization is within the divine plan, so to speak, and therefore a task imposed upon man and one to be executed by him. Fire, the helpmate in every craft without which nothing serviceable to mankind can be had, is a gift of the deity and attests his love of men and his providence. (*Memorabilia*, IV, 3, 7.) This doctrine precludes the acceptance of any primitivistic creed or the endorsement of animalitarianism (I, 4, 2 ff.) and undertakes to justify the ways of god. Caring for the happiness of men, he has given them the power to do the right; and men can carry out his intentions by learning to understand them and to yield to them.[72]

Such a teleological interpretation cannot have had wide currency as yet, however, and must have been unacceptable to the naturalists, who resigned themselves to the limits of human nature. Clinging to Xenophanes' belief that it is man and not god who makes the world over, the "Pre-Socratics" emphasized man's strength and his ability to rise above the level of his original animality.[73] It constitutes his grandeur that, once having been like the animals, he is capable of leaving them behind; but he is not omnipotent. The whim of the moment gives and takes away earthly goods, earthly rewards, earthly happiness; and, in conflict with forces greater than himself, man's only way of overcoming them is to understand them by means of contemplation. This recognition of man's limitations distinguishes classic progressivism from much of later ancient as well as modern progressive thought and gives it a tragic aspect befitting the tragic age of antiquity.[74] It is this same truth that must

[72] For the source of the passage of Xenophon see W. Theiler, *op. cit.*, pp. 36 ff. Xenophon follows Antisthenes and Diogenes but also philosophizes on his own. In my context this distinction is of no importance, for the passage from Euripides just quoted shows that teleological thought was current in the time of the historical Socrates. Cf. also Herodotus III, 108.

[73] Cf. again Whitehead, *Adventures of Ideas*, p. 115. Other passages which, in addition to those quoted above, note 7, contain the expression "brutish" are Critias, Fr. 25, 2 (Diels–Kranz); Aeschylus, *Prometheus Bound* 453; Euripides, *The Suppliants* 202; *On Ancient Medicine* chap. 3; Archelaus in Isocrates, *Nicocles* 5 ff. (Uxkull, *op. cit.*, p. 11, note 21). The frequency of the term's occurrence, observed by Kleingünther (*op. cit.*, p. 39, note 86), indicates that its use is characteristic of the literature.

[74] The epithet, "tragic," used by Nietzsche in his essay *Die Philosophie im tragischen Zeitalter der Griechen*, seems to me to describe the fifth century better than "classic."

have given men the strength to maintain their trust in progress even during the horrors of the thirty years' war at the end of the fifth century. Undoubtedly, the weaker spirits faltered in the face of events; but the leaders of the movement can hardly have done so, for what they believed in was the progress of culture, of the arts and sciences, which go their own way despite human suffering and political failure and are the true achievement of past, present, and future generations.[75]

[75] E.R. Dodds in his book, *The Greeks and the Irrational*, where he has drawn attention to a long-neglected aspect of Greek thought, comes to the conclusion that "Protagoras before he died had ample ground for revising his (belief in progress)," p. 184; and he goes on to describe the reactions to progressivism, the persecutions of intellectuals, the wartime hysteria, the reaction against immoralism, and the relapse into primitivism, one form of which he finds in the cult of Asclepius (pp. 188–193). Concerning Asclepius, who according to ancient tradition counted Sophocles among his devotees, I need not argue here (see E.J. Edelstein and L. Edelstein, *Asclepius II, passim*); but, if the belief in progress in the fifth century b.c. is not identified with the optimistic faith current in England in the nineteenth century (p. 184), the conclusion of the historian must be different from that drawn by Prof. Dodds. There may have been a temporary crisis, but that there was a decisive turn of events at the end of the fifth century cannot be asserted. This seems to be clear from the evidence quoted; and it will be corroborated, I think, by the development in the fourth century.

III

With the close of the fifth century and the breakdown of Athenian hegemony, a chapter in the political history of Greece was ended. During the fourth century the independent city-states lost power and strength and were finally superseded by the Macedonian monarchy and the world empire of Alexander. No less significant were the changes in general outlook which began in the last decades of the preceding age but assumed their full importance only now. These were in some measure both responsible for the political development and intensified by it. The community with its demands and its tasks ceased to be the center of the life of the citizen, who became conscious of himself as a free personality with views and rights of his own. More and more he looked upon the outside world not "through the medium of his city, but directly, as it were, with his own eyes and in its bearing on him individually."[1]

Transformations as far-reaching as these do not come about without bitter dissension in the field of politics as well as in that of theorizing about actual events. There must have been those who lamented the decay of the old order and those who identified

[1] J.B. Bury, *A History of Greece*, p. 560. Cf. also H. Berve, *op. cit.*, II, p. 76. There is disagreement as to when in the fifth century the political "decline" began; cf. G.C. Field, *Plato and His Contemporaries*, pp. 107 ff. On the other hand, the time from the fall of Athens to the death of Alexander, roughly speaking the fourth century, is generally recognized to be a distinct historical unit; and it is in this sense that I speak of "the fourth century."

themselves with the new. There must have been both despair and hope. Which of the two reactions was the more characteristic of the time is a question to which modern interpreters have given various answers. Some say that the fourth century was one of discouragement, the effects of which permeated philosophy, literature, and art as well as political and moral reflection. Others, far from admitting a general feeling of failure, find that the "capacity for sustained effort and constructive imagination was little impaired, as the history of Greek art, literature, and science no less than of politics and strategy declares. In fine, the fourth century was not an age of senile decay but of mature and active manhood."[2]

The student of the history of the idea of progress may at first be inclined to side with those for whom disillusionment is the outstanding feature of the period between the fall of Athens and the rise of the kingdoms of the Diadochi, for he cannot fail to be impressed by the fact that during that period the trust in human advance was challenged in an unprecedented manner by some of the new philosophical schools. The teaching of Antisthenes and Aristippus called into question the premises of civilization, the acknowledgment of the value of theoretical and practical knowledge. The Cynic doctrine condemned civilization altogether; and it may reasonably be argued that its criticism is indicative of the general response to the dissolution of inherited forms of social existence and to the political turmoil and vicissitudes which revealed the vanity of all mundane affairs.[3]

[2] M. Cary, *Cambridge Ancient History* (Cambridge, 1927) VI, 25. The thesis that Greek life and literature after 400 are deeply moulded by the conviction of failure is most forcefully upheld by G. Murray, *Five Stages of Greek Religion*, pp. 76 ff.: "The Great Schools of the Fourth Century B.C." For the various evaluations of historians see G.P. Gooch, *History and Historians in the Nineteenth Century* (Boston [Mass.]: Beacon Press, 1959), pp. 446 ff.

[3] Cf. Murray (*op. cit.*, pp. 83 ff.), who in his account does not include Aristippus. I have named him together with Antisthenes, since the philosophies of both, divergent as they are in their evaluation of the good, lead to the same negative attitude to the world in which man lives, a similarity recognized even by the ancient testimony; cf. F. Ueberweg–K. Praechter, *op. cit.*, p. 176; and Zeller, *op. cit.*, II, 1, 372 f.; and in general C.J. Classen, "Aristippos," *Hermes*, LXXXVI (1958), 182 ff. On the other hand, I make a distinction between Antisthenes' doctrine and that of the Cynics because Cynic rigorism is presented clearly for the first time in the teaching of Diogenes, whether he merely transformed the tenets of Antisthenes

It is true that Antisthenes and Aristippus, the followers of Socrates, were not opposed to all learning and education. The former stressed the importance of philosophical training, especially of logic and epistemology (Epictetus, I, 17, 12); and the latter maintained that it is better to be a beggar than to be without mental culture, "for the one needs money, the other needs humanization." (Diogenes Laertius, II, 70.) Yet both thinkers emphasized ethics to the neglect of the other branches of philosophy, and they restricted the scope of objective knowledge and thereby the sphere of scientific inquiry.[4] Moreover, they were concerned primarily with the goodness and happiness of the individual which they identified with his "self-sufficiency" (αὐτάρκεια). Antisthenes demanded a return to the simple, natural life and renunciation of everything that may endanger inner freedom. Aristippus exalted enjoyment but urged acceptance of whatever might happen, whether good or bad, without letting oneself be enslaved by either. Thus detachment was the watchword of the ascetic Antisthenes and of the hedonist Aristippus alike. Both recommended withdrawal from society and its concerns. They permitted man to continue to live in the world of civilization but left him no incentive to work for it or to contribute to its advance, for man to reach his true goal must learn to be indifferent or superior to all things. Progress in understanding, consequently, could mean only increasingly clear recognition of that form of self-contained existence for which man is destined, so that he may reduce the complexity of social activities to proportions that he considers fitting and sufficient for human dignity.[5]

(Ueberweg–Praechter, *op. cit.*, p. 168) or was the founder of Cynicism (D.R. Dudley, *A History of Cynicism* [London, 1937], p. 15).

[4] Cf. e.g., Ueberweg–Praechter, *op. cit.*, pp. 162, 174.

[5] This evaluation of culture and progress is not explicitly expressed in the preserved fragments, but the evidence seems to imply it. Scanty and inconsistent in details as this evidence is, beginning with the reports of Xenophon (*Symposium* IV, 34 ff.; *Memorab.* II, 1), a contemporary of Aristippus and Antisthenes, it shows that their aim was "*Befreiung des Menschen durch die Einsicht, Erhebung desselben über die äusseren Dinge und Schicksale*" (Zeller, *op. cit.*, p. 372). Antisthenes achieved this goal by "living with himself" (Diogenes Laertius, VI, 6), that is by renunciation; but Aristippus did so by "living with all things" (Diogenes Laertius, II, 68), that is by making use of them without "being possessed by them" (*idem.*, II, 75); cf. Zeller, *ibid.*, and p. 364. Their criticism of civilization was negative and did not advocate changes of the established institutions. R. Höistad's contention (*op. cit.*) that

Thus the doubt expressed in the fifth century that the cultivation of the arts and science had made life happier or man better came to have practical significance. Antisthenes and Aristippus, convinced that the human good whether of soul or of body need not be identical with the good produced by the unchecked process of civilization, restricted the activity of the individual. This attitude of aloofness distinguishes the doctrine of the Socratics from the teaching of their master and gives an entirely different turn even to the views they had in common with him. Socrates too had warned his pupils not to busy themselves too much with the investigation of scientific problems. He wished them to study geometry and astronomy only to the extent that these may be of practical use (Xenophon, *Memorab.*, IV, 7, 2–5); and he restricted physical studies by disapproving any attempt to discover the laws that govern celestial phenomena, since the gods had not chosen to reveal their secret. (*Memorab.*, IV, 7, 6.) His summons to return to ethics, however, did not involve a conflict with civilization, which itself is divinely ordained. On the contrary, Socrates endorsed man's obligations within the community and urged upon him greater responsibility and stricter standards in these pursuits rather than abstention and detachment from practical life.[6]

With the Cynics, the anti-progressive tendencies inherent in the teaching of Antisthenes and Aristippus take an extreme form. Not only does Diogenes deride as useless and unnecessary music, geometry, astronomy, and other studies of this kind (Diogenes Laertius, VI, 73; cf. 104), recommending concentration on ethical practice, scolding the astronomers for neglecting "what is close at hand," and inveighing against the orators because they speak about the good yet fail to do it (Diogenes Laertius, VI, 28); but he finds all civilization a positive impediment to virtue. Human inventiveness and human ability to devise technical improvements have in his

Antisthenes had a positive political theory is unconvincing; cf. E.L. Minar "Review of R. Höistad . . .," *A.J.P.*, LXXII (1951), 436 f.

[6] For Socrates on progress, cf. above, chap. II, p. 55. In the "didactic conversations" too Xenophon gives his recollections of his teacher (E. Edelstein, *Xenophontisches und platonisches Bild des Sokrates* [Berlin, 1935], pp. 95 and 131 ff.), and what he says in *Memorab.* IV, 7 may therefore be used to reconstruct the teaching of the "historical Socrates."

opinion been of little benefit to mankind, for they have been misused for the aggrandizement of pleasure rather than devoted to the furtherance of courage and justice. (Dio Chrysostomus, VI, 28 ff.) This verdict of the Cynic, he holds, is not at variance with the foresight of the gods, for they withheld fire from the human race and punished Prometheus for stealing it and, as they would not out of hatred or envy have deprived men of anything beneficial, they must have considered civilization to be the origin of all evil. (Dio Chrysostomus, VI, 25.) [7]

For the Cynic, then, progress was not a god-given task but delusion and self-destruction. Nor could he be satisfied with preaching indifference to what might become harmful, for in fact the harm had already been done and to be virtuous and achieve moral perfection one had to abandon the ways of civilized life. A revaluation of all values was imperative. It was no longer enough to live a simple, natural life without the accretions of false pleasures or merely to free oneself from all involvement. Man must return to his original state before his fall from grace and before the existence of any of his proud inventions. He must imitate the example of the animals, who follow their instincts and are happy and content with what they have by nature. (Theophrastus in Diogenes Laertius, VI, 22.) [8]

[7] Kurt von Fritz ("Quellenuntersuchungen zu Leben und Philosophie des Diogenes von Sinope," *Philologus*, Suppl. XVIII, Heft 2 [Leipzig, 1926]) has shown that Diogenes Laertius' account of Diogenes is the most authentic one, while that by Dio Chrysostomus is quite unreliable. The interpretation of the story of Prometheus he like others ascribes to Antisthenes (p. 78), for, even though in the fragment surviving from the latter's *Heracles* Prometheus teaches Heracles that exercise in worldly affairs without knowledge of "the higher things in life" is of no avail, von Fritz supposes that at the end of the conversation the rôles were exchanged and that Prometheus was represented to be the destroyer of human life even as he is by Dio Chrysostomus. This is unwarranted, however, because Antisthenes did believe that for the philosopher the things of the spirit are important; cf. above, p. 59. On the other hand, the denigration of Prometheus, the fire-bringer, which is ascribed by Dio Chrysostomus to Diogenes here and also in VIII, 33, where Heracles appears as the teacher of Prometheus, is at least in accord with Diogenes' views, for he decided "to eat raw meat" (Diogenes Laertius, VI, 34), "a raw polyp" (Plutarch, *De Esu Carnium* I, 6, 995 C–D), in order to denounce the cooking of meat, which is "contrary to nature" and "makes man's soul swell from satiety and surfeit." (Zeller [*op. cit.*, p. 319, note 1] had already compared the passages quoted with Dio Chrysostomus, VI, 25.)

[8] For Diogenes' praise of animals, cf. further Dio Chrysostomus, VI, 26 f. and Dudley, *op. cit.*, p. 32. The Cynic was consistent enough to assume that "the first men" could live without fire, houses, clothes, or any nourishment other than that

No harsher or more far-reaching indictment of progress can be imagined than that pronounced by the Cynic of the fourth century. His very life was a denial of civilization itself, of that seemingly splendid superstructure that mortals have erected above their true needs, desires, and aims. He tried to break the chains by which the individual had come to be shackled in the course of history. While progressivism early in its development had identified the rise of the arts and sciences with man's liberation from the bondage of an initially savage and animal-like existence, with his increasing humanization, Cynicism championed the superiority of the beasts, the doctrine of animalitarianism in its most outspoken form. While the anti-progressivists of earlier centuries had tended to defend old values against novel ideas and had been wary of the new and untried, Cynicism subverted all cultural values. In the hands of Diogenes it became "the first and most vigorous philosophic revolt of the civilized against civilization."[9]

How widespread was this disillusionment with culture which for the first time finds expression in deeds as well as in words? It is certain that the circle of Antisthenes, Aristippus, and Diogenes was small;[10] and it cannot be maintained that the feeling of dissatisfaction underlying their censures was a common malaise to which they merely gave exaggerated expression. In the general opinion, no matter how great the political and moral crisis, civilization itself

---

afforded by the earth herself (VI, 28). Consequently, a life according to nature was one stripped of "all the accretions of conventions, tradition, and social existence" (Dudley, *op. cit.*, p. 31); in contrast to Antisthenes he practised "absolute simplicity of living, absolute renunciation of comforts" (*ibid.*, p. 10). Any kind of law or convention he considered to be unnatural (Diogenes Laertius, VI, 72; cf. von Fritz, *op. cit.*, pp. 59 ff.).

[9] Lovejoy and Boas, *op. cit.*, p. 118. The question of the nature and degree of the difference between man and animals had, of course, been discussed before Diogenes (*ibid.*, p. 389); but the Cynics were the first to "fuse animalitarianism with primitivism by sometimes substituting animals for primitive men in their depreciation of civilized man" (p. 391). For Democritus, Fr. 198 (Diels–Kranz) see above, chap. II, note 61.

[10] Only through Crates, a younger contemporary of Diogenes, does Cynicism seem to have exercised a popular appeal, at least in Athens; and, ascetic though he was, he did not maintain the original rigor of the doctrine. He treated people with kindliness, attempted to free them from self-deception, their greatest disease in his opinion, and played the rôle of a moral counsellor to all; cf. Dudley, *op. cit.*, pp. 42–53. A criticism of culture based on the conception of self-sufficiency is perhaps to be found in a writing of Alexinus. (See Jacoby, *Fr. gr. Hist.* 70 T 31, and his commentary.)

was not in question. The first evidence of this is provided by the teaching of the three great schools that were contemporaneous with the Cyrenaics and Cynics and were all opposed to cultural primitivism.

Plato, first of all, although he was willing to grant that "the first men"—men at the beginning of a new cycle of history after the destruction wrought by some natural catastrophe—were "more righteous generally" (*Laws* III, 679 E) and also that they were "better" because the simplicity of their life and their ignorance of most things gave them less opportunity to be bad, still maintained that, if the height of villainy can be achieved only in a fully developed civilization, the same thing is true of maturity in virtue. (678 B.) It is consistent with such a view that he could let pass uncensored the remark that the "healthy city" of primitive conditions—healthy because it knows few activities in comparison with the multifarious occupations in the "fevered city" of later times—is "a city of pigs." (*Rep.* II, 372 D.)[11] The true "Islands of the Blest" (*Rep.* VII, 519 B) is for him the realm of ideas; and references to an earthly paradise or even to the reign of Cronus, occasionally introduced into his dialogues, he used as allegories (*Laws* IV, 713 C–D) or in order to suggest that what he considered to be the best policy could be put into practice (*Critias* 109 B ff.), for by saying that it once had been done in the highly developed Athens of another cycle of history remembered only by the Egyptian priests (*Timaeus* 22 A) he meant to indicate that it should not be beyond men of the present to do the same.[12]

[11] That the "healthy city" does not represent Plato's "wishful thinking" is shown by P. Friedländer, *Platon* II, 362. As he says, Plato in this passage is concerned neither with historical explanations nor with polemic against other ideals but with the principle that as prefigured in the primitive society virtue could exist only in an imperfect form. Cf. also below, pp. 85 f.

[12] After scrutinizing the pertinent passages in the dialogues mentioned, Lovejoy and Boas (*op. cit.*, pp. 156–164) came to the conclusion that none of them justifies classifying Plato as an adherent of primitivism, though certain sentences taken out of context "could plausibly be construed as giving support to cultural primitivism" (p. 158; cf. also p. 164). I fail to see that even in other passages Plato "gives a summary endorsement to the general thesis of chronological primitivism" (p. 168). Surely, he did not really believe that the gods have children (*Tim.* 40 D) or that there were heroes who were the sons of Poseidon or Zeus (*Republic* III, 391 D); and the sentence, "the men of early times were better than we and nearer to the gods" (*Philebus* 16 C), if not simply a literary reminiscence (*Republic* 391 E), can hardly

Plato's greatest rival, Isocrates, knew no higher praise to give Athens than that she had given civilization to mankind. (*Panegyricus*, 28–33.) In his many references to the development of culture he never so much as mentions the dream of a Golden Age of the past, and he frequently asserts that human existence in its initial stage was savage and therefore bad. (*Antidosis*, 254; cf. *Busiris*, 25; *Panegyricus*, 48.)[13]

That Aristotle, Plato's greatest pupil, had no patience with any primitivistic beliefs goes without saying. For him, "the earliest known human beings, whether they were 'earth-born' or the survivors of some cataclysm, were in all probability similar to ordinary or even foolish people today. (Indeed that is actually the tale that is told of the 'earth-born' men.) It would therefore be an absurdity to remain constant to their notions" (*Politics* II, 8, 1269 a 4–8), to the "barbarism," the "utter foolishness" of ancient customs. (1268 b 39 ff.)[14]

As to popular beliefs, the tale mentioned in passing by Aristotle—obviously so well known that it was unnecessary to give the details—cannot have been flattering to the "first men"; and Plato, too, speaks of the "proverbial simplicity" of early mankind. (*Laws* IV, 679 C.) Herodotus' view of the simplemindedness of archaic centuries had by this time, it seems, become a commonplace applied to the earliest times.[15] This makes it highly unlikely that even Aristotle's "ordinary" or "foolish people" of the day found much to praise in men of primitive times. To gauge their beliefs is extremely difficult because exceedingly few fragments survive from the poeti-

---

mean more than what the passage just quoted from the *Laws* (690 E) says about men at the beginning of a new period of history, concerning whose knowledge see *Laws* III, 679 C, and below, pp. 85 f. For Plato's criticism of his own time and his advocacy of the tenets of "hard primitivism," see Lovejoy and Boas, *op. cit.*, p. 167.

[13] Isocrates' endorsement of civilization is, of course, not contradicted by the fact that like Socrates he considered mathematical studies to have only limited usefulness in general education (*Antidosis* 261 ff.). He knew that the matter stands differently for the experts "who make their living" by such research (264). For details of his theory, see below, pp. 98 f.

[14] Aristotle was skeptical of the poetical tales about the "Islands of the Blest." If they exist at all, their inhabitants could not be happy without philosophy; *Politics* 1334 a 28 ff. (See E. Rohde, *Der Griechische Roman*, p. 214.) The remark is very much in the vein of Plato's *Politicus* 272 C.

[15] Cf. above, chap. II, p. 48.

cal works of the period. It is perhaps also true that the poetry of the fourth century was becoming literature to be read and so reflects the temper of the educated rather than of the general populace. Nevertheless, it is significant that such evidence as there is on the whole favors progressivism.

The fact that comedy ridicules Cynics and Cyrenaics has, of course, not much importance, for other philosophers too and notably the Pythagoreans were derided;[16] but, had there not been a fervent pride in Greek civilization, one could not account for the moving words of a barbarian slave who rejects the thought of betraying his master by recalling the benefits of his "savior" and "father": "Through him, I came to live under Greek laws, I learned to read, I was initiated into the mysteries of the gods." (Theophilus, Fr. 1 [Kock].) When the problem of man's early existence and of the value of culture is discussed at length in one of the tragedies, the answer given is definitely anti-primitivistic and has polemic overtones directed against the Cynic contention—perhaps the boldest of all their theses— that according to the law of nature nothing is bad, not even the eating of human flesh.[17]

"First I shall begin to unfold in my poem," says Moschion, "the original condition of human life. For once there was a time when men lived like beasts, dwelling in mountain-caves and sunless ravines. For there was not yet to be found either a roofed house or a wide city fortified with stone turrets. Nor was the black earth cut with curved ploughs to be a nurse of the ripening corn, nor did the pruning iron care for the exuberant rows of Bacchic vineyards, but the sterile earth lay silent and solitary. The flesh of their fellows was men's food. And Law was humble, and Brute Force was enthroned with Zeus, and the weak was food for his better. And when Time, the father and nurturer of all things, changed mortal life either by the forethought of Prometheus or through necessity or again through long practice making nature herself their teacher, then were cultivated fruits discovered, the nourishment given by chaste

[16] Cf. 58 E (Diels–Kranz), and in general A. Weiher, *Philosophen und Philosophenspott in der attischen Komödie* (Nördlingen, 1913).

[17] Diogenes defended cannibalism in his *Republic* and in his tragedies; cf. Dudley, *op. cit.*, p. 26. (The authenticity of the early catalogue of Diogenes' writings containing these works has been proved by K. von Fritz, *op. cit.*, p. 55–57.)

Demeter, and the sweet stream of Bacchus was found. And the earth, until then unsown, was now ploughed by yoked oxen; and cities were turreted and roofed houses were built; and they exchanged their savage life for one that is soft. And Law decreed that the dead be concealed in tombs and that the unburied dead be buried and not left before men's gaze as a reminder of their impious deeds." (Stobaeus, *Ecl.*, I, viii, 38 = Fr. 7, p. 633 [Nauck].)[18]

Moschion's prologue reads like a summary from a textbook on progress. The various agents that may be at work in the rise of civilization—forethought, necessity, long practice—are enumerated; and it is as if one were permitted to choose from among them and as if the choice were not very important, for in the last analysis all these powers are only handmaidens of time, which itself creates things and arranges events by its own devices. Time is, in Bacon's famous phrase, "the author of authors." (*Novum Organum*, I, 84.)[19] What truly engaged the emotions of the poet, however, is the contrast between the horrors of uncivilized life, from which he recoils, and the blessings of culture, which he treasures. His is the voice of a highly refined society. The thought of men once having eaten "their fellows' flesh" haunts his imagination; he celebrates the release from such "impious deeds" of primordial centuries through the law, order, and morality established by later generations. And one can sense his indignation at those who dare to attack the most precious achievements of mankind and to speak of a return to the dark ages, which are best forgotten.[20]

[18] The translation is taken from Lovejoy and Boas, *op. cit.*, p. 216. For the date of Moschion, cf. Christ–Schmid, *op. cit.*, I, 395.

[19] This comfortable belief, which makes progress almost an automatic outcome of time, is obviously sophistic, though in part reminiscent of the archaic concept of time; cf. above, chap. I, pp. 10 f. and chap. II, p. 46. The specific theories that Moschion had in mind cannot be determined. The tragic poet Chaeremon expressed his trust in progress in a form similar to that of Xenophanes: "There is nothing in this world that men searching for it do not find out in time." (Fr. 21, p. 788 [Nauck].)

[20] The satyr play, following the tragedy in the true Greek manner, is provided by a fragment from a work of the comic poet Athenio. According to him, it was the art of cooking that liberated mankind from cannibalism and it is really the progress in this art that led men to desire to live in communities (Athenaeus, XIV, 660 E—661 D = III, p. 369 [Kock]). The last statement incidentally testifies to the currency of the idea of continuous progress from the original state of barbarism to present civilization. Athenio's dates are uncertain. He may belong to the beginning of the Hellenistic era (Lovejoy and Boas, *op. cit.*, p. 213).

No wish was expressed to set the clock back in politics either and to revive a way of life that had been customary in the distant past, and this is true despite the fact that the slogan of the "ancestral constitution" played an increasing rôle. Demosthenes praised as "ancestral" the virtues of the fifth century (*Olynth.*, III, 35); and Isocrates, if he did not do the same (*On The Peace*, 26), imagined an early Athens that was democratic as was in reality the Athens of a much later day. (*Areopagiticus*; cf. Demosthenes, *Adv. Aristo-crat.*, 65–79.)[21] Even those who wrote the history of Athens, the Atthidographers, were not, as has often been claimed, inspired by a "romantic regret for a transformed past," as is "suitable for a time conscious of political decline." They saw the past of Athens as merely a phase in the whole development, and their interests seem to have been concentrated on the present. The "ancestral constitution" was the ideal constitution that each had drawn for himself.[22]

Furthermore, there can hardly have been a widespread belief that a better state of affairs existed among other distant peoples at the ends of the earth, a belief such as that in which the previous century had indulged itself despite its admiration of culture. At any rate, no such belief is expressed in the poetry of the fourth century. Even comedy, realistic as it had become and eager to expose the fancies of the human mind, pillories only the weakness revealed in the petty details of daily life.[23] A glorification of the Noble Savage can be detected only among historians who obviously used it for a particular purpose. Ephorus, feigning shock because his predeces-

---

[21] Burckhardt (*Griechische Kulturgeschichte* IV, 195, 337) rightly points out that the idealization of the fifth century began in the fourth. The attitude of Demosthenes and Isocrates is reminiscent of that of Aristophanes, who in fighting the democracy of his time recalled the Athens of Aristides (cf. G. Murray, *Aristophanes*, p. 56).

[22] F. Jacoby, *Atthis*, p. 112 (cf. 109) and pp. 113 ff., 213 ff.

[23] The mention of the Scythians by Antiphanes (Athenaeus VI, 226 C ff. = II, p. 75 [Kock]) might seem to be an exception, and it is treated by Lovejoy and Boas as an ironic reference to these tribes, which in his time began to be regarded as the prototype of the Noble Savage (pp. 289, 324); but, as will soon be seen, this view was at that time still unusual. Moreover, according to Athenaeus Antiphanes held the Scythians to be "the most miserable of men"; and the praise of their wisdom by his character, a fishmonger, is meant to emphasize the misanthropy of this class of people. The Scythians being barbarians, men without culture, the reference to them may be due not to the poet's wish to deride some idealization of them but simply to the traditional contrast of Greeks and barbarians, which Antiphanes mentions elsewhere. (Athenaeus, IV, 131 e–f = II, p. 81 [Kock].)

sors reported of the Scythians only "their savagery," refers on the authority of Homer and Hesiod to Scythians of another kind and tries "to set them up as an example" for their frugal living and their contempt of money, qualities responsible in turn for their justice, good government, and disdain of war and fighting. To be sure, these Scythians are not altogether ignorant of technical inventions and devices; but, "having everything in common," they are better than the rest of mankind. (Strabo, VII, 3, 9 = Fr. 42 [Jacoby].) Even if Ephorus thought that his description was true to the facts, still he introduced it in order to hold up to his contemporaries a mirror in which they might contemplate their own mistakes. His praise of distant countries, unique even among historians, was written for didactic purposes, as befitted the historian of Isocratean persuasion, criticism of the present rather than genuine belief in the values of primitive life.[24]

The romance or utopia written by Theopompus had the same purpose. A member of the school of Isocrates also, he could find only things to blame in the people whom he had occasion to mention, whether they were highly civilized or men still living in more primitive conditions. Therefore, when he wished to preach the gospel of moral truth, he, like Plato, invented a fable and one more fabulous than any of Plato's. On a continent beyond all known lands and visited only once by the Silenus Marsyas, life is entirely different from life here; it is better and happier. (Aelian, *Varia Historia*, III, 18 = Fr. 75 [Jacoby].) The story, admittedly fictitious, was invented, Theopompus declares, in order to divert

[24] Ephorus says that he follows Homer and Hesiod in his glorification of the Scythians. (According to Lovejoy and Boas, he "visited" their country [p. 288], but the word thus translated [περιοδεύσας, p. 327] can in this context mean only "having gone through the whole of Europe up to Scythia in his description.") In addition to literary sources, he is supposed to have followed Cynic teaching (cf. Jacoby, *Fr. gr. Hist.*, ad Fr. 42; also K. Trüdinger, *Studien zur Geschichte der griechisch–römischen Ethnographie* [Basel, 1918], p. 140); but, if this is true, his source can have been only Antisthenes, who found examples of right living among Greeks and barbarians alike (Diogenes Laertius, VI, 2), whereas Diogenes rejected civilization altogether, and the Scythians of Ephorus are not uncultured. Since Ephorus maintains that "the other writers" (i.e., other than Homer and Hesiod) give an unfavorable picture of the Scythians, he is unlikely to have been influenced by any contemporary author and may be justified in asserting that he was the first to introduce the Scythians as an example.

the reader's mind but also as a way of telling not what once was or now is but what ought to be.[25]

The characteristic note of thought in the fourth century, then, was not one of disillusionment with civilization itself. That human life and civilized life are one and the same and that the arts and crafts and sciences are great achievements of the human race, if not the very greatest, remained the firmly established conviction of the vast majority. Primitivism, the most dangerous enemy of progressivism, was on the wane rather than gaining in favor. It is not true that men, disappointed by the present, took refuge in a past when life had been less unwieldy and therefore less frustrating. They did not assume that mankind had decayed or that the original conditions of existence in a Golden Age had been a surer warrant of happiness.[26]

This is not very strange, for among the intellectuals, at any rate, the general conviction was that men were living in an age of incomparably great advance in all fields of intellectual endeavor. Aristotle asserted that "now" progress had been made from small beginnings within the shortest time by those concerned with geometry, logic, and the other disciplines such as had been made by no

[25] Theopompus too is said to have been influenced by "Cynic" philosophy; cf. especially G. Murray, *Greek Studies* (Oxford, 1946), pp. 149 ff. Antisthenes was, in fact, the only Socratic for whom he had any admiration (Fr. 295 [Jacoby] = Diogenes Laertius, VI, 14); but, whether or not one assumes such an influence on him as a moralist (cf. Trüdinger, *op. cit.*, pp. 140 ff.), Theopompus remains fundamentally an historian of the Isocratean school, as Murray himself admits (*op. cit.*, pp. 151, 156). For the story of the Meropians cf. E. Rohde, *Der griechische Roman*, pp. 204 ff.

[26] To be sure, primitivism did not disappear altogether; and there was admiration for other peoples and other cultures, even for those less advanced. Ctesias made India the land of fable *par excellence* and praised the justice of its inhabitants, doing so either for philosophical reasons or simply out of his love of the curious and miraculous; cf. E. Schwartz, *Fünf Vorträge über den griechischen Roman* (2. Auf.; Berlin, 1943), pp. 109 ff. Xenophon mentions the courage and outstanding strength of the Arcadians (*Hellenica* VII, 1, 22 ff.), not a highly civilized people; and Theopompus refers to their social equalitarianism (Fr. 215 [Jacoby] = Athenaeus, IV, 149 d; cf. Lovejoy and Boas, *op. cit.*, pp. 344 f.). Yet the inference that "the increasing luxury of the fourth century stimulated the development of the idea of 'natural simplicity' " (T.S. Brown, *Onesicritus*, p. 155, note 37, following Trüdinger, *op. cit.*, p. 137) is justifiable only if, like Trüdinger, one draws on the literature of Stoicism as well as of Epicureanism, movements not of the fourth century but of the beginning of the Hellenistic period, or like Brown on the historical novels and utopias written by the generation flourishing at that time (see below, chap. IV, note 16).

generation before in any of the sciences. (Iamblichus, *De Comm. Math. Scientia*, 26 = Aristotle, Fr. 53 [Rose]; cf. Fr. 52 [Rose] = Euclid, p. 28, 13 [Friedlein].) He had seen philosophy too make immense progress in a span of only a few years. (Fr. 53 [Rose] = Cicero, *Tusc. Disp.*, III, 28, 69.)[27] Plato had given specific examples of the rapidity of the progress made. In one of his earlier works, he introduced as quite recent what he considered to be the true doctrine concerning the surface of the earth (*Phaedo*, 108 C); and late in life he asserted that "not long ago" the course of the planets had come to be adequately understood (*Laws* VII, 821 E) and only "now" had the regularity of the movement of all celestial bodies and the nature of the forces controlling their movements, "before" only suspected, been fully grasped. (*Laws* XII, 967 A–D.) "Rather belatedly," he said, a theory of irrational numbers had been framed. (*Laws* VII, 819 D.)[28]

Other testimony is given in more polemic language and shows that from the height of their own achievement men looked down upon the contributions of their predecessors as a mere beginning. Thus, Aristoxenus protested loudly that before him no one had had anything worthwhile to say about music. (*The Harmonics*, I, 3, 4,

[27] The Aristotelian statements quoted are usually attributed to the *Protrepticus*, a relatively early dialogue of Aristotle; but see W.G. Rabinowitz, *Aristotle's Protrepticus and the Sources of its Reconstruction* (University of California Publications in Classical Philology, XVI [Berkeley, 1957]), 1 ff. For Fr. 52 cf. also W. Jaeger, *Aristoteles* (Berlin, 1923), pp. 97 ff. Assertions to the same effect, less sweeping in scope, but not different in spirit, appear in the Aristotelian treatises, *e.g.*, *Meteorol.* I, 3, 339 b 7 and 32 (concerning astronomy) and *Polit.* VII, 11, 1331 a 1 (concerning military science); see also Fr. 246 (Rose): "This is no longer a problem, for the facts have been seen," and *Magna Moralia* 1198 a 13: οἱ νῦν βέλτιον.

[28] E. Frank (*Plato und die sogenannten Pythagoreer*, pp. 23 ff. and p. 59) first emphasized the significance of the Platonic passages as evidence that the discoveries referred to by Plato were recent. Taylor in his translation of the *Laws* (p. 206, note 1) denies that the novelty of the theory of irrational numbers can be inferred from VII, 819 D; but cf. Frank, *op. cit.*, p. 228. Taylor himself takes *Laws* XII, 968 D and 969 B to be references to the Academy's progress in astronomy and legislation (p. 364, note 1). Details concerning the views called novel in *Phaedo* 108 C and *Laws* XII, 967 A have been variously interpreted, cf. Frank, *op. cit.*, pp. 184, 193; and, opposing him, H. Cherniss, *Aristotle's Criticism of Presocratic Philosophy* (Baltimore [Md.], 1935), pp. 395 ff.; it has also been debated whether Plato in *Laws* VII, 821 E ff., was thinking merely of the regularity of the planetary movements or anticipating the heliocentric theory (cf. the short summary by Taylor, *ad loc.*, p. 210, note 1). A resolution of these various problems seems to be unnecessary here, where the issue is only Plato's awareness of the progress achieved in his time.

6, 7). Theopompus declared that the writers who formerly held first rank in historiography were far inferior to the authors of his own time and would not be given even second place if they were his contemporaries. History, he added, had made great progress even within his own memory. (Fr. 25 [Jacoby] = Photius, *Bibl.*, 176, p. 120 b 30.) The author of the Ps. Hippocratic treatise *On Regimen in Acute Diseases* thought worthy of being put into writing "especially that which has not yet been discovered by physicians" (chap. 3). He admitted that his predecessors had dealt adequately with a great many things, but he added mordantly that these were precisely the things that even laymen might describe correctly if they only took the trouble to learn from the sick what ails them. In the truly medical interpretation of the data, that which the physician has to discover for himself and which the patient is unable to tell him, they had overlooked much in practically every field (chap. 1). It had thus far not been customary even to propose the kind of investigation that he was about to undertake, although, unless his new question was answered by physicians, medicine would not differ essentially from divination, where the same sign is interpreted as a good omen by one prophet and as a bad one by another (chap. 3, *finis*).[29]

As music, history, and medicine were thought by the workers in these fields to be undergoing revolutionary changes, the same was thought to be true of the fine arts and the art of rhetoric, so dear to the Greeks, by those who cultivated these subjects. According to Pliny (XXXIV, 65) Lysippus, the sculptor who adopted "a procedure new and hitherto not followed" and abandoned the artistic principles of his predecessors, used to say that they had represented the human body in its objective, numerical proportions, while he represented men "as they are seen to be," thereby arrogating to himself the merit of having for the first time given a lifelike quality

---

[29] The criticism is directed especially against the authors of the *Cnidian Sentences*, Euryphon and his associates; cf. J. Ilberg, "Die Ärzteschule von Knidos," pp. 4 f. Since they are contemporaries of Hippocrates, the essay can hardly be dated earlier than the first half of the fourth century. It is, I think, the work of a member of the Cnidian school of a younger generation; cf. L. Edelstein, Περὶ ἀέρων *und die Sammlung der Hippokratischen Schriften*, Problemata, IV (Berlin, 1931), 154 ff.; esp. p. 156, note 2, and below, p. 73, note 33.

and a realistic truth to the work of stone.[30] No less emphatic were the claims made by Isocrates for the originality of his rhetoric. Stating that no one had ever tried to vie in prose with the poetical encomiums on individuals as he attempted to do (*Euagoras*, 8 ff.), he justified his novel enterprise by asserting that in rhetoric as well as in the other arts and sciences and in fact in everything improvements come about not by abiding by the established tradition but by making revisions and having the courage to change matters whenever they are in a poor way. (*Ibid.*, 7.) For his political speeches, trusting that they would surpass all speeches made by previous orators both in style and in adequacy of subject matter (*Panegyricus*, 4;9), he expected the reward that should be given to all innovators, for oratory or in his terminology "the philosophy concerned with human discourse" like all arts and crafts can advance only when people cease to admire those who "have made a first start" and learn instead to honor those "who do them in the best way." (*Ibid.*, 10.)[31]

As to logic and philosophy, Aristotle in speaking of his refutation of Sophistic proofs contended that hitherto the subject had not been treated in part and partially neglected but had not existed at all (183 b 35 ff.). Of the concept of space he asserted that his precursors had not laid anything down or even formulated any problems on the subject. (208 a 34; cf. 209 b 15.) He said that generation and corruption had been dealt with superficially by everybody except Democritus (315 a 34) and that concerning growth no one had said anything that could not be said by anyone (315 b 1); and in discussing winds and waters he remarked in the same spirit that "just as in regard to the rest, so here too we have

[30] Though an anecdote, the saying of Lysippus is generally taken to be authentic and used in interpreting his workmanship; cf. e.g., Franz Winter, "Griechische Kunst," *Einleitung in die Altertumswissenschaft*, ed. A. Gercke and E. Norden (3. Auf.; Leipzig, 1922), II, 176. See also G.M.S. Richter, *The Sculpture and Sculptors of the Greeks* (New Haven [Conn.], 1950), p. 288; below, pp. 77 f.

[31] F. Dümmler (*Akademika* [Giessen, 1889], pp. 58, 272), who emphasized the importance of these two passages, also suggested that Isocrates' belief in progress is ridiculed in the figure of Hippias in Plato's *Hippias Major*. Hippias, however, was himself a defender of what is new; cf. above, chap. II, p. 26, so that, if Plato thought that a representation of Hippias was a jibe at Isocrates, the implication would be that the positions of the two were essentially the same. (Isocrates' belief in "progress" is referred to in passing by Jaeger, *Paideia* III, 152.)

not found anything said by a writer that could not have been said by just anybody." (349 a 14 f.) In his work *On the Heavens* he wrote: "This question, then, has become, as one might expect, a subject of general inquiry. But one may well wonder that the answers suggested are not recognized as being more incomprehensible than the question which they set out to solve." (294 a 19 ff.)[32]

It is in agreement with such proud self-assertion that writers of the fourth century used the term "the ancients" to include generations not far removed from their own or even the generation of their own youth. Isocrates in referring to the "ancient teachers of wisdom" meant Empedocles, Ion, Alcmaeon, Parmenides, Melissus, and Gorgias, whose "juggling devices" he thought attractive only to fools. (*Antidosis*, 268 ff.) Theopompus, so sure that the historians of his day were superior to those of old and so certain of his own accomplishments, named Herodotus, Hellanicus, and Ctesias among those whom he surpassed (Fr. 381 = Strabo, I, 2, 35). The physician of whom I have spoken meant by "the ancients" (*On Regimen in Acute Diseases*, chap. 11) or "elders" (chap. 14) whom he took to task especially the authors of the *Cnidian Sentences*, that is Euryphon and his associates or, roughly speaking, older contemporaries of Hippocrates.[33]

In Platonic and Aristotelian usage the term in question is quite precise and has a definitely dyslogistic implication. In mentioning "the famous men of old" (*Sophist*, 243 A) Plato is thinking of

[32] I owe most of these passages to R. Eucken, *Die Methode der Aristotelischen Forschung* (Berlin, 1872), p. 5, notes 3 and 4. It is interesting to note that twice Aristotle uses the same word as the Hippocratic author does (above, p. 71) to indicate that the knowledge of previous generations was that which anyone, i.e., a layman, could have.

[33] Cf. above, note 29. Democritus once speaks of "ancient views" (ἀρχαῖαι [δόξαι]) concerning the sun and moon which he charges Anaxagoras with having plagiarized (Fr. 5 [Diels–Kranz]). Diels (*ad loc.*) took this to mean that in Democritus' opinion Anaxagoras had copied Leucippus. W. Kranz ("Empedokles und die Atomistik," *Hermes*, XLVII [1912], 41, note 1) denied that Democritus could have applied the word "ancient" to the immediately preceding generation and explained Aristophanes, *Knights* 507, the parallel quoted by Diels, as a reference to a poet old in years in contrast to the young Aristophanes. The Aristophanes passage perhaps has the sense Kranz attributed to it, for the *Knights* is one of the poet's earliest plays; but, since the evidence given in the text shows that in the fourth century the word in question did include the preceding generation and since Democritus lived into the fourth century, Diels' interpretation may be correct.

Parmenides and his followers and of Empedocles and his associates. They "address us as if we were children," he says (243 C), "to whom they are telling a story," and he submits their inspired utterances to a criticism made even sharper by the professions of awe and reverence that he intersperses in it. "The ancients," as he puts it elsewhere, are the philosophers since Thales, including the "later" Anaxagoras. (*Hippias Major* 281 C; 283 A.)[34] For Aristotle they are the philosophers from Thales to Anaxagoras and Democritus—the Pre-Socratics, as they are now called. (*Metaphysics* I, 1069 a 25; *On Generation and Corruption* I, 341 a 6; *On Parts of Animals* 640 b 5 ff.) Their knowledge was only the "stammering" and "vague" expression of the truth (*Metaphysics* I, 993 b 15), although in some of these early philosophers, notably in Anaxagoras and Democritus, something "newer" or more modern can be detected (*Metaphysics* I, 989 b 6; *On the Heavens* 308 b 31); but on the whole their insight is antiquated and out of date.[35]

This general indictment is specified in the emphasis frequently placed upon the ancients' lack of knowledge. The physician and historian Ctesias, for example, in words that have a familiar ring to

[34] Cf. Also *Gorgias* 518 E—519 A, where "the old statesmen" are Themistocles, Cimon, and Pericles; and *Laws* XII, 967 B and D, where Anaxagoras is certainly included among the thinkers who "then" divined what is "now" known. There is no reason, therefore, to doubt the authenticity of the *Hippias Major* on the ground alleged by M. Pohlenz that Plato could not have spoken of Anaxagoras as one of the ancients (*Aus Platos Werdezeit* [Berlin, 1913], p. 125 and "Review of D. Tarrant, *The Hippias Major Attributed to Plato*," *Gnomon*, VII [1931], 305.) On the other hand, I am not convinced by P. Friedländer (*Platon* II, 291, note 31) that in this dialogue Anaxagoras is not included among the ancient philosophers, for the πρότεροι (283 A) with whom Anaxagoras is ranked are surely the ἀρχαῖοι, as the sentence immediately preceding shows. Pohlenz's further contention that Plato could not have attributed a theoretical ideal of life to a Pre-Socratic is hardly reconcilable with the mention of Thales in the famous excursus in the *Theaetetus*, on which see Friedländer, *Platon* II, 436 ff.

[35] Although the Aristotelian usage of the term "the ancients" is generally recognized, its dyslogistic connotation (see also *Problemata* 922 b 3 and 918 a 13) is not always remembered. (The exception occasionally made with respect to Anaxagoras and Democritus is emphasized by E. Frank, "Mathematik und Musik und der griechische Geist," *Logos*, IX [1920–21], 243; cf. also the expression "the more recent of the ancients," *Physics* 185 b 29.) This usage must be distinguished from the eulogistic connotation that the word has when Aristotle treats the knowledge of the ancients as a survival of what was found in earlier highly developed civilizations; cf. *Metaphysics* XII, 8, 1074 a 38—b 14; *Meteorology* I, 3, 339 b 20; *On the Heavens* I, 3, 270 b 16 and 9, 279 a 23; II, 1, 284 a 2 and 284 b 2.

modern ears condemns the shortcomings of medicine before his time: "In the generations of my father and my grandfather no physician prescribed hellebore, for they did not know how to mix a potion of it or the measure and amount in which to give it; and, if a physician ever dared to prescribe a potion of hellebore, he first asked the patient to make his will, since he was facing great danger, and of those who took the potion many were choked to death and only few survived. Now, however, hellebore seems to be a perfectly safe remedy." (In Oribasius, *Collect. Medic. Reliquiae*, VII, 8.)[36] Aristotle has variations on the same theme. "Parmenides did not yet know," he asserts (*Physics* I, 3, 186 a 32), or "dialectic was not yet well-known then" (*Metaphysics* XIII, 4, 1078 b 25); and in the same spirit as that of Galileo and Kepler, who felt sure that they could have convinced Aristotle of his mistakes if they could only have communicated their new discoveries to him, the latter exclaims: "[my predecessors] . . . would perhaps have left off holding their childlike opinions, had they been able to contemplate what mathematical research now has shown conclusively to be true." (*Meteorology* I, 3, 339 b 32–34; cf. 339 b 30.)[37]

The fourth century, then, was surely not given to adulation of the past but, if anything, was more self-consciously modern than the fifth. Not only did it carry on the battle between the ancients and the moderns that the fifth century had initiated, but it took a much more aggressive stand. Instead of merely claiming the right to be themselves, men rejected the inherited tradition as obsolete. It had forfeited its right to exist and had been supplanted by the new science. On the whole, such was also the outcome of the *Querelle* that began in the seventeenth century. One cannot fail to notice, in fact, how much more radical and in a way more modern were the moderns of ancient times than those of the "battle of the books." The ancients whom the seventeenth and eighteenth centuries were intent on driving from the scene were authors who had lived two thousand years earlier or more; but the criticism of the fourth century B.C. did not spare even the works of those great men of the

[36] *Corpus Medicorum Graecorum* VI, 1, 1 (ed. J. Raeder, 1928), p. 261, 12–25.
[37] For Kepler and Galileo cf. E. Cassirer, "Die Antike und die Entstehung der exakten Wissenschaft," *Die Antike*, VIII (1932), 279.

fifth century who only recently had wrought a transformation of all intellectual life. Plato's Eleatic, beginning his refutation of his spiritual father Parmenides, fears that he will appear to be a "parricide." (*Sophist*, 249 D.) It is, indeed, an epithet suitable to all the moderns in the fourth century.[38]

Their claim to superiority will seem to be pretentious, of course, to the devotee of the fifth century, for whom that age is the classical century *par excellence*. Yet with regard to the sciences their attitude was certainly justified, and so it was regarded by ancient historians until their judgment of the past was perverted by classicistic prejudices and all discoveries began to be attributed to a few great individuals who lived at the beginning of the scientific enterprise, while the names of those who came afterwards were condemned to oblivion. In the older accounts of mathematical discoveries not Pythagoras but Theaetetus and Eudoxus, Plato's contemporaries, are given preeminence. The early Alexandrian tradition still ranked Praxagoras and Chrysippus with their predecessor, Hippocrates; and Diocles was "second in fame as well as in time" to Hippocrates. (Pliny XXVI, 10 = Fr. 5 [Wellmann].)[39] One cannot quarrel with this judgment if one considers Theaetetus' theory of irrational numbers, his "invention" of stereometry, Eudoxus' astronomical investigations, or the achievements of the three physicians, which can still be gleaned from the fragments, scanty though they are; and, if one adds the hypothesis of the rotation of the earth on its axis and its revolution around the sun, Aristotle's creation of biology, the mathematical studies of the so-called Pythagoreans, and Euclid's establishment of mathematics

[38] I need hardly add that the passages quoted refute Bury's assertion that the people of Plato's age were not "self-consciously modern" (*The Idea of Progress*, p. 8). They were, if anything, even more conscious of their modernity than were those of the seventeenth century, for which see Lynn Thorndike, "Newness and Novelty in Seventeenth Century Science and Medicine," *The Roots of Scientific Thought*, ed. P.P. Wiener and A. Noland (New York, 1958), pp. 443 ff.

[39] For Diocles as a contemporary of Aristotle, cf. W. Jaeger, *Diokles von Karystos*, *passim*, and L. Edelstein, "Review of W. Jaeger, *Diokles von Karystos*," A.J.P., LXI (1940), 487. For Hippocrates, Praxagoras, and Chrysippus, cf. L. Edelstein, Περί ἀ , pp. 123–126. For the early Greek view of the history of science, cf. e.g., Mekler, *Academicorum Philosophorum Index Herculanensis* (Berlin, 1902), pp. 15–17, or the fragments from Eudemus' history of mathematics, especially Fr. 133 (Wehrli) = Proclus, *In Euclidem*, p. 64, 16 ff. (Friedlein).

as a systematic science, the modern verdict too must be that the progress achieved in the fourth century or from the time of Anaxagoras to that of Aristotle was incomparably greater than was that of the period from Anaximander to Anaxagoras and that the work done in the late fifth century only hinted at the beginning of things to come.[40]

The ancient critics and a strictly historical point of view can help one to understand the pride of the historians, artists, and rhetoricians of the fourth century, also. Ephorus composed the first universal history, which Polybius did not hesitate to praise. (V, 33, 2 = T. 7 [Jacoby]; XII, 28, 10 = T. 23 [Jacoby].) The replacement of the annalistic scheme by treatment according to subject matter required a more sophisticated technique of narration, and understanding of the individual was immeasurably enhanced by the new genre of historical biography. As Dionysius of Halicarnassus says (*Epistula ad Pompeium*, 6, 7), Theopompus in his analysis of human motives excelled all who had come before him and all who wrote later. His bold appraisal of earlier historians and of his own contemporaries is therefore not without foundation. One can recognize Herodotus and Thucydides as peerless in their insight into the objective forces determining the fate of states and individuals without for that reason decrying as mere oratory or declamation the work of their successors in the fourth century who greatly refined the methods of historiography.[41]

As for sculpture, when Lysippus contrasted his art of lifelike representation to the older art and claimed to have done what

[40] Cf. A. Rehm and K. Vogel, *Exakte Wissenschaften*, in *Einleitung in die Altertumswissenschaft*, ed. A. Gercke and E. Norden, (4th ed.; Leipzig, 1933), II, 5, p. 28.

[41] Jacoby in his commentary on Ephorus, T 11, has drawn attention to some of the work on historiography done between the time of Thucydides and that of Ephorus (p. 37, 19–23), material often overlooked by modern interpreters. Concerning Theopompus' verdict he says: "*Die Polemik gegen die Vorgänger war von ruhiger, vom Standpunkt seiner Zeit selbstverständlicher Uberlegenheit*" (p. 360, 6–9; cf. 360, 3; *Nachweis der befähigung* [*Prototyp Thuk.*, V, 26, 5]). J.B. Bury (*The Ancient Greek Historians* [New York, 1909], pp. 160 ff., esp. p. 165) exaggerates the pernicious influence of rhetoric on history, though naturally he too stresses the "limitations" of Thucydides' work (pp. 146 ff.). The ancient discussion concerning the relative merit of Thucydides and Theopompus is sketched by H. Bloch, *Harvard Studies in Classical Philology*, Suppl. I (1940), 311 ff. For the Peripatetic historical writings and the beginnings of biographical writing cf. below, pp. 94 f.

earlier artists never did, it is clear from the context in which Pliny quotes the statement (XXXIV, 65) that he spoke as one who had increased the potentialities of his craft by the invention of new means, illusory representation. The wonder at the conquest of illusion—the ability of "sculptors or painters whose works are of colossal size" to reproduce not "the true proportions of a well-made figure" but "those that will appear beautiful"—is echoed in Plato's analysis of the art of the imitator. (*Sophist*, 235 E ff.)[42] In other words, the fine arts were still preeminently techniques. A technological theory of art being still predominant, art was judged in technological terms. The day had not yet come for assuming that different art-forms represent different ways of seeing the world and that the genius of the artist is decisive for the greatness of his accomplishment, which itself is timeless.[43] In fact, a technological history of art prevailed down to the first century after Christ; and even then the development of sculpture was viewed in the main as a development of techniques, and Lysippus was accordingly assigned his place within it. (Cf. Quintilian, XII, 10, 3–6.) The same is true of the development of painting. The work of the fourth-

[42] See Plato, *Hippias Major* 281 D—282 A, where it is said that today the statues of old are ridiculed. The Ps.–Aristotelian *Problemata* pass a similar judgment in stating that among the "old painters and sculptors there was no excellent painting or statue anywhere, but many inferior," for, as has been said before, "the full realization is not the first step, but it is hard to achieve," and "the same principle applies to works of nature as to works of art" (X, 45). Incidentally, E.H. Gombrich, who explains the importance of the conception of mimesis for ancient art by the interest in the correct representation of illusion, maintains that progress towards the conquest of illusion was to the ancients what technical progress is to the moderns, "the model of progress as such." (*Art and Illusion* [New York, 1960], p. 11.) In view of the material on progress referred to in my analysis this would seem to be an exaggeration. (I owe to Charles Singleton my knowledge of Gombrich's view.)

[43] For the term "technological theory of art," taken from A. Riegl (*Stilfragen* [Berlin, 1893]), see E. Rothacker, *Logik und Systematik der Geisteswissenschaften* (Bonn, 1926), p. 32. There is no need here to discuss the opposite view, according to which the past is to be understood in categories such as classical or romantic. For the "romanticism" of fourth-century art, see e.g., L. Curtius, *Die Antike Kunst* (Berlin, 1923–39) II, 1, pp. 326 ff. I should, however, observe that B. Schweitzer, emphasizing the fact that the fine arts down to the fourth century were considered as crafts, i.e., as mastery of the technical rules ("Der bildende Künstler und der Begriff des Künstlerischen in der Antike," *Neue Heidelberger Jahrbücher* [1925], pp. 63 ff.) ascribes to Lysippus the rejection of τέχνη as artistic tradition because he is said to have imitated not artists but nature (Pliny, XXXIV, 61). Even if the story is not an invention of Duris, the pupil of Theophrastus, it does not contradict the interpretation that I have given of the other anecdote, which is certainly genuine.

century painter Apelles marks the high point of portraiture after the small beginnings made in that genre in the fifth century.[44]

Isocrates' rhetoric was to the ancients an art comparable with poetry. Even Plato and Aristotle paid him the compliment of regarding him as an extraordinary stylist, although they recognized that his new prose, which replaced the prose of Protagoras and Gorgias as a model of writing, was merely the vehicle of his "pragmatism" and that this in the form of rhetorical education was the one kind of intellectual training that competed with their philosophical instruction. Throughout antiquity and in many phases of later European history there was to be rivalry between rhetoric and philosophy, a bitter struggle over the question whether the Isocratean or the Platonic ideal was the better guide to right living; and this not without reason, for Isocrates too believed in reforming human nature by training in the art of words that transcends the boundaries of nationality as do philosophical and scientific training and maintained that participation in Greek culture made everyone, even barbarians, Greek. (*Panath.*, 26.)[45]

In fields where the practitioners do not themselves testify to their feeling of superiority there is at least evidence of the opinion that their contemporaries had of these innovators. At the hands of Philoxenus the dithyramb underwent changes similar to those that Timotheus had introduced into cithara-playing, and Antiphanes considered this to be the "true music." (Athenaeus, XIV, 613 e–f = II, p. 102 [Kock].) In general, the chromatic mode was now

[44] Polygnotus and Aglaophon were the first painters whose works deserve to be looked at "not merely for the sake of antiquity"; Zeuxis and Parrhasius added a great deal (the former invented the art of light and shade, and the latter improved the art of delineation); and in the age of Philip painting reached its climax (Quintilian, XII, 10, 3–6). Apelles' "inventions" helped all other artists (97; cf. 79). Through the doors opened by Apollodorus Zeuxis entered into the sanctuary of art (Pliny, XXXV, 60 ff.). In these late authors the conception of the fine arts as techniques is already combined with other criteria of historical development, for example that the fourth century was the climax of ancient art. (The Mausoleum, the tomb erected for Mausolus who died in 351 B.C., was in their opinion "among the Seven Wonders" [Pliny, XXXVI, 30].)

[45] For the conflict between rhetoric and philosophy see H. von Arnim, *Leben und Werke des Dion von Prusa* (Berlin, 1898), pp. 4 ff.; and for Isocrates see W. Jaeger (*Paideia* III, 46 ff.), who stresses the difference between his teaching and that of the sophists and his claim to being considered the forerunner of the humanistic movement.

preferred to the enharmonic one. The "sweet" music so-called, which originated with Agathon and in its passionate pathos and sensual charm was parallel to the style of Praxiteles and Scopas, provoked Plato's violent censure (*Rep.* 396 B), though even he had to admit that the musicians of his time were gifted. (*Laws* III, 700 D.)[46] The drama developed new forms, not displeasing at least to Aristotle. (*Poetics* VI, 1450 a 25 f. and *Rhetoric* III, 12, 1413 b 12 f.) Comedy of the fourth century, in the opinion of later critics, was far superior to that of the fifth, which they denounced as indecent as well as aesthetically imperfect. The middle comedy renounced the foul language of "obscenity" (Aristotle, *Eth. Nic.* IV, 14, 1128 a 22 ff.); and there is no reason to doubt that the public thought this an improvement, as did Isocrates (*Ad Nicoclem* II, 42 ff.; *On the Peace* 14), Plato (*Laws* XI, 935 E–936 A), and Aristotle. (*Politics* VII, 17, 1336 b 3–5 ff.)[47]

That Plato and Aristotle, the idols of many ages, did not sway their own age is clear from the contemporary criticism still extant. It also follows from the fact that most of their students thought themselves able to devise new systems superior to those of their scholarch. Still, although for them as "modern thinkers" philosophy "became mathematics" (Aristotle, *Metaphysics* I, 9, 982 a 32 f.), they took their start from the advances made by Plato and Aristotle; and so they cannot have accorded the Pre-Socratics the admiration that in recent times it has become customary to pay them but must have thought of them instead as their teachers had done. The reason for this is not far to seek. Whether materialism or idealism provides the true answer to the philosophical riddle, the Platonic and Aristotelian systems obviously integrated the novel scientific knowledge and were more in accord with the data of experience then available and with mathematical research as it had been developed than were the pictures of the world drawn by Anaximander or by Anaxagoras or even by Democritus, all of which

---

[46] For the development of music, cf. Frank, *Plato und die sogenannten Pythagoreer*, pp. 6–10.

[47] The later criticism of the old comedy is preserved in Plutarch's *Comparison of Aristophanes and Menander* and in Aristides' *Oration* XIX. For an interpretation of its aesthetic principles, cf. Schmid–Stählin, *op. cit.*, I, 4, 447 ff., and for the general character of the Middle Comedy *ibid.*, pp. 445 f.

must have looked naïve compared with those of Plato and of Aristotle.[48] Moreover, Platonic and Aristotelian philosophy is imbued with a power of abstract reasoning and logic unknown to the Pre-Socratics. The interpreter who tries to understand early Greek speculation in categories suited to the time of its origin and not borrowed from Plato or Aristotle can hardly contradict the latter's verdict that the chief cause for the difficulties encountered by his predecessors in discussing philosophical issues was "their putting the matter in an archaic manner." (*Metaphysics* XIV, 2, 1089 a 1–2; cf. XIV, 6, 1093 a 26–28.)[49]

So much for the intellectuals and their progressivism, but to understand the attitude of the fourth century it is important to recognize also that, whatever the decline in the political power of the city-states, archaism was overcome in daily life too by a rationalization and control of the environment hitherto unknown. The number of large factories and industries increased; division of labor was intensified; a banking system was developed; export and import trade was greatly expanded with improvement of shipping facilities and technical devices that made seafaring at all times of the year more secure than it had ever been. In short, the economy was refined and modernized. Reforms of the tax system and of military training made the administration of public affairs more effective. Most important, governmental offices began to be entrusted to specialists, and it was no longer considered feasible for every citizen regardless of training to be entrusted with any and every state function. The professional military leader of an army of citizens or of a standing army of professional soldiers, the financial expert, and the diplomatist made their appearance.[50]

[48] It is the merit of E. Frank to have stressed the "modernity" of Plato's and Aristotle's picture of the world and to have explained it by the influence exercised by scientific mathematics on philosophical thought, *Logos*, IX (1920–21), 243 f.

[49] One example of the progress in logical analysis is Plato's recognition of the immaterial substantiality of qualities; cf. H. Cherniss, *Aristotle's Criticism of Pre-socratic Philosophy*, pp. 369 f. In general see W.A. Heidel, "The Logic of the Pre-Socratic Philosophy," in *Studies in Logical Theory*, Decennial Publications of the University of Chicago, (2d. series; Chicago, 1903), XI, 203–226; also Ernst Hoffmann, "Die Sprache und die archaische Logik," *Heidelberger Abhandlungen zur Philosophie und ihrer Geschichte*, III (1925), an analysis of Pre-Socratic logic from the point of view of its archaism.

[50] Cf. H. Berve, *op. cit.*, II, 76 ff. and Bury, *A History of Greece*, pp. 570 ff.

By accident the evidence preserved most clearly illustrates the trend toward modernization and its effects in matters of warfare. New weapons and new artillery had made obsolete the old method of conquering cities. Instead of laying siege to a stronghold one could now take it by storm. Archidamus, the King of Sparta, confronted by the Sicilian catapults, is said to have exclaimed: "By Heracles, human courage has gone." (Plutarch, *Moralia* 191 D and 219 A.)[51] The invention and improvement of such instruments was not haphazard either. When Dionysius of Sicily prepared for the war with Carthage, he summoned specialists from all over Greece to construct new machines for him and to strengthen the resources of his power by land and sea. He himself supervised their work, and the citizens were drawn into it too. Philistus, the historian who reports the events (Diodorus, XIV, 41–43), insists that, had Dionysius not mobilized this army of scientific experts, his enterprise might have ended in disaster almost at the beginning. (51, 7.)[52]

That such an attitude, such consciousness of the manageability of things, was not restricted to individuals, whether political reformers or enlightened tyrants, is proved by the general rationalization of the environment just mentioned. It shows that the expert had begun to find a place in daily life.[53] This itself would not have been possible, had there not been an increasingly large number of people willing to forgo political responsibility and renown and to become specialists. Politics no longer held men in bondage. Withdrawal from the life of the city had been rare in the fifth century even among philosophers, but it now became quite common. Plato assumed that anyone who had seen the realm of Ideas would enter into the service of the state only if forced to do so.[54] Whether or not the philosopher ought to be concerned with politics, the growing individualism did benefit research in philosophy no less than in

[51] Cf. Burckhardt, *Griechische Kulturgeschichte* IV, 322 ff.; and for naval warfare in particular cf. *s.v.* Seewesen, *R.–E.*, Suppl. V (1931), col. 939.

[52] cf. A. Rehm, *Archiv für Kulturgeschichte*, XXVIII (1938), 142.

[53] The new belief in experts as contrasted to the ideal of the citizen is well illustrated by Aristotle's discussion of the question whether in the matter of elections the decision should not be left in the hands of experts (*Polit.* III, 1282 a 7 ff.).

[54] For the philosopher's withdrawal from politics and for the individualism of the fourth century see Burckhardt (*Griechische Kulturgeschichte* IV, 286, 348, and 366), to whose analysis of the period I am much indebted.

the humanities and sciences. Freed from their old loyalties and no longer primarily citizens, men sought private occupations and made their own chosen interests their main concern. If the Cynics denied the value of culture altogether, there also arose a class of intellectuals whose lives were centered in cultural activities. Undoubtedly, it was still a small group, consisting mainly of the rich or men of independent means, for there were no "positions" to be had. The relation between student and teacher was a voluntary one. Support was given by the state rarely and only if need arose.[55] One was no longer an outcast or socially condemned as useless, however, if one transferred one's desire for distinction and applied one's gifts to the pursuits of the mind. A human ideal not inferior to the ideal of citizenship began to be established. The place of the *homo politicus* was taken over not only by the *homo economicus* but also by the *homo intellectualis*. Thus the political decay by giving men free rein prepared the way for further progress.[56]

It is time to turn from this attempt to explain the self-assurance of the age of Plato and Aristotle and its condescension towards earlier generations to its conception of the process of advance itself. Xenophanes had expressed his notion of progress almost in the form of an aphorism. The Pre-Socratics had discovered the laws of progress. Isocrates, Plato, and Aristotle made the general conception specific and elaborated a theory of progress, which is most fully expressed in the Aristotelian writings.

The framework of the theories of these three writers was provided by the teaching of Democritus. Hence the acknowledgment by all of the rôle played at first by human need and later by superabundance in the creation of the arts and crafts.[57] There are certain refinements, however. According to Plato and Aristotle "lei-

[55] The rise of an intellectual class was observed by Burckhardt, *op. cit.*, IV, 391 ff. The body politic reacted to scientific work just as it had in the fifth century (see L. Edelstein, *J.H.I.*, XIII [1952], 597). It is true that schools were now coming into existence, but they were private organizations and were maintained by the contributions of their members.

[56] For the importance of the concept of culture in evaluating the fourth century, see below, p. 130.

[57] For the influence of Democritus on Plato cf. K. Reinhardt, *Hermes*, XLVII (1912), pp. 504 ff. and Theiler, *op. cit.*, pp. 81 ff. As regards Isocrates' *Panegyr.*, cf. Kleingünther, *op. cit.*, p. 121. (See also *Antidosis* 252 and *Nicocles, init.*) For Aristotle, cf. e.g., *Metaphysics* I, 1, 981 b 20 ff.

sure" gives birth to the disinterested regard for truth and theoretical knowledge.[58] Plato, Aristotle, and Isocrates agree that progress comes about "little by little" (ἐπὶ μικρόν) or "bit by bit." Things do not happen "suddenly" but "over a very long period of time" (Plato, Laws III, 678 B); they do not become "immediately" what they are "now." (Isocrates, Panegyricus, 32.) The forward movement is slow and gradual; and from problems that "lie near at hand" one ascends to those that have "broader implications." (Aristotle, Metaphysics I, 2, 982 b 13–15.)[59]

No explanation for the adoption of this latter thesis is ever offered; but it is unlikely that the greater emphasis on the gradualness of progress came from research into what had happened in earlier times, for the analysis of prehistory always remained in antiquity a philosophical construction based on analogies, studies of proverbs that were taken to be relics of prior wisdom, and similar data and never became historical in the modern sense.[60] Perhaps, as in the seventeenth century, the interdependence of the sciences strengthened the conviction that in the process of advance each step is indispensable for the next. For Aristotle the working of Nature may have afforded a significant parallel, for Nature too "progresses little by little from things lifeless to animal life." (History of Animals VIII, 1, 588 b 4 ff.)[61] Whatever the origin of the conception common to Plato, Aristotle, and Isocrates, they recognized the organic character of the development. It did not have to wait for recognition by Lucretius, whose famous pedetemptin (V,

---

[58] Plato (Republic II, 373 A) distinguishes between what is necessary and what is the superadditamentum of pleasure and luxury. In Critias 110 A he speaks of interests that come with leisure, as Shorey has noted (ad Rep. II, 373 A). The Aristotelian theory of leisure as the origin of disinterested investigation is found e.g., in Metaphysics I, 1, 981 b 23 ff.; for him, of course, "wonder" is the origin of knowledge.

[59] Aristotle uses the phrase κατὰ μικρόν in his analysis of the development of specific arts also; cf. Poetics IV, 1449 a 13.

[60] See Jacoby, Atthis, pp. 133 ff.

[61] Meteorology I, 14, 351 b 8–38 speaks of the gradual changes in the configuration of the earth. That "certain stages of theoretical knowledge and practical skills must have been reached before the next higher step could be taken" was clearly recognized by Hobbes, and the idea was fully developed by Comte; cf. E. Frank, Philosophical Understanding and Religious Truth (London/New York, 1945), p. 136 and note 10.

533 and 1453) merely rephrases an insight gained in the fourth century.[62]

Beyond this the several theories differ. The essential of Isocrates' opinion can be stated briefly. Faithful to Democritus' belief that life was initially savage (*Antidosis*, 254; *Busiris*, 25), he deviates from atomistic philosophy in attributing decisive importance to the power of speech. It is in fact speech that distinguishes man from the animals and allows for the growth of civilized life. Through persuasion reasoned discourse unites men in cities; it constitutes moral values; it produces arguments convincing to others and to oneself. (*Antidosis*, 253–57; cf. *Panegyricus*, 47 ff.; *Nicocles*, 5–9.)[63]

Plato's view is more circumstantial. According to him the human race has always existed. When he discusses its beginnings it is, as in the case of the beginning of the world, in categories of mythology; and then he assumes that men, "bereft of the guardian care of the Daemon who had governed and reared them," lacked "all tools and all crafts in the early years." (*Politicus* 274 B–C.)[64] This, of course, is mere poetical fancy. In those beginnings that follow upon one of the periodic destructions of mankind (*Laws* III, 677 A; cf. *Timaeus* 22 C, 23 A–B and *Critias* 109 D) the few survivors, "the scanty embers of humanity," lead the life of mountain shepherds (*Laws* III, 677 B) and possess only some primitive

[62] Shorey explained Isocrates, *Paneg.* 40—the only passage he considered—as rhetorical amplification (*Class. Philol.*, VI [1911], 89) and believed Lucretius to be the first for whom the concept of gradual progress is attested, for he thought the presumptions against ascribing it to an early Greek writer. It is possible, however, that the principle given expression by Plato, Aristotle, and Isocrates is derived from Democritus, to whom they are indebted in other respects (cf. above, note 57), for Democritus (Fr. 5 [Diels–Kranz] = Diodorus, I, 8) spoke of progress κατ' ὀλίγον (7) and ατὰ μικρόν (8). It is true that Diodorus' account is influenced by later sources, and it therefore remains uncertain whether the idea of a gradual ascent can be traced to Democritus; but it should be observed that the author of the Ps.–Hippocratic treatise *On Ancient Medicine* had already assumed the necessity of beginning from earlier discoveries in order to make further advances in science (chap. 2).

[63] The same notion is expressed by Aristotle, *Politics* I, 2, 1253 a 7–18. Isocrates sometimes attributes all inventions to one person, an Egyptian (*Busiris*), sometimes to one city, Athens (*Paneg.*, 32–50). Such different representations of the topic are determined by different rhetorical aims, as was the case with the earlier sophists; cf. above, chap. II, note 10.

[64] The evidence for the assertion that according to Plato the human race had always existed is discussed by F.M. Cornford, *Plato's Cosmology* (London, 1937), pp. 145 f.

crafts such as pottery and weaving (679 A); but then conditions change as the result of time and an increase of population, for initially there was a "frightful and widespread depopulation." (677 E–678 B.) "Nomadic" existence is superseded by the stage of agricuture (680 D), which is in turn replaced by the founding of cities. (681 C.) In the first phase of this development men, ignorant of wars and conflicts but also of the art of writing and of laws and of all forms of legal government, live like the Cyclops of Homer under a patriarchical system. (679 D–680 B.) In the agricultural stage groups are organized with particular customs and laws (680 D ff.); and in the "third type of polity" the process of legislation goes even farther, and society exhibits "all varieties of form and fortunes." (681 D.)[65]

The *Epinomis* elaborates Plato's scheme of the rise of culture. In this work there are among the arts those demanded by necessity (974 D), and next the imitative arts providing pleasure (975 D), and finally "the arts that ward off evil" (975 E) such as generalship, medicine, navigation, and jurisprudence. Undoubtedly, the necessary arts, invented first, were once of greatest importance, for they humanized life, and consequently men who were skilled in them were considered "wise." (974 E.) Today, this is no longer true (974 B; 976 A); and it is rather abstract science or theoretical speculation that constitutes true wisdom. (976 C ff.) In other words, history brings about a reversal of values. What comes first in time and, being necessary, is at first prized loses status when conditions improve; its dignity and worth fade in the light of goods discovered later. Furthermore, not only in material progress but in enlightenment also there are distinct stages. At first a mythical explanation of the data of experience was given; next the Pre-

[65] Plato's recognition of nomadic life as the first stage of human existence continues and improves upon the speculations of Protagoras and Hippias; cf. above, chap. II, note 7. His whole construction is determined by the question concerning "the first beginnings of a State" (676 A), or "how laws came to be needed" (679 E). Like Thucydides he draws inferences from primitive conditions still obtaining within and without Greece (680 B). His notion that the increase of population and the rise of culture are interrelated is a kind of inverted Malthusianism and quite different from later ancient theories. I restrict myself here to Plato's theory in the *Laws* because his *Republic* does not purport to give an historical account; see above, note 11.

Socratics gave a rational account but one that was still far removed from truth (988 C—D);[66] and finally certain sciences arose in countries favorable to their development. So astronomical observations began in Egypt and Syria because there the stars are almost always visible, the skies being clear and cloudless. (987 A.) This knowledge then spread to other countries; and the Greeks too learned from the Orient, but the geographical position of their land enabled them successfully to bring everything to the point of perfection, so that whatever they received from the barbarians "they completed and improved upon." (987 D–E.)

The *Epinomis* abandons some of Plato's presuppositions but gives more concreteness to his picture of the past in its relation to the present. At the same time, it answers questions which the fifth century had raised but had failed to answer satisfactorily. It overcomes the externalization of history by restating the diffusion theory of Herodotus in terms that do more justice to the give and take in the interdependence of the various nations that have contributed to the rise of civilization. The Greeks, the latecomers in the development, finally appear in the rôle of masters of "the art of fruitful borrowing from others," to express the opinion of the Platonists in the language of one of the most penetrating modern interpreters of the Greek mind.[67]

Aristotle unlike Plato or the author of the *Epinomis* does not give even a brief sketch of the whole development of civilization but merely touches upon a few of its outstanding features. He also notices the fact that the first discoveries seemed to be not only useful but also the work of wisdom, while later the epithet "wise" was given to those who developed knowledge not concerned with

[66] In this account of the *Epinomis* Plato's general position and Aristotle's criticism of earlier philosophers seem to have been systematized in a form similar to that of Comte's law of the three stages.

[67] Nietzsche, "Philosophie im tragischen Zeitalter der Griechen," p. 155. The author of the *Epinomis* despite his general agreement with Plato seems to deviate from him in at least two points. The dialogues never imply that in the beginning men lived like animals and even resorted to cannibalism (975 A), nor do they mention a reversal of value-judgments. Plato, though extolling the theoretical life, shows no contempt for the practical life, and instead of separating the arts from wisdom he tries to infuse them with wisdom. The interest of the *Epinomis* in the Orient may be Academic, but see Jula Kerschensteiner, *Platon und der Orient* (Stuttgart, 1945), p. 196.

usefulness; and he too traces some of the sciences to the Orient, where a whole class of people had leisure for research. (*Metaphysics* I, 981 b 13–25.)[68]

Nevertheless, he insists that at least in social institutions "inventions" are made independently in different places and at different times. The diffusion theory does not provide a full explanation of all phenomena, for that which is indispensable for life necessity produces in all places and at all times. On the other hand, it would be foolish to duplicate inventions, which should rather be adopted, when discovered, and improved upon. (*Polit.*, VII, 10, 1329 b 25–35.)[69]

Having dealt cursorily with these general points, Aristotle carefully considers the way in which the arts and sciences are established and perfected. The beginnings, he thinks, must be clearly distinguished from the later development. Everything new advances slowly and with difficulty, but first steps forward are the most important: "The first beginning is the main thing, as the saying goes." Afterwards, it is easier to make additions and to attain considerable knowledge or skill (*Soph. Ref.* 34, 183 b 17–28), for, once a project has been well-outlined, anyone can promote it, and at this stage time itself becomes "the inventor or [at least] a good partner in the enterprise; it is in such a way that the arts and crafts grow in perfection." (*Nic. Eth.* I, 7, 1098 a 22–25.) Time, which for the Sophists was the essential condition of progress, for Moschion the true inventor, and even for Plato one of the two basic factors responsible for the transformation of human life, was for Aristotle less important. He like Xenophanes emphasizes instead

---

[68] On the scientific merit of the Oriental peoples cf. also *On the Heavens* II, 12, 292 a 7–9. The reflections on the σοφός in the *Metaphysics* passage referred to are similar to those found in a passage in Philoponus' commentary on Nicomachus' *Isagoge*, which was held to be an Aristotelian fragment by I. Bywater, "Aristotle's Dialogue on Philosophy," *The Journal of Philology*, VII (1877), 64 ff; but see, on that passage of Philoponus, H. Cherniss, *Gnomon*, XXXI (1959), 38 and W. Haase, *Synusia: Festgabe für Wolfgang Schadewaldt* (1965), pp. 323 ff.

[69] E. Barker (trans.), *The Politics of Aristotle* (Oxford, 1946), p. 306, note DDD, drew attention to the importance of this passage and considers it possible that the section at the end of which it occurs (1–8) is "an antiquarian interpolation"; but, since he admits that "it has certainly an Aristotelian flavor," I have not hesitated to attribute to Aristotle the theory that it proposes. (With Barker and others I read εὑρημένοις [1329 b 34] instead of the εἰρημένοις adopted by Becker and Newman).

88

the significance of the individual especially at the inception of the arts and crafts. It is as if he had tried to distinguish between the genius of the true or "first" inventor and the talent of the mere improver.[70]

On the other hand, in Aristotle's opinion he who comes first is in some ways inferior to those who come later. Those who first tried to search for truth and the nature of all things were diverted from the right path and followed another because of their "lack of experience." (*Physics* I, 8, 191 a 25–27; cf. 191 b 30–34.) Previous ages failed because the earlier philosophers behaved "like untrained men in fights, rushing around and often striking smart blows but not fighting on scientific principles; and similarly these thinkers do not seem to know what they are saying, for it is clear that as a rule they make little if any use of their own principles." (*Metaphysics* I, 4, 985 a 14 ff.)[71] When Aristotle after having surveyed the philosophy of the Pre-Socratics says that with them knowledge was "young," "in its infancy," and "only in its beginnings" (*Metaphysics* I, 10, 993 a 16 ff.), one is reminded of Bacon's paradoxical assertion: *antiquitas saeculi iuventus mundi.* (*Novum Organum*, I, 84.) For Aristotle too the truly "old" were those living in his time.

Yet, had the present effort not been preceded by that of others, today's generation would not have the knowledge that it actually possesses. "No one," says Aristotle, "is able to attain the truth adequately, while on the other hand we do not collectively fail; but each one says something true about the nature of things, and, while individually we contribute little or nothing to the truth, by all of us together a considerable amount is amassed." (*Metaphysics* II, 1, 993 a 31–b 4.)[72] In fact, the present is indebted not only to the

[70] The conception of genius became important only later in ancient historiography.

[71] In the same way Aristotle distinguishes between the unscientific attempts to deal with a subject, which necessarily precede the establishment of an art, and the true foundation of the art; cf. e.g., *Soph. Refut.* 34, 184 a 3 (τὰ ἀπὸ τῆς τέχνης). That any kind of perfection presupposes long effort for many generations is implied also in *Poetics* 4, 1448 b 27–30, on which cf. A Gudeman, *Aristoteles*, Περὶ ποιητικῆς (Berlin, 1934), pp. 122 ff. This assumption that there must have been poets before Homer reappears in the assumption of Theophrastus that Thales cannot have been the first philosopher (*Physic. Opinion*, Fr. 1 [Diels]).

[72] *Metaphysics* α, from which this quotation and the following are taken, may be a later addition to the Aristotelian work by Pasicles; but its thought and language are "thoroughly Aristotelian." See W.D. Ross (ed.), *Aristotle's Metaphysics* (Oxford, 1924), I, xxv. Its tenor is certainly the same as that of *Sophistic Refutations*, chap.

correct solutions of the past but to its mistakes as well; and therefore "it is fair that we should be grateful not only to those with whose views we may agree but also to those who have expressed more superficial views, for these also contributed something by developing before us the power of thought." (993 b 11–14.) Using as an example the work of Timotheus, whose claim to originality and novelty and whose blunt rejection of the old typify the attitude of the fifth century and that of many authors of the fourth also, Aristotle concludes: "It is true that, had there been no Timotheus, we should be without much of our lyric poetry; but, had there been no Phrynis, there would have been no Timotheus. The same holds for those who have expressed views about the truth, for from some thinkers we have inherited certain opinions, while others were responsible for the appearance of the former." (993 b 15–19.) [73]

How, then, do things develop and reach greater perfection? As regards men, the agents of progress, their knowledge is not merely additive but cumulative. Great individuals start out on the way but do not advance very far. Subsequent generations go farther not only because they follow their predecessors but because they are their heirs; their strength is in part the strength of those who lived earlier, for the past with its truths as well as its falsehoods makes the present what it is. Civilization is the work neither of god nor of heroes, half-human and half-divine, but of men cooperating throughout the course of history, helping one another, and bound to one another like the links in a chain. [74] In Aristotle's grandiose metaphor "those who are now renowned have taken over as if in a relay race (from hand to hand; relieving one another [ἐκ διαδοχῆς]) from many predecessors who on their part progressed,

34, where Aristotle gives an historical appreciation of his own "invention" and of the process of discovery in general (cf. above, pp. 72, 88; and below, pp. 90 f.).

[73] This chapter of the *Metaphysics* prompted Dilthey to say that *"die Alten (besassen) shon ein klares Bewusstsein des geschichtlichen Fortschritts der Menschheit in Bezug auf Wissenschaften und Künste"* (*Gesammelte Schriften* I [1922], 281).

[74] G. Simmel showed that the alternative of god or hero still haunted the eighteenth century and was overcome only when a third possible explanation of inventions was found in the modern concepts of society and history. See *The Sociology of Georg Simmel*, trans. and ed. K.H. Wolfe (Glencoe [Ill.], 1950), pp. 12 ff. In my analysis of Aristotle's discovery that history accounts for progress, I have made use of some of Simmel's categories.

and thus have made progress themselves." (*Soph. Refut.* chap. 34, 183 b 29–31.) The "torch of learning" is passed on from one generation to the next succeeding one; and that is why its brightness always increases. It is the insight embodied in the "immortal aphorism" of Pascal: "The entire succession of men through the whole course of ages must be regarded as one man, always living and incessantly learning."[75]

If this is so, the time and place in which the individual finds himself are important factors of his accomplishment and limits of what he can accomplish. When a new civilization begins—and, though for Aristotle as for Plato the human race is eternal and strictly speaking there is no beginning of culture, individual civilizations do rise and fall and are destroyed by natural catastrophes— there are "benefactors of the people in connection with the invention of arts or with regard to warfare," the founders of heroic kingships. (*Politics* III, 14, 1285 b 6; cf. 1286 b 10.)[76] With the gradual rise of civilization the general intellectual level also rises (II, 8, 1269 a 4–6). While in the beginning few men of outstanding merit, few benefactors, are found, later their number increases greatly. (III, 15, 1286 b 8–13.)[77] Moreover, the discoveries made are enlarged and perfected. No matter how great the accomplishment of the first inventor, his successors are bound to excel him. The different positions men occupy in the development of the arts and sciences determine the value and rate of their achievement.

[75] *Traité de vide* (the translation is taken from Teggart, *The Idea of Progress*, p. 167). This is the aphorism which, according to Comte, was the "first ray of light" in the modern debate (Introduction, note 17). (Dilthey [see above, note 73] observed the general similarity of Aristotle's concept of progress and that of Pascal, who he thought followed Bacon.) The usual translation of the expression ἐκ διαδοχῆς is "in a succession of learning," but in *Physics* 228 a 28 Aristotle exemplifies the consecutive by "a torch passed from hand to hand" (οἷον ἡ λαμπὰς ἐκ διαδοχῆς); see also the Ps.–Aristotelian *On the Cosmos* 398 a 33, where the unity of the cosmos is likened to a relay race; and last but not least, Plato, *Laws* VI, 776 B, where it is said that the torch of life is handed from one generation to another to perpetuate the service of God.

[76] That in speaking here of the repeated destruction (and reinvention) of the arts and sciences Aristotle is thinking of their disappearance because of sudden natural catastrophes was shown by J. Bernays, *op. cit.*, p. 48, and note 27. For the conception of recurrence see below, p. 121. Other passages referring to the survival of ancient views are cited above, note 35.

[77] I take the Aristotelian "benefactor" as corresponding to Plato's "god or divine man," which is used in the same context (*Laws* II, 657 A).

Within the realm of progress a certain law of historical relativity obtains.[78]

Neither the notion that knowledge is cumulative rather than additive nor the contention that the individual is subject to historical determination is quite original with Aristotle. As to the former, the common assertion that development takes place "step by step" itself implies awareness of the interdependence of discoveries and inventions, and further evidence that this truth was generally accepted is to be found in the language that Aristotle like Plato, Isocrates, and Xenophon uses when dealing with the ascent of the arts and sciences. While earlier authors had no term that corresponds to the word progress and the various phases of the historical process, these writers of the fourth century speak of the "growth" or "the increase" (ἐπίδοσις) of the arts and sciences, or say that they themselves "grow" or "increase" (ἐπιδιδόναι).[79] Such an expres-

[78] R. McKeon ("Plato and Aristotle as Historians," *International Journal of Ethics* LI [1940–41], 97) denies that Aristotle had a conception of the historical relativity of knowledge; and Bury, on principle denying that the Greeks had any such notion, says "the judgment of a wise man at any time might be final or absolutely valid" (*The Ancient Greek Historians*, 251, 1 [although he exempts Thucydides and Eratosthenes from this verdict, 252, 2]). The passages that I have quoted from Aristotle appear to prove that he was an historical relativist; and it is probably as such that he condemned the naiveté of the Pre-Socratics, who thought that they had found the whole truth (see above, chap. II, p. 26). How this relativism goes with Aristotle's eternalism will be discussed presently.

[79] Cf. Plato, *Hippias Major* 281 D and 282 B; Aristotle, *Nic. Eth.* I, 7, 1098 a 24 f. and *Soph. Ref.* chap. 34, 183 b 19, 21; Isocrates, *Paneg.*, 10; Theopompus, Fr. 25, 1, 28 (Jacoby); Xenophon, *Hiero* IX, 7. ἐπιδιδόναι in the sense of "to grow" is to be found even in the literature of the fifth century but there usually with a prepositional phrase (e.g., Herodotus, II, 13; Thucydides, VI, 60; VIII, 24 and 83) whereas in Plato Comicus, Fr. 213 (Kock) it is used absolutely. In the *Protagoras* (318 A) Plato applies the word to the improvement of man's inner faculties, his soul (cf. *Laws* III, 694 B; Aristotle, *On the Soul* II, 5, 417 b 6 ff.; Isocrates, *Antidosis* 267). In Hippocrates, *Aphorisms* I, 3 it refers to bodily states (cf. also Ps.–Aristotle, *Problemata* XX, 7, 923 a 37; Plato, *Laws* III, 679 B). In short, it appears in almost as many senses as does the term progress in modern usage (cf. Baillie, *op. cit.*, pp. 1 ff.). Synonymous with ἐπιδιδόναι and ἐπίδοσις are αὐξάνειν and αὔξησις, e.g., Aristotle, *Politics* VII, 10, 1329 b 29 f. and *Soph. Ref.* chap. 34, 183 b 22 and 31 (συναύξειν [183 b 26]); Plato, *Rep.* IV, 424 A and VII, 528 C; and these too are words that occur in earlier literature in contexts similar to those of ἐπιδιδόναι and ἐπίδοσις (e.g., Thucydides, I, 12, 1; 16; Heraclitus, Fr. 115 [Diels–Kranz]), but the latter seem the more typical and the more generally accepted. Προαγαγεῖν "is the transitive verb corresponding to ἐπιδοῦναι," cf. J. Burnet (ed.), *The Ethics of Aristotle* (London, 1900), p. 38 *ad Nic. Eth.* I, 7, 17, and the parallels collected there.

sion would not have been coined and have found favor if the continuous character of the forward movement, the concatenation of events, that aspect of the temporal progress which turns it into an organic whole, had not been visualized, for that which increases or grows is something that is at once the same and not the same, something that exhibits persistence and change, identity and difference.[80]

There was also a growing awareness of the fact that the individuals, who were thought by Xenophanes and the other Pre-Socratics to act as isolated personalities, creating out of nothing or simply taking over and adapting to their purposes what others equally isolated had created, are in fact contributors to a common cause, each doing his own particular share. The so-called Pythagoreans ascribed to their master their new-found insight and remained anonymous because they believed that they were only carrying out the intentions of the founder of their school and that therefore their knowledge was in truth his. The Platonic dialogue drew the great men of the past into the conversation of the day and in examining their views carried the inquiry further.[81] Earlier inventions and inventors were made the subject of special investigations in the fourth century and were no longer merely mentioned by general historians within a broader context or in passing references. Monographs on ancient poets and musicians had been written from the end of the fifth century; and by 380 B.C., as is clear from a speech

[80] For the later Greek term "progress" and its difference from the term here discussed see below, chap. IV, p. 146. At any rate, it is not true even of the fourth century that the Greek language had no word "which really corresponds to our word Progress" (above, Introduction, note 54).

[81] For the Pythagoreans' ascription of their own theories to their master and the significance of this for the idea of progress, see Edelstein, "Platonic Anonymity," A.J.P., LXXXIII (1962), 12 f. Aristotle's debt to Plato for his conception of history was noticed by W. Jaeger (*Aristoteles*, p. 387); but his dependence is not restricted to his acceptance of certain data or to his wish "to include [earlier Greek speculations] in the construction of his own system," as Jaeger formulated it later ("Review of H. Cherniss, *Aristotle's Criticism of Pre–Socratic Philosophy*," A.J.P., LVIII [1937], 354). Plato, by turning away from the direct study of phenomena to the scrutiny of human opinions and insisting that the dialogue is the only right method of philosophizing, gave the authors of the theories greater dignity and value than they had ever had before. They were made partners in a great conversation in which Plato tried to ferret out their opinions and thereby to ascertain the truth. This represents the beginning of historical consciousness and is therefore the starting-point of Aristotle's approach to the past. See also below, pp. 96 f.

of Isocrates (*Pan.*, 10), a literature of inventions had already been well established. Indeed, the past had become an object of scholarly interest and study more than it had ever been before; and this was only natural in an age that was proud of its own advance and yet conscious that it was not making a beginning altogether new, an age that measured its own achievement by constantly comparing it with that of its predecessors, an age that was, in fact, not merely revolutionary but truly progressive.[82]

Aristotle, then, can be said to have progressed in his understanding of progress because others before him and contemporary with him had progressed in their understanding of progress. Aspiring to be the arbiter of thought (*Physics*, III, 6, 206 a 13), he analyzed with his usual lucidity the issues raised, giving a full hearing to each party and eventually passing a balanced judgment on the case under consideration. Past and present are given their just deserts, and pride and humility assigned their right places. No one carries off the full prize, but each receives the share that is his.

It is in this spirit that Aristotle had others make large collections of historical material, such as the collection of old constitutions, and inspired his pupils to write the history of culture as a whole and that of the various arts and sciences. In the Peripatetic analyses of the various civilizations the evolutionistic point of view prevailed. The "life" of each particular culture was regarded as a unit stretching from its early beginnings to the present. Customs and institutions were not enumerated or represented as details to be remarked with astonishment, admiration, or disdain but were recorded as having come to be one after the other by human decision and action depending largely on geographical and physical factors.[83]

[82] Collingwood observed that without comparing two ways of life and judging one to be better than the other there can be "no conception of the change as a progress" (see above, Introduction, note 22), and that the revolutionary "can only regard his revolution as a progress in so far as he is also an historian, genuinely re-enacting in his own historical thought the life he nevertheless rejects" (*The Idea of History*, p. 326).

[83] Cf. K. Trüdinger, *op. cit.*, pp. 47 ff. Dicaearchus' *Life of Greece*, the outstanding example of this type of history, will be discussed below, chap. IV, p. 134. (Pausanias' account of the history of Arcadia [VIII, 1 ff.] may show Peripatetic influence; see Trüdinger, p. 51 and Nestle, *Vom Mythos zum Logos*, pp. 145 ff.). In connection with these studies should also be mentioned Aristotle's own analysis in the *Politics* of the sequence of social organizations; cf. Lovejoy and Boas, *op. cit.*, pp. 174–177.

In the historical accounts of the various sciences compiled by Aristotle's pupils the development of the intellectual achievement was presented in accordance with the belief in continuous progress. Few as the extant fragments are, they suffice to show that the contributions of the outstanding scientists were arranged chronologically and that the whole achievement was represented as a steady advance from an incomplete and limited understanding to a wider mastery of the respective subjects, i.e., to a greater perfection.[84]

It may be objected that there is another Aristotle much less given to historical objectivity, and that in what has been said above too much emphasis has been put upon his thoughts about progress. It is true that through his writings are scattered remarks about previous discoveries and that there are frequent historical surveys written with the fairness of the critical observer and made the starting-point of his investigations;[85] but just as often in his systematic works and especially in the famous introductory book of his *Metaphysics* he uses or misuses historical data for the purpose of proving that his own insight was already implied by earlier philosophers, who are in this way suborned witnesses to the truth of his own theories. This dialectical method, it has been argued, is the antithesis of a true historical appreciation, which gives to each age its peculiar truth, and it tends to place Aristotle alongside Plato in his intention "of eliciting the typical or universal aspects from these imperfect particular manifestations (of the thought of the past)."[86]

There is no gainsaying the assertion that Aristotle was inclined to

---

[84] Cf. Eudemus, Frs. 133–150 (Wehrli), and Wehrli's general introduction to his commentary on the various passages (*Die Schule des Aristoteles* [Basle, 1944–1959] VIII, 113 ff.) Frs. 133 and 145 are characteristic of Eudemus' procedure. In general, see F. Leo, *Die griechisch–römische Biographie* (Leipzig, 1901), p. 100 and Jaeger, *Aristoteles*, pp. 358 f. Cf. also Strato, Fr. 144–47 (Wehrli), who wrote against the Isocratean Ephorus from the point of view of the Peripatos. Jacoby correctly observed that it is no longer possible to determine the principles followed by the Isocrateans and Aristotelians respectively (the former may have stressed the share of the barbarians, the latter that of the Greeks [on Ephorus, Frs. 2–5, p. 41, 39–41]).

[85] *The Constitution of Athens* 9, 2, illustrates Aristotle's willingness to interpret earlier views according to the intention or position of their authors.

[86] H. Cherniss, "The History of Ideas . . . ," p. 45. How often Aristotle distorts historical data or gives a correct interpretation, a problem with which the article by W.K.C. Guthrie, "Aristotle as a Historian of Philosophy," is mainly concerned (*J.H.S.*, LXXVII [1957], 35 ff.), is not here relevant, for in this context it is important only that both distortions and correct interpretations do occur.

look at the past as the repository of that same insight, though imperfectly expressed, that is elaborated in the present. It was only natural for him to do so, especially with regard to philosophical truth, for truth in his opinion exists irrespective of the individuals who find it. They do not make it but merely come to discover it. Every investigation, therefore, has an objective as well as a subjective aspect. If a question is considered from the latter point of view, it is men who in the course of time and "little by little" bring about the realization of the truth; and, if looked at from the objective point of view, it is "Truth itself" that drives the philosopher to pose further problems. (*Metaphysics* I, 984 b 9–11; cf. 984 a 18 ff.)[87] This does not mean, however, that the truth now accessible to everyone was accessible at all times.

Consequently, it is wrong to maintain that for Aristotle as well as for Plato ideas have no history. Their history is the history of their discovery.[88] Still less can it be assumed that by Aristotle, as by Hegel, with whom he has much in common in his interpretation or misinterpretation of the past, the temporal sequence of philosophical systems was taken to be identical with the logical sequence or deployment of concepts. Aristotle held that the truth comes into sight gradually, is purified in the act of being visualized, or is hewn out like a statue and emerges slowly in its fullness. He certainly would not have said that "what the spirit is in itself, it has always been," that "the difference (in the formulations reached in pre-

[87] See also 984 a 18; 1091 a 9; 188 b 30; 642 a 19. Eucken, *Die Methode der Aristotelischen Forschung*, p. 1, note 3 and G. Teichmüller, *Aristotelische Forschungen* (Halle, 1867–73), II, 377 ff. and 383 (for examples in the history of art and for the development of the arts). Here too Aristotle followed a Platonic lead, for Plato held that the investigation constrains (ἀναγκάζει) the investigator to raise certain problems and imposes upon him certain solutions (*Republic* 518 ff.; 523 D; 524 C–E; 525 D).

[88] Cherniss ("The History of Ideas . . . ," p. 45) says that "to Aristotle as well as to Plato the very possibility of what we call a history of ideas would have seemed incompatible with philosophy." This is undoubtedly true if one has in mind, as Cherniss does, the modern conception of a history of ideas (as defined by Lovejoy), i.e., a historical synthesis in which implicit assumptions, dialectical motives, susceptibilities to diverse kinds of metaphysical pathos, philosophical semantics, and so forth are categories of interpretation. Plato as well as Aristotle was concerned with the truth of past ideas; but that their philosophy "implied an objective and eternal truth discernible by each human mind directly" (*ibid.*) does not mean, as I have attempted to show for Aristotle, that the truth was always equally accessible to all men.

vious ages) is but the unfolding of this essence."[89] How much more of an historian Aristotle was than Hegel, how conscious of history he remained throughout, is symbolized by the fact that when he called earlier philosophy the "stammering expression of his insight," he remembered that the men of the past could not yet have known what he knew. It is, after all, at the end of his survey of Pre-Socratic thought that he speaks of their beginnings as "the youth of mankind."[90]

The only charge one can bring against him is that despite his progressivism he did not abandon the idea of an objective and common truth; but progressivism and relativism are not necessarily identical, and an historical approach need not turn into historicism. Aristotle's standards of criticism, though to be sure they do not satisfy the modern historian, would have been acceptable even to the greatest writers on history in the eighteenth century; and,

[89] *Vernunft in der Geschichte*, p. 165 [Lasson], quoted by E. Frank, *Wissen, Wollen, Glauben* (Zürich, 1955), p. 240. A comparison of Aristotle's approach and Hegel's is made by Jaeger in his *Aristoteles* (p. 396), who later stated that what Aristotle, at any rate in the *Metaphysics*, "seeks in the historical process is the successive development of truth, a view which was renewed by Hegel in his *History of Philosophy* (*A.J.P.*, LVIII [1937], 353), whereas in his later period he took a more historical attitude (*ibid.*, pp. 353–355). Yet, though according to both philosophers philosophical truth is progressively developed in the succession of various systems, the historical moment, which was important for Aristotle even in the *Metaphysics* (cf. below, note 90), has no part in Hegel's discussion; and besides Hegel's conception of "subjective truth" differs from the Aristotelian notion of "objective truth" (Frank, *op. cit.*, pp. 236–238), while the reconciliation of opposing opinions by Aristotle, the "arbiter" (cf. above, p. 94 and further passages in Eucken, *Die Methode der Aristotelischen Forschung*, p. 10), is quite different from Hegel's reconciliation of thesis and antithesis in a "higher" synthesis. The evidence for Aristotle's "historicism" comes from "earlier" and "later" writings alike; and it is therefore unnecessary to speak of different stages in his understanding of history, even if it should prove to be true that historical statements occur more frequently in his "later" works, something that to prove would presuppose a soundly established chronology of the various treatises (cf. R. Weil, *Aristote et l'histoire* [Paris, 1960], p. 89).

[90] Cf. above, pp. 89 f. Moreover, in the first book of the *Metaphysics* Aristotle repeatedly touches upon the question of the first to formulate a specific insight (984 b 31 f.; 985 a 9 ff.; b 24; 986 b 21; 987 b 4) and tries to determine how his predecessors came to formulate their opinions (983 b 22 and 985 b 32, passages to which Eucken [*Die Methode der Aristotelischen Forschung*, p. 10, note 3] draws attention, citing also from later books 1010 a 1 f., 1012 a 17, 1062 b 20, 1078 b 13, 1084 b 24, 1090 a 20 f.); and besides he observes some historical periodizations (985 a 10 f.; 987 a 29 and b 32; 992 a 33). He says himself that *Metaphysics* I is not intended to be a straight "history of philosophy" (983 b 4–6; 988 b 16–19; 993 a 11–13), but this does not mean that he is innocent of an historical approach.

whatever qualification may be found necessary, it still was he who definitely refuted the "naïve" belief of the Pre-Socratics that one man by himself could achieve the truth.[91]

But what about development in the future? The evidence thus far examined testifies to so much concern with an historical assessment of the past and to such certainty that the present had moved far ahead of the past that one almost expects to find little interest in the future or at least little ambition for it. What Bacon says with regard to progress in the mechanical arts could well be said with regard to all progress: "When a man looks at the variety and the beauty of the provisions . . . brought together . . . he will certainly be more inclined to admire the wealth of man than to feel his wants." (*Novum Organum*, I, 85, cf. 88.)[92] In fact, the situation was quite different. Further advance was so much taken for granted and assumed to be possible as well as desirable that the discussion seems to have been largely concerned with the ways in which it could be consciously assured. This is especially clear in the writings of Isocrates and Xenophon, who certainly reflect the general situation or at least the attitude of the intellectuals to these matters.[93]

Isocrates puts the case in his usual personal manner, saying that despite the general unwillingness to reward progress he has not been disheartened and has not relaxed his efforts. (*Panegyr.* 3.) He asks for public rewards, however, for all who labor for the common

[91] A similar combination of historicism and eternalism occurs in Kant, for whom—though for reasons different from Aristotle's—"contingency and the character of having a history" belong "not to the doctrines themselves but to their appearance at a particular time and as as a result of favorable conditions." Kant's position is rightly stated by E. Bréhier ("The Formation of Our History of Philosophy," *Philosophy and History*, ed. Klibansky and Paton [Oxford, 1936], p. 165); the parallel is not a perfect one, however, because Kant would have to assume that the historical characteristics "do not really concern the philosopher at all" since the diversity of philosophical systems rests on "the a priori possibilities of thought" and could "in the last resort have [been] discovered without history, since they arise from the natural laws of the mind" [Bréhier, *ibid.*].

[92] It is not without interest that Bacon, thinking of Aristotle, adds, "the thought that nothing or nothing much can be done naturally presents itself to grave men and of great judgment." Aristotle, I think, would not have agreed, for the hero of scholasticism was not a scholastic.

[93] The poetry of the fifth century tells a good deal about the common attitude to the dreams concerning the future (cf. above, chap. II, pp. 42 f.), but that of the fourth is silent on the matter. This makes the testimony of Isocrates and Xenophon even more important.

good because then and only then will progress be made (*Panegyr.* 1 f. and 10 f.); and he censures the Athenians for failing to acknowledge this truism. (Cf. Aristotle, *Rhetoric* III, 14, 1414 b 33–35.) Xenophon takes up the issue quite objectively in an essay on government and argues that rewards be offered for inventions, since honor (τιμή), praise (ἔπαινος), and love of distinction (φιλοτιμία) are the characteristics that distinguish men from animals (*Hiero* VII, 2–3) and, if men are encouraged by the ruler and many people are induced to ponder what may be useful, more things will be discovered and more will be accomplished. (IX, 10.)

The suggestion made by Isocrates and Xenophon was not new. Xenophanes had asked to be rewarded; and Hippodamus too had demanded that innovators in the political field be honored in recognition of their public merit and their contributions to the welfare of the community.[94] Nevertheless, the remarks of these writers of the fourth century have different overtones. Their predecessors asked for the reward that by right belongs to the inventor and the withholding of which may disappoint the individual. For both Isocrates and Xenophon, however, reward is not so much an honor due after the effort has been made as an incentive to do what should be done. Recognizing the individualism of their period and the doubt about any obligation to the community, they wished to harness self-interest to common interest. Thus the contest is no longer one for victory alone, no longer one fought in the cause of good Eris that "stirs up even the shiftless to toil," no longer the wholesome strife in which "potter is angry with potter, and craftsman with craftsman, and beggar is jealous of beggar, and minstrel of minstrel." (Hesiod, *Works*, 20–26.) Instead, "the spring of action" is love of honor or pride, that passion which in the later seventeenth and eighteenth centuries, in a somewhat similar intellectual climate, came to be called "the craving for distinction," the *fureur de se distinguer.*[95]

[94] Cf. above chap. II, p. 30.
[95] Cf. A.O. Lovejoy, *Essays in the History of Ideas*, p. 62. Burckhardt, who first spoke of the agonistic type and its significance for Greek culture, characterized the victory in the agon as a noble victory without passion (*Griechische Kulturgeschichte* IV, 94). He based this interpretation on a late anecdote in which Pythagoras asked that all rivalry be like that of the stadium, where those who fight do not harm one

Xenophon also envisaged to some extent the scope of inventions and their influence on life. Not unnaturally, military matters were uppermost in his mind. In this regard he knew that it is not enough for a political leader to acquaint himself with all there is to learn and to rely upon knowledge hitherto accumulated. In warfare new things must be invented also just as musicians do not merely repeat what they have been taught but create melodies of their own, for, as in music the new and the original are highly esteemed, so even more highly esteemed are new inventions in warfare (*Cyropaideia* I, 6, 38) no doubt because, as Thucydides had said, the new wins out over the old.[96] Xenophon himself suggested reforms of the Athenian cavalry (*Hipparchus* III, 5); but he also proposed a new system of taxation and a novel distribution of state income, which would eliminate the poverty of the Athenian citizenry, poverty that was held responsible by some for the sad state of current affairs. (*On Revenues*, chap. 1.) Acceptance of such a program, he hoped, would make the city safe and ensure the happiness of its inhabitants (6, 1); and, should the measures to be taken find the approval of the Oracles, he added in his typical fashion, the city should grow "forever in a more desirable and better way." (6, 2.)[97] The language but not the import of his message is altered when he addresses not his fellow citizens but a tyrant. Improvements to be made will in the first place be of practical usefulness, for example in commerce (*Hiero*, IX, 9–10) or in agriculture (X, 7); but indirectly they will have some moral effects also, for, if an individual's income

---

another, but aim only at victory (Iamblichus, *Vita Pythagorica* IX). The story is no doubt a fiction; but *si non è vero, è ben trovato.*

[96] Cf. above, chap. II, p. 31. In the closing chapter of Xenophon's book, which deals with the decay of the Persian monarchy but which may not be genuine, new inventions that serve only the increase of luxury and injustice are described (VIII, 8, 15–18).

[97] The need for divine sanction is expressed by other writers too, though not because of the conventional piety that motivates Xenophon. When the author of the *Epinomis* expresses his confidence that with the support of the Delphic Oracle and the traditional cults the Greeks will one day arrive at a proper worship of the divine (987 E—988 A), he expects a reform of the traditional religion along the lines of his proposals; and, when Plato, in the *Laws* (VI, 772 D), makes the future changes in the constitution dependent on the confirmation of the oracles of all the gods, it is most probably because he wishes to avoid any rash alteration of the prevailing state of affairs; cf. below, pp. 103 f.

rises, he will have more leisure, and consequently will improve by gaining in judgment and moderation (IX, 8). Poverty, Xenophon seems to think, is the mother of immorality. Banish the one and be rid of the other.[98]

Not everyone would have agreed with Xenophon that the pursuit of happiness and of ever more happiness depends so exclusively upon the development of efficient technological devices and the improvement of social conditions; but, though less sanguine in this respect, most people must have shared his basic optimism, for the plans outlined in his political pamphlets, which were written for the public of his day, and in theoretical works embodying the principles of statecraft only expatiate and project into the future the rationalization of human existence that the fourth century had brought about.[99] It is also likely that most progressivists were willing to follow Xenophon and Isocrates in their endorsement of a system of rewards as an incentive to greater advance. Even Plato in the *Republic* suggested that scientific studies would be accelerated if they were supervised and held in esteem by the state (VII, 528 B–C), and in the *Laws* proposed to establish prizes for discoveries.[100] Aristotle seems alone to emphasize the fact that the great forward movement of the recent past had come about "although there was no reward in sight" (Proclus, *In Eucl.*, p. 28, 13 [Friedlein] = Fr. 52 [Rose]), and he seems nowhere to consider rewards necessary. In the *Problemata* (XXX, 11) it is asked who

[98] Xenophon's programme is cast in the form of a dialogue between Simonides and Hiero, the tyrant of Sicily. He may have been thinking in reality of the tyrant Dionysius, with whose policies the proposals may agree (cf. above, pp. 82 f.) and with whom he may have been acquainted, for according to ancient tradition Xenophon visited Sicily and was a guest at the court of the tyrant (Athenaeus, X, 427 f.); but what he says and especially his notion of the spring of human actions is surely not determined by the fact that it is addressed to a tyrant whose subjects are all the enemies of their master (*Hiero* VI, 14), for the remarks of Isocrates show that even in a democratic regime the self-interest of the citizen had come to be regarded as predominant.

[99] Cf. above, pp. 81 f.

[100] To explain Plato's statement by the dramatic date of the dialogue, i.e., by assuming that when the *Republic* was composed the studies mentioned had not yet been far developed (J.B. Skemp, *Plato's Statesman, a translation of the Politicus of Plato* [London, 1952] p. 207, note 1), hardly does justice to Plato's words; but, on the other hand, the evidence cited above refutes the notion that Plato's is "perhaps the earliest demand in literature for the State-encouragement—we might almost say the State-endowment—of pure science." (Adam, *op. cit., ad* 528 C.)

the judge would be if the wise were competing in wisdom and what prize could be better than wisdom itself.

The proposals made by Xenophon and Isocrates remain within the realm of generalities; they take the fact of progress at face value and assume that progress is unquestionably for the better. It is different with Plato and Aristotle, who analyze, distinguish, and weigh arguments, dealing not only with principles but also with concrete issues; but they give their opinions almost incidentally when in the movement of the dialogue or in the course of the lecture the occasion arises, and it is consequently not immediately obvious where they stand themselves. Nevertheless, the attempt to ascertain this must be made, not because their answers were those of the fourth century but because their discussions clarify many problems at which the other evidence available only hints and because their thoughts had a decisive influence on later generations.[101]

The dialogues concerned with political theory contain the main evidence for this part of Plato's doctrine. In the *Republic*, which provides the outlines of "the best state," he has a good deal to say about progress; he discusses it in principle in the *Statesman*, where he gives an abstract analysis of politics; but he speaks about it most concretely and in the greatest detail in his description of the "second-best state," which gives flesh and blood to the picture of the constitution that he had in mind. It is easiest to exhibit this part of his doctrine, therefore, by beginning with what is said in the *Laws*.[102]

Improvements of the constitution after the state has been founded are not only to be expected, Plato thinks, but to be sought. The existing laws are meant to be permanent, but selected observers must be sent abroad to travel "with a view to the confirmation of such practices as are sound and the amendment of any that are

[101] For this reason in what follows I depart from my principle of interpretation (cf. above, Introduction, p. xxviii), and deal with the Platonic and Aristotelian material for the purpose of reconstructing the teaching of Plato and Aristotle.

[102] According to the opinion now prevalent the *Republic* and the *Laws* reflect two different stages of Plato's political thinking. I believe that the two works form a unit, the later supplementing the earlier; but for the purpose of the present analysis the question of the unity of Plato's thought is not important, and I treat the two dialogues as two different discussions of the same subject, which they certainly are.

102

defective in their own community." (*Laws*, XII, 951 B–C; 953 C–D; cf. 961 A [ἐπὶ ζήτησιν].) The observations or personal reflections (952 B) of these emissaries must then be submitted to the official ruling body; and, if accepted as useful, their authors are to be rewarded during their lifetime and after their death as are the rulers of the best state (*Rep.*, VII, 540 C). Similarly selected observers from foreign states are to be brought together with the magistrates or outstanding citizens of the Platonic community for the purpose of "imparting and acquiring knowledge" and are to be dismissed at the end of their stay "with suitable parting gifts and distinctions" (953 D), for, as Plato solemnly declares before laying down this ordinance, "a state unacquainted with mankind, bad or good, will never in its isolation attain an adequate level of civilization and maturity, nor will it succeed in preserving its own laws permanently so long as its grasp of them depends on mere habituation without comprehension." (951 A–B.) Plato, then, thought that future improvements are desirable and necessary, and he would reward "inventors" for valuable suggestions approved by the state.[103]

The principle by which Plato is guided in prescribing such supervision of the progress he expects is somewhat clarified in *The Statesman*. It embodies the "second-best method of government" (300 C), obviously chosen for the second-best state, and is based on the assumption that the first requirement is the preservation of the existing laws; but, Plato hastens to add, the true statesman or "man with real knowledge" will and must always follow "the dictates of his art," i.e., be free to do "what seems better to him, to try to achieve something different with a view to something 'better' "

[103] Cf. above, p. 101. Barker (*Greek Political Theory*, p. 304) speaks of a "retouching" of the code of laws and says that in *Laws* XII, 951 E—952 A a power of revision "seems to be implied" (p. 305, note 1), but in fact such revision is required rather than implied, and it is not restricted to any particular part of the constitution or its ordinances. According to Jaeger (*Paideia* III, 260) Plato in the *Laws* "is endeavoring to avoid the danger of allowing his state to become fossilized and to combine authoritative regulation of life within it with the power freely to adopt valuable suggestions from outside." Such a statement minimizes the significance of the law that requires further search and "amendment" (ἐπανορθούμενον) of what is defective (951 C) in a community recognizing the need "for the presence of loyalty to law in the soul, or rather for the abiding preservation of its law" (960 D).

(300 C–D), and "an individual or a group in possession of a code of laws and trying to introduce a change in it because they consider this to be an improvement are doing the same thing according to their light as the true statesman" (D). They do it "scientifically" as long as they copy "the true original," but no "large group of men" is capable of doing this (D). The provision in the constitution of the *Laws*, according to which improvements are decided upon by the small gremium of the nocturnal council, is a provision for the "scientific" way of making progress.[104]

At this point, one attuned to the modern concept of progress may object that progress as envisaged by Plato can be called progress only by courtesy. He will observe that Plato even when discussing improvements that may become necessary (VI, 769–773; esp. 772 A–D) makes change extremely difficult and goes out of his way to plead for the stability of political institutions, and he will cite the inflexibility of the rules laid down in the *Laws* for all human pursuits, whether gymnastics or music, whether poetry or sculpture. In short, he is likely to feel that Plato, though he endorsed progress in principle, was in fact the arch-enemy of what has lately come to be called "the open society," a society that permits or favors unbridled progress.[105]

To such a society Plato was certainly opposed but not because he was opposed to all progress. As the passages already quoted show, he was far from thinking that the arrangements which he advocated would need no further improvement. The only question is why he felt bound to set limits to progress; and this does at first seem to be a puzzling question because in the very dialogue in which he expounds "the second-best method"—in fact, immediately before this exposition—he speaks of progress in a manner that would lead one to expect from him a full and unqualified endorsement of progressivism.

[104] This solution is not given in the *Politicus*, where the second-best method described is really the second worst, the worst being that of having the arts and sciences supervised by one individual elected by lot, for he could never be impartial (300 A–B). Obviously the *Laws* avoids the difficulty by the stipulation that new proposals must be submitted to the council.
[105] K.R. Popper, *The Open Society and Its Enemies* (London, 1945), *passim*. Plato's insistence in his "political" writings on an unchanging order of society has always been recognized; cf. e.g., Barker, *Greek Political Theory*, pp. 205 and 304.

He assumes for argument's sake that an ordinance has been introduced requiring that "for all future time" (*Politicus* 298 B. ff.) medicine and navigation be practised according to written—that is, fixed—rules (298 E) and forbidding any "searching further" (299 B) or "theorizing on one's own" in defiance of such rules. Then, extending this assumption to the practice of all other pursuits, he asks what the consequences would be. "Suppose," he says, "that all the arts are treated likewise, generalship, hunting, painting, and the imitative arts in general, building and the manufacture of all types of implements, farming or any cultivation whatever, the rearing of horses and other animals, divination and similarly ministerial functions, draught-playing, simple arithmetic, plane geometry, stereometry, kinematics—what would happen?" (299 D–E.)[106] The answer is: "Clearly, the arts would be annihilated and could never be resurrected because of this law which puts an embargo on further search; and the result would be that life, which is hard enough as it is, would be quite impossible then and intolerable." (299 E.)

There can be no doubt of Plato's assertion here that inquiry should continue for all future time and that there is no limit to be established for it. The search is infinite, although it cannot be "infinite" in exactly the sense in which this word is used in modern times. For Plato all the works of men, though not men themselves, are destroyed by recurrent natural catastrophes. Infinite advance, then, means advance without end within the several cultures that come into being; but, on the other hand, in each of these it is a unique process. The statement that time "revolves according to number" (*Timaeus* 30 A) implies merely that it comprises within itself a "cycle of becoming" through which life moves, passing from birth to death and rebirth and exhibiting the inevitable coming-into-being and passing-away of everything. Plato's conception of time is not cyclical. Even the end of the "great year" or the "perfect year" (39 D), the moment when the planets return to their original configuration, does not mark the complete destruction of the

---

[106] I have quoted the passage in full to illustrate the extent of the conception of the arts and sciences, for it shows that such a treatise as *On the Equestrian Art* would be classified as a "scientific" treatise along with essays on stereometry for instance.

natural or human world and the recommencement of another identical with the former one.[107]

The verdict of *The Statesman*, then, marks a decisive turn in the thought of the ancients about the arts and sciences. The Pre-Socratics had held that human inventiveness could not go very far. For them, the horizon of the future was limited.[108] Plato revealed that the task is one without end; and he also recognized that freedom and independence are indispensable to the development of the arts and sciences, for, as he says, they must be practised not "according to written rules" but "according to [the rules of] the art itself." (299 E.) The decision as to good or bad in the performance of the respective arts depends solely upon "the nature of the mean" (283 E; cf. 284 A–B), by which excess and deficiency can be measured objectively and the existence of which is a postulate inherent in the very existence of the arts. (284 B–C, D.)[109] In other words, the arts and sciences have their own standards to which alone they are subject *qua* arts; and, rightly practised, they themselves "guard against exceeding the due measure or falling short of

---

[107] As is assumed e.g., by Bury, *The Idea of Progress*, pp. 9 f. For the interpretation of the "Platonic Year," see A.E. Taylor, *A Commentary on Plato's Timaeus* (Oxford, 1928) pp. 216 ff., especially p. 217, whose view is substantially accepted by F.M. Cornford, *Plato's Cosmology*, p. 117. I follow the latter for Plato's conception of time (*ibid.*, pp. 103 ff.). Adam (*The Republic of Plato*, Appendices to Book VIII, pp. 295–302) tries to identify the "two harmonies" of the *Republic* with the two periods of world history distinguished in the *Politicus* and attributes to Plato the belief that his age falls into the age of dissolution (p. 297, note 4); but the *Politicus* myth is not evidence for Plato's adherence to the dogma of a Golden Age (see above, p. 63), and Book VIII of the *Republic* does not contain a theory of history; cf. below, note 113.

[108] Cf. above, chap. II, pp. 28 f.

[109] The exposition of "excess and deficiency" is prefaced by the assertion that what turns out to be the right kind of measurement operates κατὰ τὴν τῆς γενέσεως ἀναγκαίαν οὐσίαν (283 D). These words, "meant to be enigmatical" (L. Campbell, *The Sophistes and Politicus of Plato* [Oxford, 1867], *ad loc.*), have been variously translated. Whatever rendering is accepted (Schleiermachers' "*des Werdens notwendiges Wesen*" is rightly favored, I think, by Friedländer, *Platon* II, 547, note 2), the later discussion is concerned with "the nature of the Meet" (283 E), as Campbell translates (*ad loc.*), or "the just proportionate in estimating excess and defect," as Taylor puts it (*Plato*, p. 399), i.e., the artist or scientist must avoid the "too much" as well as the "too little," and this he does by observing "the right mean," "the appropriate," "the seasonable," and "the needful" (284 E). I depart from Taylor's translation of the fourth and last of these terms as "the *morally* necessary" (*Plato*, p. 399); δέον is the "*Seinsollende*" (Friedländer, *op. cit.*, p. 548). In the *Politicus* the conception of value, whether aesthetic or moral, is consciously left aside; cf. 257 B with 266 C; also *Sophist* 227 B.

it" and achieve "effectiveness and beauty in all they produce." (286 A.) That they do so is evidently to their interest as well as to that of society, for, as *The Statesman* so emphatically puts it, the arts and sciences must be left to their own devices and they must go on forever without any restraint, not only because otherwise there would be no possibility of their survival, but also because life itself would no longer be possible or livable.

If this is true, one wonders how it can be reconciled with the position that Plato takes as political reformer. It is surely paradoxical to assert that the freedom of the arts and sciences is indispensable to their survival and to a tolerable life for men and at the same time to ask that they be restricted by written laws. The statement in *The Statesman* is unique. May Plato here have given expression to a passing thought, the consequences of which he did not fully see?[110] Indeed, is this statement not contradicted by others? At least for the fine arts, which *The Statesman* includes in the demand for freedom of growth (299 D), the *Republic* and the *Laws*, it has been argued, implicitly or explicitly assume a high point of development that can never be surpassed; and in the last analysis the arts and sciences, like all other human efforts, are in Plato's opinion subject to an inexorable law of rise and fall.[111]

Now the latter contention is undoubtedly in conflict with Plato's assertion that "the scanty embers of humanity," from which the

[110] Only in this passage of the *Politicus* does Plato, so far as I know, speak of infinite progress. Taylor in his commentary on the *Timaeus* (*ad* 27 D 5–29 D 3; cf. also Taylor, *Plato*, pp. 440 f.) finds in that dialogue the recognition that "all natural science is 'provisional,' whereas arithmetic for instance is 'final,' or to put it in a more complimentary way . . . natural science is 'progressive' in a sense in which pure mathematics is not" (p. 60). I do not believe that Timaeus' characterization of natural science as 'mythos' is open to such an interpretation (for the myth in Plato's natural philosophy, cf. Edelstein, "The Function of the Myth in Plato's Philosophy," *J.H.I.*, X [1949], 467 ff.). Aristotle's proposition that physical theories must change in accordance with newly observed facts (cf. below, p. 120) seems to me to be the first formulation of the modern concept of progress in the physical sciences. However that may be, the *Timaeus* certainly does not imply that progress is necessary in all the arts and sciences. On *Republic* IV, 424 A, see below, note 120. B. Schweitzer (*Plato und die Bildende Kunst der Griechen* [Tübingen, 1953], p. 87, note, finds that *Politicus* 298 C–300 E grants a "certain freedom" to the arts and sciences, but this formulation does not do justice to the passage.

[111] J. Stenzel, *Platon der Erzieher* (Leipzig, 1928), p. 133. In a general way, Plato's opposition to the idea of perpetual progress is asserted by F.M. Cornford, *The Republic of Plato*, p. 112, note 2 (*ad Rep.* 424 C). Bury connects it with "the tendency characteristic of Greek philosophical thinkers to idealize the immutable as possessing a higher value than that which varies" (*The Idea of Progress*, p. 11).

fire of civilization is rekindled after one of the periodic natural catastrophes, have views which Plato approves about "things called fair or foul," just as he is in sympathy with their belief in the tales inherited from their ancestors. (*Laws* III, 679 D.) So, even though men at the beginning of the new era are "bound by comparison with the age before the Deluge or with our own to be rude and ignorant in the various arts" (679 D), not everything can have been debased at the end of the previous civilization.[112] Nor does Plato in his analysis of the various forms of government (*Republic* VIII, 545 ff.) presuppose a theory of general decline. The "decline" that he there describes concerns "divergencies from an ideal rather than an historical process," and no philosophy of history is intended.[113]

On the other hand, the *Republic* provides no warrant for assuming that Plato believed in the superiority of certain forms of poetry or music that can at best be retrieved after having been lost. As in the *Laws* so here too he passes judgment and makes his selection according to moral and educational effects rather than according to the principles of the arts. The effect of such restrictions on the arts he does not discuss and need not discuss, for he is concerned not with the highest development of poetry and music but with their greatest usefulness for his purposes.[114] Even the admiration expressed in the *Laws* for Egyptian art and music on the ground that

---

[112] Cf. above, pp. 63 and 85 f. The chief passages are *Timaeus* 22 C and 23 A–B; *Critias* 108 E–109 A; *Laws* III, 677 A–B.

[113] Shorey, *ad Rep.* VIII, 545 B. The impossibility of reconstructing Plato's historical views from *Republic* VIII and IX (they are to be found in *Laws* III instead) is recognized by G. Rohr, *Platos Stellung zur Geschichte* (Berlin, 1932), p. 84. Barker concedes that "it would be a mistake to claim an historical intention for this sketch," but he nevertheless refuses to "deny its historical bearing" (*Greek Political Theory*, p. 245). The analysis considers real states, however, merely as "perversions of the right polity," to use Aristotle's terms (*Politics* IV, 7, 1293 b 25 f.), and depicts their relations genetically, just as Book II characterizes the nature of the state by showing its development from small beginnings. More recently R.G. Bury in "Plato and History" (*Classical Quarterly*, XLV [1951], 86 ff.), in agreement with A.E. Taylor and J. Adam, has again tried to make a case for a Platonic philosophy of history that "condemns all that is mundane, all that is phenomenal, however seemingly perfect, however temporarily stable, to ultimate decay and transformation if not actual destruction." (p. 88)

[114] In the *Politicus*, however, which investigates the art of politics as one art among many, an analysis of the arts and sciences and their own laws is appropriate. The different statements do not reveal a difference of opinion but a difference in the subjects investigated.

108

Egyptian artists were forbidden to deviate from the models, the inventory of standard types drawn up in that nation (II, 656 D–E), does not prove that Plato intended to establish a canon of artistic perfection. What interested him, the "thought-provoking fact," as he expresses it, was not the aesthetic value of Egyptian art (even the Egyptians had made their choice for the benefit of the young, recognizing "the truth we are now affirming" [656 D]) but rather "that it has actually proved possible in such a sphere to canonize melodies which exhibit an intrinsic rightness permanently by law"; and so he feels himself encouraged in his own legislation to reduce the arts "to law and system without misgivings" according to "the intrinsically right in such matters," i.e., according to their educational value. The Egyptians' example proves that it can be done. (657 A–B.)[115]

Nowhere, then, does Plato contradict the assertion that the arts and sciences considered by themselves should proceed in their search "for all future time." In fact, the passage last mentioned incidentally affirms not only the possibility of this in the case of the fine arts but also its actual occurrence to the satisfaction of everyone, for the daring venture of canonizing one kind of music is to be undertaken against the admittedly natural instinct to deride it as "archaic," as "the cravings of pleasure and pain inspire a continual chase after new forms of music." (657 B.) Moreover, Plato the philosopher, if not Plato the political reformer, always admits that the possession of truth is beyond human reach. Except for that rare moment of exalted vision in which the mind beholds the Idea of the Good any understanding of Being is dialectical, i.e., partial and incomplete. Philosophy is love of wisdom, search for that which in a sense one has but in a sense has not and certainly will never entirely have Here and Now. God alone is wise. (*Phaedrus* 278 D.) Insight, even if clearly caught, cannot be confined adequately in written words, because dead letters do not take account of particular circumstances and individual situations; and it is the fate of men

[115] That this is the meaning of the passage in question was briefly explained by A.E. Taylor, *Plato, the Man and his Work* (4th ed.; London, 1937), p. 469; but I have argued it in more detail because the contrary view is still defended in recent literature (e.g., Schweitzer, *Plato und die Bildende Kunst der Griechen*, p. 87).

in their attempt to translate the archetype of truth and perfection into human deeds always to fall short of the goal. Fitting the ideal pattern of the state to the phenomenal world, the lawgiver must reduce its size, as it were, in order that it may assume more of that likeness of humanity (ἀνδρείκελον) that Homer also called, when it appears in men, the image and likeness of god. (θεοείκελον *Republic* VI, 501 B.) The best, as reason envisages it, cannot be realized, for it is impossible that anything be realized in deed as it is spoken in words, and the only state that can be constituted in fact is the one "most nearly answering our description." (V, 473 A.) This "second-best state," when it is described in the *Laws*, does provide for future progress, as has been shown. It does fulfill the prescription of *The Statesman* for the second-best method, to have written laws and yet to permit the true statesman to follow "the dictates of his art."[116]

All the evidence, therefore, seems to support the conclusion that Plato is very much in earnest when he argues that the end of search would mean the virtual death of the arts and sciences. It cannot be imagined that he should have ascribed to them the power denied to reason itself, the power to translate into permanent form the model of truth, the Ideas that they imitate. Like all imitations—those of reason, and even those of nature—the imitations of the arts and sciences can never represent their models adequately. Why, then, should they not be permitted to continue their quest, create values ever new, and make life endurable and livable? Why should the political reformer Plato wish to place them under constant supervision? The answer must be that in his opinion the arts and sciences,

[116] Cf. above, pp. 103 f. For the Platonic conceptions of knowledge and learning and of philosophy it is superfluous to specify the evidence of particular passages in the *Symposium* and the *Phaedrus*. For Plato's conception of dialectic cf. E. Frank, *Wissen, Wollen, Glauben*, pp. 90 ff., and for instruction as a process of "begetting," *ibid.*, pp. 229 ff., esp. p. 232. The Platonic insistence on eternal search for truth is not adequately taken into account by those who ascribe to the Greeks in general and to Plato in particular a "veneration for the past and the ever-present" and from this infer that the Greeks could not conceive the idea of progress. Cf. Löwith, *op. cit.*, pp. 111 and 238 with reference to H. Weiss, *Philosophy and Phenomenological Research*, II (1941–1942), 173 ff. Cf. also the writers mentioned above, notes 78 and 86.

though, if rightly practiced, they will not destroy themselves, may well become destructive of the "just life" that political leadership is designed to provide.

That the several arts shape man's character and that discoveries in the sciences determine his actions, these observations had been made long before Plato. The *Querelle des anciens et des modernes* in the fifth century was a dispute about two ways of life. The new was asked to justify itself before the old, to show cause why it should be preferred and considered "better." Some modernists contended that the new is better because it is the new, or the necessary, or the stronger. Others, though aware of the fact that the arts and sciences had transformed man's originally brutish existence into human existence, still doubted that mankind had become happier or morally better by advancing ever further in all fields. The Cynics, insisting that civilization is irreconcilable with a moral life, opted for morality and sacrificed culture.[117] Plato was obviously not satisfied to welcome the new as a brute fact or merely to record the outcome of the development, just as he was unwilling to adopt a radical nihilism that would destroy the precious work of man's hand and mind. Instead, he attempted to save both culture and morality by placing the arts and sciences under the guidance of moral consciousness.

If such guidance is needed, however, whence can it come? In Plato's time the various human activities were becoming independent and autonomous. In the pursuit of artistic or scientific ends all other ends were obliterated, while, as the incipient rationalization of life clearly shows, society was becoming more and more dependent on the expert's competence and advice.[118] The expert or the specialist, however, in Plato's opinion knows only what is good for his art and does not know what is good for men (*Charmides*, 169 D ff.; cf. *Laches*, 195 C–D), so that in order to assign each particular discipline and each particular skill its appropriate place within the scheme of the whole another art is needed (*Euthydemus*,

[117] For the Cynics, cf. above, pp. 60 f.; for the fifth century, cf. above, chap. II, pp. 52 f.
[118] Cf. above, pp. 81 f.

286 ff.), a "kingly" or "political" art. (291 B.) Otherwise, there will be no fixed values, truth will be unobtainable, and there will be chaos instead of a cosmos.[119]

This art, without which the just life is impossible, is provided by philosophy and embodied in political theory. To distinguish between the philosopher Plato and the political theorist Plato is in the last analysis otiose and even invidious. It is, then, only natural that as a lawgiver too he should be concerned not merely with the routine questions of so-called politics but also with the issue between morality and the arts and sciences. So he condemns the "advance" that pays no attention to value and endorses that which keeps an eye upon changing circumstances and increases skill and knowledge to create and maintain "the good life." It is as if he were to say that the "new" as such has no specific meaning and that to know whether it is better one must first ask in what respect it is supposed to be better and for whom, for man or for the arts and sciences themselves, since what is better for the latter may prove to be worse for the former. If this should be the case, one must decide in favor of human improvement, for in the larger view progress is "growth in virtue." Therefore, the new, although valuable in its way, might have to be abandoned, for it might turn out not to be an improvement in the true sense of the ambiguous word "better," which is to be defined by the ultimate aim of life, that of becoming a morally responsible agent and of achieving the insight of the mind. Advance need be true improvement no more than change need be true advance. This is the truth to be acknowledged; and, if it is not, one may well say with a play on Plato's own words that the point will soon be reached where life, which without "progress" in the arts and sciences is not "livable" (ἀβίωτος), will no longer be "worth living" (οὐ βιωτός).[120]

Now, the degree of supervision depends on the situation. In ideal conditions, in the best state, all citizens would be "artisans of

[119] Cf. Friedländer, Platon II, 74–77.

[120] Skemp, whose translation I have followed in my quotations from the Statesman, renders ἀβίωτος (299 E) "not to be endured." I have rendered the word "not livable" in order to bring out the contrast to the famous remark of Socrates (Apology 38 A), which is noticed by Skemp also and which Plato must have intended to be noticed.

virtue." The lawgiver could be sure of their constant moral progress because a development, "if it once starts well, proceeds, as it were, in a cycle of growth" (*Republic* IV, 424 A) and thus has a cumulative effect. It is necessary merely to preserve the framework that has been erected for education, to guard against any changes in the principles of gymnastics and music, so that the moral fibre of men will remain uncorrupted, to have "new songs but (not) a new way of song." (C.) The rest can be left to the citizenry. Being good men, they will do what is right. (425 D–E.)[121] It is a different matter in the "second-best" state, the state nearer to reality, for this is open to a "double progressive development of a city in virtue and vice" and which tendency will prevail depends on the course followed by the arts and sciences in their growth and development. (*Laws* III 676 A.) Here the lawgiver must not only prescribe for all activities in his legislation but must approve the changes to be made and all the innovations to be expected, deciding each case on the basis of its bearing on the purpose of human existence.[122]

The progressivism advocated by Plato would not have been called such at all in the nineteenth century. Even today it is anath-

---

[121] I follow Shorey, *ad* 424 A. (Adam's explanation [*ad loc.*] is unconvincing, for Books VIII and IX, to which he refers, do not prove or imply that the circle "narrows to the inevitable end" [see above, note 113].) The passage, which is neglected by those who deny that Plato envisaged any kind of progress, is amusingly illustrated by Socrates' contention that his citizens, if properly educated, will easily discover by themselves all the principles that he is to propose and others that he passes over (423 E–424 A). On the other hand, E.O. Bassett, "Plato's Theory of Social Progress," *International Journal of Ethics*, XXXVIII (1927–28), 476, goes too far in concluding from the statement in question that according to Plato "society executes an infinite progression," that "progress must be perpetual." The *Republic* is not a blueprint for reality. For progressing "little by little" see above, p. 84.

[122] Cf. above, p. 63. Commenting on *Laws* 678 A 9, E.B. England (*The Laws of Plato* I [Manchester, 1921]), remarks: "He means, as he explains immediately, that virtue and vice, like the details of civilization, take time to develop and can only develop in their company. How this applies to vice is explained at E 6 ff. He does not give a corresponding explanation of the rise of virtue, because a virtuous development (the ἐπί δοσις εἰς ἀρετήν) is *natural*. The object of the whole treatise (*sc.* on the emergence of laws and constitutions) is to show how to avoid and obviate the *accidents* which give rise to vice." (p. 348) I am not sure that England's use of the terms 'natural' and 'accidental' fits Plato, but essentially his explanation is surely correct and may be extended to the *Laws* in general. In the *Republic* too, vices and virtues grow with the growth of the civilization, with the development from the "healthy" to the "fevered" city; and it is Plato's main aim to secure for his city a truly moral life.

ema to the defenders of the open society. In practice, however, no modern statesman, no "third" lawgiver charged with framing the constitution of the city of reality, can afford to neglect the problem that Plato poses[123]; and there may now be a growing understanding of Plato's attitude and of the need that he felt, when confronted with the alternatives, "better for science" and "better for man," to decide for man. It will be the more important not to misinterpret his proposals or to take them in a spirit contrary to that in which he made them. Having discovered the infinity of the human task, he not only counseled caution and restraint but also asked for constant change and was eager to apply the spur to man, a sluggish horse by nature (*Apology*, 30 E), and to drive him on. He wanted him to do his utmost to improve himself and his environment for evermore.

It is true that the contemplative life, which Democritus and others had sanctioned, was given the highest rank by Plato too. It makes the soul invulnerable and brings eudaemonia, which can never be gained in the active life where pain and pleasure are inextricably interwoven. (*Phaedo*, 60 B.) In theoretical speculation the philosopher is transported to the "Islands of the Blest" (*Republic*, VII, 519 B), where he finds the true and timeless Golden Age, the state of felicity that many of Plato's predecessors had hoped to find and some of his contemporaries still hoped to find at the ends of the *oecumene* or among the primitives.[124] The Platonist is constrained to return, however, from the realm of Ideas to the realm of Becoming (519 D) and to toil "in the service of the state and [hold] office for the city's sake, regarding the task not as a fine thing, but as a necessity" (540 B). He must reshape the world in the light of the new knowledge. Plato's own writings, to use an

---

[123] As already stated (above, note 102), the *Republic* and the *Laws* are in my opinion complementary and not contradictory. Moreover, both outline a theory of the constitution; but even the *Laws* does not give a blueprint for an actual city, which will have to be provided by the third lawgiver, who must reduce the theory of the *Laws* to what is possible under the circumstances, just as the *Laws* reduces the construction of reason in the *Republic* to the humanly possible.

[124] Cf. above, note 26 and chap. II, p. 50 for the primitives; Boll (*op. cit.*, p. 33 [*ad* p. 16]) emphasized the importance of the passage in the *Republic* in which Plato identifies the state of knowledge with life on the isles of the blessed.

114

expression of Aristotle's, are distinguished by "novelty of view" (*Politics* 1265 a 12; cf. 1266 a 35); but whether the realization of his proposed reforms or of any reform is possible, this question too Plato anticipated and answered by analyzing human possibilities just as he had analyzed the possibilities of the arts and sciences. In doing so he brought to light another and equally important aspect of progressivism.[125]

His first concern in his investigation is what may be called a psychological prejudice. As he puts it in the *Republic,* any true craftsman "feels the difference between impossibilities ($τὰ ἀδύνατα$) and possibilities ($τὰ δυνατά$) in his art and attempts the one and lets the other go" (II, 360 E). For the philosopher and his art feeling would of course not be enough. He must define the possible, which is not necessarily identical with the best, "for one might doubt whether what is proposed is possible and, even conceding the possibility, one might still be skeptical whether it is best" (V, 450 C). On the other hand, one must not think that the best is impossible just because it seems to be ridiculous in the present conditions (452 B). So people often do think; but experience shows that the ridiculous, which seemed better or the best to reason, is accepted by everyone when once it has become a fact. The criterion of a serious evaluation of the possible is nothing other than the good. (C–E; cf. 457 B.)[126]

Bacon thought that "lack of hope is the greatest obstacle to the progress of science," greater than veneration of the ancients or false planning; and so in his "plan for preparing man's mind" for the task of progress "preparation to give hope is no unimportant part," for the most serious despondency is due to the fact that "men despair and think things impossible." (*Novum Organum,* I, 92.) [127] The hopes of the fifth century had been dimmed not only by its conception of the nature of the arts and sciences but also by its

[125] I leave aside the question whether Plato ever engaged in political activities; but, even if he did not advise Dionysius and counsel reforms, it was still appropriate for him to deal with the problems of human possibilities in his theoretical writings. For the question of the Seventh Letter see below, note 130.

[126] These remarks of Plato's are reflected, I think, in the history of Tacitus.

[127] The passage follows immediately upon the one quoted above, chap. II, p. 28.

conception of human nature. To avoid the impossible and to cling to the possible had been the teaching that it cherished.[128] Plato tried to raise man's hopes by showing that in all too many cases what is regarded as impossible is simply the unaccustomed, which for that reason alone is ridiculed as unrealistic. He felt about the wits of his time the way the author of the *History of the Royal Society* did about those of the Restoration: "I believe the New Philosophy need not (as Caesar) fear the pale or melancholy as much as the humorous and merry."[129]

After having prepared the ground for his argument, Plato could proceed to "the chief topic of contention" (457 D), the possible itself. Complete realization of the best must be recognized to be beyond human power. (472 E–473 D.) Man can achieve it only "in the measure of the possible" (VI, 501 B) or "as far as it is possible for man," to quote the famous Platonic phrase (cf. *Theaetetus* 176 B and *Timaeus* 90 B–C). This is not a phrase of meek humility, for, granting the difficulties involved in doing even the possible (VII, 540 C), it must be assumed that, if there is the wish to achieve it, "it has been, is, or will be achieved." (VI, 499 D.) "In all the course of time" it can happen (502 A–B), or in the words of the *Laws* time is "vast and incalculable," and infinite changes have taken place during infinite ages in the past. (III, 676 A–B; cf. VI, 781 E–782 A; also *Republic* VI, 499 C.) Customs and especially sexual mores have during the course of history been altered to an almost incredible degree under the impact of social institutions, which subjugate the instincts. (*Laws* VIII, 838 C–D.) Men are readily inclined to deem further changes impossible (839 C), but in fact they are not "beyond human nature." (D.)

So Platonic idealism was not so niggardly in drawing the limits imposed upon man as were the Pre-Socratics. The Beyond, the new dimension of the realm of Ideas which it added to the world of phenomena, showed human nature to be stronger than does the experience of what men call reality. Reference to what is is there-

---

[128] Cf. above, chap. II, pp. 27 ff. For Democritus in particular cf. Frs. 191 and 58 (Diels–Kranz), and for Gorgias cf. his *Palamedes*, p. 300, 23 and 7 ff. (82 B 11 a).
[129] M.H. Nicolson, "Two Voices, Science and Literature," *The Rockefeller University Review*, IV (June, 1963), p. 7.

fore not an argument against what could be. *De non esse ad non posse non valeat consequentia.* Man is free to make an ever greater effort to gain knowledge and to produce ever more beautiful and useful things. Perfection is denied to him, but to strive for it continually is his prerogative. Perfectibility is his from his birth and dies only with his death.[130]

In the light of this Plato's position with regard to progress should be clear. The constant change to which man's views are subjected by the endless progress of the arts and sciences is matched by the changeability of his own nature, which of itself offers no resistance to the novel but is malleable and like society in need of receiving shape and form. Both man and society must use whatever knowledge may be available as an instrument with which to model themselves; and, since knowledge progresses, this process will necessarily go on forever. It will take the right direction only if time is allowed for criticism and for careful consideration of the new. That is why one must supervise progress and transform unconscious adaptation to what is new into conscious acceptance; or, in Plato's words, just as the individual must mould himself so the legislator must "practice stamping on the plastic matter of human nature in public and private the pattern that he visions there" (*Rep.* VI, 500 D). Nothing can be left to chance, for otherwise what could be a beautiful work of art might become ugly and distorted;[131] but, if man uses reason, if in human affairs he does not feel himself to be at the mercy of chance and opportunity or leave everything to god,

[130] The peculiar nature of Plato's interpretation of the humanly or objectively possible and of his ethico-practical conception of the possible is clearly recognized by A. Faust (*op. cit.*, I, 47 ff.) and is contrasted to his concept of ontological possibility, which acknowledges the really existent as a limit in the explanation of the world of sense-phenomena (pp. 56 ff.). J. Stenzel (*s.v.* Speusippos, R.–E., III A, 2, col. 1651, 11 ff.) finds in the seventh Platonic Letter "the infinity of *paideia*"; but I do not believe that the letter is genuine (cf. Edelstein, "Plato's Seventh Letter," *Philosophia Antiqua*, XIV [Leiden, 1966]).

[131] This activity of the legislator in the end includes the true education by which the little soul, if it is "hammered from childhood," is "struck free of the leaden weights, so to speak, of our birth and becoming, which attaching themselves to it by food and similar pleasures and gluttonies turn downwards the vision of the soul" (*Republic* VII, 519 A). Adam in his commentary on 518 C aptly compares Plato's theory of education to the thought frequently expressed by Michelangelo "that every block of marble contains a statue and that the sculptor brings it to light by cutting away the encumbrances by which the 'human face divine' is concealed."

117

"if there is art as well," things will get better. (*Laws* IV, 709 B ff.) With the Platonic ethos of infinity comes a measured optimism, a tragic optimism, as it were, superseding the tragic pessimism of the Pre-Socratics. In terms of human time men are "the playthings of the gods"; but in terms of "everness" teleology prevails. This creed can issue in a shallow overconfidence and did; but this was not so in the beginning when Platonic "futurism" generated the hope that the further search first envisaged by Xenophanes would lead men to heights of which they had hardly dreamed.[132]

Aristotle's initial approach to the problem of progress is very much in the Platonic vein, for like Plato he considered it in principle within the framework of political theory. When he discusses the law proposed by Hippodamus, he first makes a number of general objections: such a proposal to reward inventors might encourage informers; it might lead to political commotion; more important, it may be asked whether changes, even changes for the better, are not inexpedient for other reasons and in fact destructive of the constitution. (*Politics* II, 8, 1268 b 22–31.) He observes that something can be said for both sides of the case. It is certain, on the one hand, that in politics as well as in the arts and sciences changes have been advantageous, that the relics of ancient customs still in existence here and there are "utterly absurd" and illustrate the benefit of change from traditional usages to new practices, that further improvement of political institutions will be necessary if for no other reason than that the law in its universality cannot cover all the particular circumstances that may arise. (1268 b 31–1269 a 13.)[133] On the other hand, however, changing the laws lightheartedly may create distrust in the rulers, a disadvantage greater than the possible benefit, and also weakens the power of the law and obedience to it, which is grounded solely in the force of custom, custom that takes a long time to establish itself. All this, he observes, is quite otherwise in the arts and sciences; and furthermore, if a change of laws is to be recommended, the questions arise whether all laws are to be altered and whether they are to be altered

[132] Cf. below, pp. 126 ff.
[133] This argument is Platonic in origin (cf. *Politicus* 294 A–C), and Plato himself makes use of it in his *Laws* in order to explain why in fixing penalties and fines the law must give some freedom to the courts (III, 875 D—876 A).

by anyone whomever or only by certain persons, for it makes quite a difference which alternative is chosen. (1269 a 13–27.)

At this point Aristotle breaks off the argument because, he says, it properly belongs to another occasion (1269 a 27 ff.);[134] and unfortunately the discussion, the only continuous one of this kind preserved from the fourth century, is not taken up again in his works. The drift of his reasoning emerges clearly, however. The proposal of Hippodamus, "specious to the ear" (1268 b 24), is seen to be fallacious as soon as one recognizes the fact that the *modus operandi* of progress varies in the various fields of human activity. Politics, to be sure, is an art like other arts; and yet in political life the conditions are different from those that exist in medicine or other crafts and sciences. The analogy with other arts and sciences therefore is partly right (1268 b 34–38; 1269 b 8–10), and partly wrong (1269 b 19; cf. also III, 16, 1287 a 33).

This is Aristotle's characteristic method of clarifying the vague comparisons made by the Pre-Socratics and thus of avoiding the errors that arise from their unrestricted use of analogies.[135] It preserves the force of the analogy on which his predecessors had based their belief in progress but specifies it and delimits its use. Political advance thereby gains a certain autonomy, for here the particular exigencies of the art outweigh the advantages of improvement at least to some extent. Thus mainly by logical analysis Aristotle arrives at a conclusion not unlike that of the moralist Plato. The current economic system, he thinks, can and should be improved "through correction of human behavior and through the enactment of right laws"; and, ironically enough, only then will it be superior to the communism advocated by Plato. (II, 5, 1263 a 21–24.) The measures to be taken, however, will have to be adapted to the specific political conditions. Restraint is as essential here as is the will to make innovations.[136]

[134] Barker in his edition assumes that a few words of Aristotle's discussion have been lost from the text, and this is not impossible.

[135] For the Aristotelian conception of analogy and the way in which it differs from that of the Pre-Socratics cf. O. Regenbogen, *Quellen und Studien zur Geschichte der Mathematik*, B: I (1930), 150–152 and 148 ff. For the Pre-Socratics, see above, chap. II, p. 31.

[136] Aristotle's hesitation is due in part to his belief that the past can teach the present; see below, p. 123.

In matters other than politics Aristotle apparently saw no reason to warn against unchecked progress. After speaking of the circularity of the heavens and proposing his own views, he adds that "whenever anyone should succeed in finding proofs of greater precision, gratitude will be due him for his discovery; but for the moment, we must be content with a probable solution." (*On the Heavens* II, 5, 287 b 34–288 a 2.) Anticipating the modern conviction that theories must change in accordance with new data, he also recognizes that regarding certain biological problems the facts "have not yet been sufficiently grasped: whenever they are, credence will have to be given to observation rather than to theories, and to theories only if what they affirm is in agreement with the observed facts." (*De Generatione Animal.* III, 10, 760 B 30–31.) Elsewhere he expressed the conviction that in some fields not even the first steps had been taken. (*Rhetoric,* I, 2, 1358 a 6 ff.)[137]

Aristotle seems not to have agreed, however, with the belief of his friend and master that encouragement by the state is necessary for the advancement of scientific studies. In his opinion, as has been indicated, the sciences had recently progressed more than ever before, more even than the arts and crafts, and this despite the fact that scientists and philosophers were not rewarded by the community and were often discouraged rather than encouraged in their work. The gains made nevertheless were due to the greater worth of theoretical studies (Fr. 53 [Rose] = Iamblichus, *De comm. math. scientia,* 26; cf. Fr. 52 [Rose] = Proclus, *In Euclid.,* p. 28, 13 [Friedlein]).[138] No matter whether it is the approval of society or the personal initiative of the individual that is responsible for progress, however, there is much to be improved, and one must certainly go on without fear of possible disadvantages, for, as he says in defending himself and his attempt to turn rhetoric into an art: "If it is argued that one who makes an unfair use of such faculty of speech may do a great deal of harm, this objection

[137] Other passages in which Aristotle deplores the insufficient results thus far achieved in the solution of particular problems are collected by Eucken, *Die Methode der Aristotelischen Forschung,* p. 5, note 4; cf. also *Meteorology* II, 5, 362 b 12 ff.

[138] Aristotle's description of the situation is quite accurate: like the city–states of the fifth century those of the fourth, if not opposed to scientific studies, were at least disinterested in them; cf. Edelstein, *J.H.I.,* XIII (1952), 596 ff.

applies equally to all good things except virtue and above all to those things which are most useful, such as strength, health, wealth, generalship, for as these, rightly used, may be of the greatest benefit so, wrongly used, they may do an equal amount of harm." (*Rhetoric* I, 1355 b 1 ff.)[139]

As for Plato this future progress for Aristotle is progress within a single civilization, for both of the founders of Greek idealism assumed the incidental destruction of human civilizations by the blind forces of nature and the rebuilding of cultures after nature had wrought its havoc and both believed that some of the insights gained in the earlier period survive into the later one. The wisdom of a former culture and its insights into the truth are reflected in the inspired sayings of the early poets. (*Metaphysics* XII, 8, 1074 a 38–b 14.) Not all knowledge can have become extinct or degenerate before the destruction of the people;[140] and Aristotle did not believe either in an eternal recurrence of the same things. The metaphor of the cycle of time denoted for him, as it did for Plato, the mutability of all things or as he expresses it himself: "We say that human affairs and those of all other things that have natural movement and become and perish seem to be in a way circular because all these things come to pass in time and have their beginning and end as it were 'periodically,' for time itself is conceived as 'coming round'; . . . to call the happenings of a thing a circle is to say that there is a sort of circle of time." (*Physics* IV, 14, 223 b 24–29.) The theory of recurrent world-cycles he rejected; or rather, admitting an identity in kind but not in number, he believed in no more than "a continuous repetition of the same generic types of entities or states," that is in what is called "theory of endless

[139] A similar argument was later used by Seneca; cf. below, chap. IV, p. 172. Indirectly Aristotle's remarks refute the Cynic position, of course.

[140] Cf. Aristotle, *Metaphysics* XII, 1074 b 10, and the passages quoted by W.D. Ross, *Aristotle's Metaphysics* II, 396 *ad loc.*; and in general cf. Jaeger, *Aristoteles*, pp. 138 ff. As Bernays showed (see above, note 76), one cannot conclude from the passage that the arts themselves were destroyed or that they decayed in the preceding civilizations; for the expression εἰς τὸ δυνατόν cf. below, p. 125. Knowledge also survives from one civilization to the other in the form of proverbs (Bernays, *op. cit.*, p. 49); and the Aristotelian theory on the whole goes well with that of Plato, as Bernays also noted, though Plato believed in destructions that affect the whole world, while Aristotle had in mind partial devastations.

undulation."[141] If absolute decay has no place in cosmic history, it is absent also from the history of the arts and sciences and of political institutions. These too are mutable, no doubt; but the direction in which they change depends upon free human decisions. Aristotle did not favor any more than Plato did an absolute determinism or absolute causality which would prescribe an inexorable course of events.[142]

Did he, then, also share Plato's expectation of endless progress as long as man is at work undisturbed by the threats of hostile nature? Surely Aristotelian philosophy, so much more involved in the study and explanation of natural and historical data than was that of Plato, ought to have been predisposed to give free reign to the inquiring mind; and its pathos of historicism and experience seems to call for unlimited progressivism. It has consequently been as-

[141] Lovejoy and Boas, *op. cit.*, p. 173; cf. p. 172; and G. Boas, "Some Assumptions of Aristotle," *Transactions of the American Philosophical Society*, N.S. Vol. XLIX, Pt. 6, p. 55, note 10. On Aristotle's conception of time cf. W.D. Ross, *Aristotle's Physics* (Oxford, 1936), p. 612 (*ad* 224 a 2): "Aristotle here points out that the sayings which describe time as the motions of the heavenly sphere, or as a circle, are natural exaggerations due to the close relation between time and its primary measure, which is the circular motion of the heavens." In *Physics* IV, 13, 222 b 17–27 Aristotle says expressly that time is only incidentally the cause of things, that things are destroyed not by time itself but by changes that occur concurrently. E. Frank maintained that he understood time to imply world cycles similar to the cycles of Empedocles (cf. above, chap. II, p. 46 and note 54); cf. E. Frank, *Philosophical Understanding and Religious Truth*, p. 82, note 41 and Baillie, *op cit.*, p. 47. The "Great Year" is mentioned by Aristotle perhaps once (*Meteorology* I, 14, 352 a 30) but without any reference to periodic destruction of the earth or of civilization. For the relation of these considerations to the problem of progress see above, Introduction, pp. xx ff.

[142] I cannot agree with Lovejoy and Boas, who on the basis of *Metaphysics* XI, 1074 b 10 assume that there is "a process of development and decline in the case of each art" (*op. cit.*, p. 173), for this passage like others refers to destruction by sudden catastrophes (above, note 76), which take place at any time. The same authors, having analyzed Aristotle's opinion concerning the sequence of the forms of social organization (pp. 174–177), conclude by saying that of constitutions "those which are faulty and perverted are necessarily subsequent to those which are perfect" (*Politics* III, 1275 b 1–3); but Aristotle's ideal state like Plato's has no existence in time and space, and his account of the changes that take place "is not really historical, but rather, like Plato's account, logical," or "rests . . . on ethical preconceptions" (Barker, *Greek Political Theory*, p. 245, note 3). Aristotle's and Plato's conceptions of freedom of action and of causality are hardly ever considered in connection with the law of decay attributed to them, and yet these conceptions seem to make it a priori unlikely that such a law could have been accepted by either one.

122

serted that in the spheres of investigation and speculation at any rate Aristotle recognized "no end within the view of any man."[143]

It is precisely in Aristotle's appreciation of the past and of experience, however, that there are indications of his having abandoned Plato's position. As he writes in a biting criticism of the latter's political dreams, "We are bound to pay some regard to the long past and the passage of the years in which things (advocated by Plato) would not have gone unnoticed if they had been really good. Almost everything has been discovered already, though some of the things discovered have not been coordinated, and some, though known, are not put into practice." (*Politics* II, 5, 1264 a 1–5.) In other words, here the pathos of human experience and of history becomes a hindrance to the extension of experience rather than a stimulus to further experience.[144]

Again, in discussing the development of tragedy, Aristotle seems to imply that there is in fact also a high point in the development that cannot be surpassed. To be sure, this may not be the meaning of the famous statement that tragedy, having undergone many alterations, "stopped because it had found its natural form." (*Poetics* IV, 1449 a 14 ff.) In all skills and disciplines, Aristotle contends almost paradoxically, artistic or scientific products (τὰ ἀπὸ τῆς τέχνης) can be created even before the art itself has been acquired (*Soph. Refut.*, chap. 34, 184 a 2–3), for the capacity to do things artistically, in the strict sense of the word, exists only when the reason for what is done by custom or chance has been recognized and understood. (*Rhetoric* I, 1, 1354 a 6–11.) Consequently, the passage of the *Poetics* may mean only that the great Attic poets established tragedy in its essentials, just as they eliminated from

[143] R. McKeon, *Ethics*, LI (1940–41), 95; cf. 96. (I have been unable to consult W.R. Krug, *Dissertatio de philosophia ex sententia Aristotelis plane absoluta, nec tamen unquam absolvenda*, 1827.) The opposite view is taken e.g., by Eucken, *Die Methode der Aristotelischen Forschung*, p. 5 and H. Meyer, "Zur Lehre von der ewigen Wiederkunft aller Dinge," *Beiträge zur Geschichte des christlichen Altertums und der Byzantinischen Literatur* (*Festgabe Albert Ehrhard* [Bonn and Leipzig, 1922]), pp. 363 ff.

[144] Only where observation has not yet yielded sufficient data does Aristotle expressly refer to the value of a more far-reaching exploration; cf. above, pp. 120 f. Barker goes too far, however, when he speaks of Aristotle's "deep respect for the general wisdom of the ages" (*The Politics of Aristotle*, p. 72, note 1).

this art certain metres and other features not properly belonging to it though formerly part of it (1449 a 15–31); and so improvements may still be possible even after the right technique of composing tragedy and its appropriate subject matter have been discovered. In fact, Aristotle himself, before admitting that tragedy had reached its "natural form" in the fifth century, raises the question whether or not it is "fully developed by now in all its various species." (*Poetics* IV, 1449 a 7 f.) He does not answer this question, but the question itself shows that he reckoned with the possibility that such full development might be achieved at a particular moment.[145]

Warned by Aristotle himself that analogies must be used with caution and that what is true in one field of human activity need not be true in all, one should hesitate to regard these statements about the arts of politics and poetry as evidence for his general outlook on future progress; and yet they are confirmed by other statements of his that put the matter beyond any reasonable doubt.[146] Aristotle expected "philosophy to be completely worked

[145] That the words ἔσχε τὴν αὐτῆς φύσιν (1449 a 15) refer to the constitution of the tragic art as art and not to its perfection was shown by M. Vahlen, "Beiträge zu Aristoteles' Poetik," *Sitzungsberichte der Kaiserlichen Akademie der Wissenschaften, Phil.–Hist. Classe* (Wien), L (1865), 379 f., who rightly compared the definition of art in *Physics* II, 1, 193 a; cf. also Franz Susemihl, *Aristoteles über die Dichtkunst* (2. Auf.; Leipzig, 1874), p. 225, note 43. Contrary to Meyer, *op. cit.*, p. 364, the passage does not show that for Aristotle all arts have a predestined end. A. Gudeman interpreted the sentence in question in its relation to the preceding statement concerning the possible completion of tragedy (*op. cit.*, pp. 135 f.); and, believing that when it had found its natural form it had indeed been perfected, he says: "*Sobald aber der Begriff der φύσις einer Sache eine Bereicherung erfährt, ist auch ihr τέλος gleichsam vorgeschoben. Deshalb konnte A. oben die Frage aufwerfen, ob die Tragödie nicht dennoch einer weiteren Entwicklung, d. h. über Sophokles hinaus, fähig wäre*" (*ad* 1449 a 15). Even though the φύσις of a thing is its τέλος (thus Gudeman, comparing *Politics* I, 2, 1252 b 32), it does not follow that, once this τέλος is apprehended, nothing further can be added. Thus Aristotle despite his conviction that he had founded the art of logic admits that his investigations remain incomplete (*Soph. Refut.* chap. 34, 184 b 6 ff.). On the other hand, no passage supports the assumption that the τέλος can ever be changed or extended. The brief characterization of the development of tragedy down to Sophocles describes, I take it, the constitution of tragedy as an art form rather than the supposedly final perfection of all its rules.

[146] Parallels drawn from the development of the fine arts are especially dangerous, since the belief in absolute aesthetic standards is not at all irreconcilable with a belief in the endless advance of science. This is true of later centuries in antiquity and in modern times, for example, of the ardent progressivist Fontenelle (cf. Bury, *The Idea of Progress*, p. 105).

124

out within a few years." (Fr. 53 [Rose] = Cicero, *Tusc. Disput.* III, 28, 69.) Even if this prophecy was made by the youthful philosopher in a burst of exuberant enthusiasm befitting his age, in his later years looking back on past civilizations he maintained that the arts and philosophy had been developed many times "to the extent possible" or "to the umost." (εἰς τὸ δυνατόν; *Metaphysics* XII, 8, 1074 b 10 f.)[147] Remarks on the manner in which advance is brought about in all arts and sciences also show that he foresaw an end to their possible improvement. Once the right approach has been determined, he says, "the remainder" can easily be added (*Soph. Refut.* chap. 34, 183 b 25 f.); or, as he puts it elsewhere, "anyone is capable of carrying on and articulating what has once been well outlined . . . anyone can add what is lacking [in the arts]." (*Nic. Eth.* I, 1, 1098 a 21–25.) As soon as the methodological problem has been solved and the aim established, the rest, he apparently thought, is child's play.[148]

As for infinity, there are three distinct kinds according to Aristotle. First, although the means by which the end of an art is reached are always limited by the end itself, the latter is indeed "infinite" (εἰς τὸ ἄπειρον) in so far as each art seeks to achieve of it "as much as it can" (ὅτι μάλιστα). The art of money-making, for example, recognizes no limit in the acquisition of wealth, just as medicine knows of no limit. (*Politics* I, 9, 1257 b 23–30; cf. 8, 1256 b 34–37.) To the technician or the expert the end of his specialty is the end of all ends, and he tries to produce it in infinite measure. This is obviously a specious infinity, for the positing of aims lies with philosophy and not with any art or science, the activity of which must be limited by values outside the art itself.[149] Secondly,

[147] For δυνατόν in the sense of the limit to which one can go, cf. e.g., *De Caelo* II, 13, 294 b 7.

[148] For the interpretation of these passages, cf. also above, pp. 70 and 121. Aristotle's only admission that research will continue in uncertainty is, so far as I know, his assertion that the fundamental questions of philosophy were raised long ago, are still being raised, and will always be raised (*Metaphysics* VII, 1, 1028 b 2–4; cf. above, chap. I, p. 5 on Xenophanes' similar statement); but even this statement hardly justifies the conclusion that he considered metaphysical problems to be insoluble, for questions do not necessarily cease to be asked even after the solutions have been found.

[149] Aristotle mentions medicine among others as one of the arts for which "progress" is beneficial (cf. above, p. 118). The determination of the aim by

while men who are satisfied even "with a modicum of virtue" (VIII, 1, 1323 a 36) seek for external goods *in infinitum* (εἰς ἄπειρον; 1323 a 38), all external goods are in fact limited, for they are nothing but instruments for achieving an end. It is men who "are never contented until they get to infinity, for it is the nature of the desire to be infinite" (II, 7, 1267 b 2–4). There is only one true kind of infinity: of the goods of the soul it can be asserted that the greater they are the more useful they become, "if indeed it is proper to predicate 'utility' at all here, and we ought not simply to predicate 'value.' " (τὸ καλόν [1323 b 11–12].) In other words, while philosophy and ethics can be perfected, there is no quantitative limit to the individual's improvement in moral and intellectual virtues, contemplation and its "growth into itself [its own full nature and actuality]." (*On the Soul* II, 5, 417 b 6 ff.)[150]

One must conclude, then, that in the development of every art and science there is for Aristotle a stage of excellence not to be surpassed. Since in earlier civilizations this was attained only "many times" (πολλάκις; *Metaphysics* XII, 8, 1074 b 10), there obviously is no certainty about its being attained in every civilization. Once it is attained, men are privileged to maintain perfection in knowledge and to practice it throughout the time allotted to the flowering of their culture.[151] Man's craving for infinity can be satisfied not by striving endlessly for more things and new insights but only within the confines of his inner life by thinking the truth, i.e., thinking immortal thoughts. (*Nic. Eth.* X, 7, 1177 b 31 ff.)[152]

Why is it that Aristotle substituted for the Pre-Socratic pessimism concerning the future not Plato's expectation of ever further

philosophy is illustrated e.g., *Eud. Eth.* II, 12, 1227 b 25 ff. (see L. Edelstein, "The Relation of Ancient Philosophy to Medicine," *Bulletin of the History of Medicine*, XXVI [1952], 310.) Aristotle transfers to the individual the responsibility that Plato puts on the state (see above, pp. 112 f.).

[150] For other aspects of Aristotle's thoughts on infinity (disregarding space and time) see J. Burnet, *The Ethics of Aristotle*, xlvi, note 3.

[151] As has been pointed out (above, p. 121 and note 141), Aristotle recognized a recurrence of generic and not numerical identity (so did his school, Ps.–Aristotle, *Problemata* XVII, 3). This is confirmed by the fact that, speaking in the *Metaphysics* of the possible perfection of philosophy and the arts, he uses the word πολλάκις, whereas the reestablishment of civilizations and of the same opinions he calls a phenomenon that occurs "not once or twice or rarely, but infinitely often" (*Meteorology* I, 3, 339 b 27–30).

[152] Cf. below, p. 128 and note 155.

advance, an expectation audacious enough, but rather an even more daring anticipation of actual perfection in the arts and sciences? Some have found an explanation of this in his "empiricism," in his reliance upon sense-perception, or in the fact that when the study of nature depends upon the naked eye instead of instruments like the microscope or the telescope, what is easily observed is likely to be taken for the complete nature of being and to satisfy the observer.[153] Factors of this kind may have been responsible in part for Aristotle's attitude; but the ancient scientists, for whom these factors were the same, were not influenced by them to draw the same conclusion. Moreover, even if science instead of creating such instruments as it needs is limited by those at its disposal, this would account at most for Aristotle's attitude to the natural sciences, whereas the perfection that he envisaged is perfection in all fields. In the last analysis, therefore, his attitude must have been caused by his specific way of thinking, his metaphysics, and more especially its essential difference from Plato's.

Aristotle rejected the notion that the Ideas exist in a Beyond and insisted instead that they are immanent in matter. The existence of particular things is in his language synonymous with that of the Ideas or rather of universals and separable only in thought. While for Plato "possibility" extends to that imitation of the true reality which can never be the latter's adequate representation and for the Pre-Socratics is limited by the factual data, for Aristotle the "potential" is only the "actual" as yet unrealized. The latter, it is true, is not always realized completely, for failures occur in nature no less than in the arts and sciences (*Physics* II, 8, 199 a 15 ff.); but the actual, the universal, the essence of what is, preexists, as it were, for

---

[153] Cf. Eucken, *Die Methode der Aristotelischen Forschung*, pp. 138 ff., especially p. 140 (also 6). Aristotle may have expressed his hope for the completion of philosophy in the *Protrepticus;* cf. Jaeger, *Aristoteles*, p. 97. Cicero, quoting Aristotle, implies that he did not see or expect to see the day when his prophecy would come true, for he did not complain about living in a state of "non-wisdom" (*Tuscul. Disput.* III, 28, 68). According to Lactantius (*Inst. Div.* III, 28), however, Aristotle thought that philosophy would be completed by his successors (*a posterioribus*), in which expectation, Lactantius adds, he was refuted by the facts. Lactantius said this in the light of later skepticism, whereas Cicero interpreted Aristotle's statement in the light of Stoicism. Whatever Aristotle may have felt in his youth, however, he must have known as the head of his school that he was leaving some work to be done by his pupils.

it precedes the act of realization and, determining the development of things in time, shapes them towards their final goal.[154]

Like any other potentiality, therefore, the potentiality of the arts and sciences moves towards a predestined end. Artisans and scientists "either on the basis of nature carry things further than nature can or they imitate nature." Natural and artificial processes are both purposeful, "for the relation of antecedent to consequent is identical in art and in nature." (*Physics, ibid.*) Instead of being based on hypotheses for which they are incapable of giving a sufficient explanation, the sciences are securely grounded on self-evident axioms, and perfectibility after a prolonged struggle turns into perfection at a definite moment of time. Man is able to attain to the truth; and in such a universe as this of Aristotle's "those who know will spend their time more pleasantly than those who inquire." (*Nic. Eth.* X, 7, 1177 a 26 ff.)[155] Thus the quest for knowledge ceases to be an endless search and comes to rest in its secure possession. The flight to the There is transformed into its contemplation in the Here. With the breakdown of the theory of Ideas the pathos of infinity vanishes, and is replaced by the *non plus ultra*.[156]

[154] Concerning the Pre-Socratics and Plato, see above, pp. 116 f. and chap. II, pp. 27 ff. In my account of Aristotelian metaphysics I follow E. Frank (*Wissen, Wollen, Glauben*, pp. 86 ff.). For the conception of possibility in particular, see Faust, *op. cit.*, I, 83 f.

[155] While Plato does not allow the philosopher to stay on the "Islands of the Blest" (above, p. 114), the Aristotelian may dwell there (cf. Fr. 58, p. 68, 3; p. 69, 1 [Rose], and Boll, *op. cit.*, note 34 *ad* p. 16). If Lessing's God had offered Aristotle the choice between infinite search and possession of the truth, he would have chosen the latter.

[156] This seems to be true also for other associates of Plato. So Xenocrates is said to have taken the same attitude as Aristotle (Cicero, *De Finibus* IV, 6, 15 ff. = Fr. 79 [Heinze]), but too little is known about him to be sure that this assertion is correct and is not just part of the attempt to elaborate a common dogma for the generation after Plato. The system of Speusippus, who remained more faithful to the founder of the Academy, looks as if it had made room for Plato's progressivism, for Speusippus held that "the more perfect forms are always produced from those which are indeterminate and imperfect" (Fr. 34 e [Lang] = *Metaphysics* XIV, 5, 1092 a 9) and in such a cosmic evolutionism, based as it was on biological analogies, perfection might have been represented as an unattainable goal. In fact, however, Speusippus like the Pythagoreans merely asserted that "perfect beauty and goodness do not exist in the beginning" (Fr. 34 a [Lang] = *Metaphysics* XII, 7, 1072 b 30–34) but contrary to Aristotle's opinion are the outcome of development rather than its determining and limiting factors.

The same philosophy that deprived the arts and sciences of what was to be their greatest dignity in later centuries gave them, nevertheless, a new and honored place in the understanding of the world and of man. Isocrates had thought a little knowledge of the sciences to be a prerequisite for the cultured but that for the rest their worth is merely pragmatic. Plato had seen in certain sciences, if studied in the way that he proposed, the stepping-stones to the absolute; but he had not thought it to be their business to comprehend the phenomena, for this the philosopher does according to his own method, which integrates the data available into a unity. With Aristotle the arts and sciences acquired a value peculiarly their own. The philosopher does determine their limitations; and research itself cannot be separated from metaphysical considerations, so that the educated person can have a critical estimate of its principles. (*On the Parts of Animals* I, 639 a 1 ff.) Insight into the phenomena themselves, however, is given only by the arts and sciences, which must not shun any object "be it ever so mean" (645 a 8)—"the mean and even filthy things" of Bacon—for "there are gods even here." (645 a 22.)[157] This was to set a pattern for the further development of all scientific studies; and Aristotle's endorsement of experience and insistence on the collection of data and the scrutiny of details lent him an importance for later progressivism almost equal to Plato's, despite his rejection of those Platonic concepts which were to lend the movement its most daring aspirations.

This analysis of Plato's thought and Aristotle's must incidentally have made it clear that in the debate during the fourth century different aspects of progress were accentuated. While Isocrates thought of progress in terms of human culture and Xenophon in terms of social and economic improvement, Plato and Aristotle maintained that man by continually making greater efforts in all fields of activity reaches out for an objective realm of Being, the truth of metaphysics. It should also be noticed that the evidence

---

[157] For Isocrates cf. above, note 13. For the Aristotelian conception of culture in contrast to Speusippus' (and Plato's) cf. Stenzel, *s.v.* Speusippus, *R.–E.*, col. 1651, 44–1652, 15. Concerning the seventeenth-century worship of the little things, Bacon's attitude, and the "literature of vermin," see M.H. Nicolson, *The Rockefeller University Review*, IV (1963 [June]), p. 6.

for the topic of progress in this century and especially the topic of future progress comes from books written by men who were reactionaries rather than liberals in politics. Plato and Aristotle and Isocrates and Xenophon, none of them shared the prevalent creed of their age, the trust in complete democracy. Their ideals were constitutions resembling the form of government that existed in Greece in the fifth century and earlier or even the monarchical rule of countries outside Greece. Nevertheless, they were not deluded into romanticism. They preferred political principles that had found recognition in the past, but they did not wish to revive the past. None of them preached or hoped for the return to a life that was gone forever. Intent on reviving values that they thought had been mistakenly discarded, they adapted those values to the requirements of their own day and fused them with values that were new.[158]

That men of various political creeds all bowed to the idea of progress is the strongest proof of the fact that it was now the vogue. The saying of Aristotle's that "all men as a rule seek to follow not the line of tradition ($\tau\grave{o}$ $\pi\acute{a}\tau\rho\iota o\nu$) but the good ($\tau\grave{o}$ $\grave{a}\gamma a\theta\acute{o}\nu$)" (Politics II, 8, 1269 a 3 ff.) seems to express a belief especially characteristic of his age. An amazing change had taken place since the time when Xenophanes had first spoken of progress and only a very few had been daring enough to trust in man's strength against the almost solid opposition of the old. The transformation could not have come about had not the city-state broken down and men been set free to go their own ways and to cherish their individuality.[159]

The progressivism of the intellectuals which expressed itself in works designed to surpass earlier achievements is, nevertheless, like a bright spot in an otherwise dark picture. Some of the new ideas,

[158] E.A. Havelock in his book, The Liberal Temper in Greek Politics (London, 1957), contends that a pure liberalism favoring progress was found among the Pre-Socratics (p. 377), that Plato was not "a liberal thinker in politics" (p. 19), and that Plato and Aristotle are responsible for the authoritarian trend in Western thought (pp. 259, 376). Plato and Aristotle were not antiprogressivist, however, whatever label one chooses to apply to their political systems. For the general thesis of Havelock's book see L. Strauss, "The Liberalism of Classical Political Philosophy," The Review of Metaphysics, XII (1959), 390 ff. (esp. pp. 394 ff.).

[159] Cf. above, p. 57. The individualism of the time is best characterized by the invention of the autobiography; cf. G. Misch, Geschichte der Autobiographie I 1³, chap. 2, esp. pp. 168 ff. Isocrates himself emphasized the novelty of the genre (Antidosis 1).

to be sure, made their way into common life. People were no longer disturbed by philosophers who called the sun and moon material rather than divine bodies. (Plato, *Laws* XII, 967 A; cf. *Epinomis* 983 C.) Learning was disseminated far and wide. In Aeneas' book, *On the Defense of Fortified Positions*, it is stated as a matter of course that in cases of emergency "citizens of neighboring states residing in the city for the purpose of education" should be registered (X, 10.) The artists of the period created the most humane and refined types of divine statues ever to come from Greece. Yet on the whole, it appears that what was most cherished in the progressive rationalization of life was the greater economic gain, the principle of the division of labor, the improved chances for successful maritime trade. The life of the upper classes lost its simplicity; and luxury not only increased but became respectable. A man acquired fame, if not as an athlete or a citizen any longer then as a gourmand or, if not rich, as a parasite, as the man who went wherever he was given a free dinner and in exchange sang the praises of the host. Actors and hetaerae were as notorious as generals or kings.[160]

Nor can it be denied that there was moral decay which was largely the result of the new individualism. Licentiousness prevailed despite the fact that there were exemplars of all "Panhellenic virtues," such as Epaminondas, Pelopidas, and Demosthenes. The recriminations of orators, statesmen, and philosophers may be tinged by partisanship; but, when one finds in Aeneas' book that "more than half his military admonitions are directed toward preventing treachery and forestalling revolution," and when one reads his reports of the horrible crimes that were committed (e.g., XVII, 2 ff.), one must admit that the poor and the rich lived together "always plotting against one another," as Plato says (*Republic* VIII, 551 E), and that because of lust for material gain internal enmity had become more threatening than all external perils.[161] If

---

[160] Cf. in general Burckhardt, *Griechische Kulturgeschichte* IV, chap. IV ("Der Mensch des IV. Jahrhunderts").

[161] The characterization of the book of Aeneas and the comparison of the pictures of contemporary life given by it and by Plato are borrowed from W.A. Oldfather's introduction to the translation by him and Pease, The Loeb Classical Library, pp. 16 ff.

later progressivism taught the *"homo homini deus,"* this progressivism of the fourth century proclaimed the *"homo homini lupus."* This immoralism was not even the immoralism of strength and independence. The Olympian religion had lost its influence; but Oriental cults had made inroads (Demosthenes, 18, 259), and magic now was practiced. There were those who clung to the mysteries of Demeter, "whose initiates are blessed with sweeter hopes concerning the end of life as well as all eternity" (Isocrates, *Paneg.* 28); but the time was soon to come when men, whose ancestors had turned away from leaders aspiring to deification, would be lavish in deifying generals and rulers because their help was near at hand, while the gods—if they existed at all—were far away and did not give succor. (Athenaeus, VI, 253 d ff.)[162]

It is difficult to say and perhaps even gratuitous to ask whether people were happier in their freedom from tradition than their fathers had been under the authority of the law. A verdict passed upon the happiness or unhappiness of past generations instead of being objective usually states the preferences of the judge; [163] but, no matter how much the *laudatores temporis acti* said in the fourth century about the preceding age or how much may be said in its favor today, one could not wish away the change that had come about. A great world had come to its end; but a new world was being created, the greatness of which was to be open to all. Athens, the school of Hellas (Thucydides, II, 41, 1), was on its way to becoming the school of humanity; and the idea of progress was not the least of the teachings that men educated in this school were to receive.

[162] For the interpretation of the passage from Athenaeus, the Athenian hymn to Demetrius Poliorketes, see V. Ehrenberg, "Athenischer Hymnus auf Demetrios Poliorketes," *Die Antike*, VII (1931), 279 ff. Dodds (*op. cit.*, p. 194) calls the revival of magic a phenomenon provoked by the Enlightenment. The practice of magic may have increased in the fourth century—more evidence of it is extant from this period than from the fifth century—; but I suspect that this happened because of a stronger emphasis on empiricism, for throughout antiquity it was the empiricists who favored acceptance of the experience of magical or sympathetic effects. See Edelstein, "Greek Medicine in Its Relation to Religion and Magic," *Bull. Instit. Hist. Med.*, V (1937), 229 ff. Concerning the Asclepius religion as "regression" see above, chap. II, note 75.

[163] Cf. Burckhardt, *Weltgeschichtliche Betrachtungen*, ed. J. Oeri (Berlin and Stuttgart, 1905), chap. VI, and for the modern evaluation of the period cf. above, p. 58.

IV

The new age of great empires beginning at the turn from the fourth to the third century opens with a setback to progressivism. At least in philosophical circles, no brief was held for the idea of progress during the first half of the Hellenistic period before the conquest of Greece by Rome.[1] Cynicism and its primitivistic mode of thought gained in influence, and skepticism increased and found its first systematic expression in the doctrine of Pyrrho. An atmosphere hostile to confidence in man's power to understand and shape his environment pervaded the teaching of Plato's followers, the members of the so-called Middle Academy.[2] Even when the significance of the progress made by the human race in the past was

[1] In the use of the term "Hellenistic age" I follow W.W. Tarn, who defines it as the time "from the death of Alexander in 323 to the establishment of the Roman Empire by Augustus in 30 b.c." (*Hellenistic Civilization* [3d. rev. ed.; London, 1952], p. 1). Like him (cf. p. 2, note 2), I rely on Latin as well as Greek writers of the period in my analysis of the development. This material can sometimes be supplemented by documents composed in the first century after Christ but clearly dependent on earlier works; cf. below, p. 168. My subdivision of the era into two periods (323–146 and 146–30 b.c.) is an attempt to do justice to the two phases in the development of the idea of progress that I think are indicated by the evidence.

[2] For Cynicism in the first half of the third century, cf. D.R. Dudley, *op. cit.*, pp. 59 ff. Crates may have toned down the austere dogma of Diogenes but only for the general public and not for the true "devotees of the Cynic life" (Dudley, *op. cit.*, p. 49). The Skeptics' view of human culture and progress is not attested. Pyrrho and his immediate followers, however, rejected the possibility of all knowledge derived either from experience or from reasoning (cf. e.g., Diogenes Laertius, IX, 114). Arcesilaus, the founder of the Middle Academy, was at least an adherent of probabilism (L. Robin, *Pyrrhon et le scepticisme grec* [Paris, 1944], particularly p. 67). From both points of view a favorable estimate of civilization or an endorsement of progress seems to be impossible.

acknowledged, less value was attached to it in the final estimate of man's position in the present.

The Peripatetics, for example, evinced a feeling of disillusion and a sentimental longing for an irretrievable past. To be sure, in analyzing the history of astronomy, mathematics, music, medicine, and philosophy, they gave due attention to "who invented what" and emphasized the continual improvement discernible in the course of scientific research; but Dicaearchus or Theophrastus, in whose work the historical studies of the Peripatos culminated, when dealing with the beginnings of mankind or the results achieved both speak in a rather pessimistic tone.[3]

Primeval man, says Dicaearchus, "akin to the gods," a "golden race in comparison with the men of the present," were best by nature and lived the best life. They were, in fact, that "golden race" in the age of Cronus of which the poets sing; at least, he adds cautiously: "if it is to be taken as having really existed and not as an idle tale, by eliminating the exaggerated mythical parts of the story one must give the whole a natural meaning by means of reason." (Porphyry, De Abstinentia, IV, 1, 2 = Fr. 49 [Wehrli].) At that time, presumably, none of the arts was yet invented; but men lived an easy life "of leisure, of freedom from care about the satisfaction of their needs, of health and peace and friendship." No wonder, if this be true, that the Golden Age "came to be longed for by men of later times who because of the manifoldness of their demands had become subject to many evils," that is to say by men who had become civilized.[4] Such a picture of the initial stages of human existence is utterly at variance with the tenets of Aristotle's philosophy, and its unreserved embellishment of primitive men is also quite un-Platonic. Here for the first time, in fact, the dream of a Golden Age in the past is made part of an historical account, and that too by a philosopher and historian who with a keen eye for facts and unusual discernment about prehistoric problems traced out "the life of Hellas."[5]

[3] For the historical studies of the Peripatetics, see above, chap. III, pp. 94 f.

[4] I use the translation of the fragment given by Lovejoy and Boas, op. cit., pp. 94 ff.

[5] For the material surviving from Dicaearchus' works see Frs. 47–66 (Wehrli); and for the principles of his historiography cf. Wehrli's Commentary on these fragments.

Dicaearchus' position was probably determined by the fact that he had given the ideal of practical life precedence over that of contemplation. Life and true philosophy, he held, consist of deeds and not of words; and he seems to have called "the ancients" to witness against the moderns or at least against his fellow philosophers in the Peripatos, where dedication to the furtherance of knowledge reigned supreme.[6] In the last analysis, he apparently meant, all the efforts made had not improved the human lot, and what really counts for men, a good and virtuous life, had become more and more difficult to achieve ever since the beginning of the world. Strangely enough, Theophrastus, a staunch defender of the theoretical life, was also inclined to regard primitive times in a eulogistic manner and betrayed some doubt at least about the moral improvement of mankind during the course of history. He did not deny that life under primitive conditions had been "full of sufferings"; but he nevertheless thought aboriginal men superior to posterity in goodness of heart and purity of habits. They had been truly pious, he believed, and their sacrifices had been simple, bloodless, and therefore more in conformity with the spirit of the divine than the religious customs of later ages. (Porphyry, *De Abstinentia*, II, 21 5 ff.)[7]

The founders of the two new schools, which were to play the dominant rôle in Hellenistic thought, though not detractors of progress, were also in favor of the practical life. Epicurus in his analysis of the development of civilization certainly followed the earlier progressivist view and even refashioned it boldly with additions of his own.[8] He believed that Nature, the "stepmother" of

---

Dicaearchus despite his primitivism does not reject culture; its achievements can be used well or misused (cf. Fr. 24 and Wehrli's *Commentary*; also below, p. 172). For Dicaearchus as a scientist see the appreciation by G. Murray (*Five Stages of Greek Religion*, ch. III, note [pp. 115 ff.]); also below, note 17.

[6] For Dicaearchus' ideal of the practical life, cf. W. Jaeger, "Über Ursprung und Kreislauf des philosophischen Lebensideals." *Sitzungsberichte der Preussischen Akademie der Wissenschaften, Phil.–Hist. Klasse* (Berlin, 1928), p. 413. B. Snell in *Die Ausdrücke für den Begriff des Wissens in der vorplatonischen Philosophie* (Philologische Untersuchungen, XXIX [Berlin, 1924], p. 2) pointed out the connection between Dicaearchus' endorsement of practical life and his return to the "natural conditions" of ancient times, when philosophers were dedicated to practical aims.

[7] Cf. Bernays, *op. cit.*, pp. 39 ff.; also, R. Hirzel, *op. cit.*, pp. 88 f.

[8] For the theory of Epicurus I use only attested fragments. Though by no means numerous, they do at least give the general features of his doctrine of culture.

man, had lavished her care on animals, while she had created the human being weak and unprepared for the hardships of life. (Lactantius, *De Opificio Dei*, 2, 10 = Fr. 372 [Usener].) Human nature "was taught and constrained to do many things of every kind merely by circumstance; and later on, reasoning elaborated what had been suggested by nature and made further inventions, in some matters quickly and in others slowly, at some epochs and time (making great advances) and lesser again at others." (*Epistula* I, 75.) [9] Epicurus, then, seems not to have believed in the steady advance of evolution. He stressed the chance occurrences that determined the course of events, alternately halting and speeding up the forward movement. He thought that nature guides man in a haphazard way and that action and reaction and individual and racial responses to the challenge presented account for what has been achieved.[10] Physical factors, perceptions, and feelings peculiar to "men's natures according to their different nationalities" were supposed to explain the origin of language (*Epistula* I, 75 ff.); and similarly knowledge was supposed to depend upon physical and ethnic qualities, as Taine was to contend much later. "Not every bodily constitution or every nationality would permit a man to become wise" (Diogenes Laertius, X, 117); the Greeks alone, for example, were able to philosophize. (Clement of Alexandria, *Strom.* I, 15 = Fr. 226 [Usener].) In the words of Lucretius, "it was a man of Greece" who first dared to combat the blinding power

Lucretius' description of the early history of mankind, which is usually assumed to be a faithful transcription of the master's opinions (cf. e.g., C. Bailey, *The Greek Atomists and Epicurus* [Oxford, 1928], p. 376; also *Lucretius, De rerum natura* III, p. 1473), contains many features which in my opinion cannot be attributed to Epicurus himself; cf. below, pp. 162 ff.

[9] The translation is Bailey's (*Epicurus* [Oxford, 1926] p. 247), whose constitution of the text of the difficult passage seems to me to be the most plausible.

[10] In discussing Epicurus' doctrine as it is briefly presented in *Ep.* I, 75, N.W. DeWitt in *Epicurus and his Philosophy* (Minneapolis [Minn.], 1954), p. 129 stresses Epicurus' emphasis on the "priority of Nature over reason." (Cf. also Bailey, *Epicurus*, p. 246, who in addition notes the conjectural character of Epicurus' statement.) Bailey holds that the main feature of Epicurus' construction is his distinction between a first stage, in which necessity is operative, and a second, in which inventiveness and reason are at work (*Lucretius* III, p.1448). This feature was not new, however; cf. above, chap. III, pp. 83 f. In my opinion, the peculiar merit of Epicurus' analysis is the recognition of distinct situations and varying phases in the development. The earlier analyses of the past of mankind had usually had an abstract and generalized character without individual shadings and qualifications.

of superstition and who started mankind on the road that led to insight into the laws of the universe and thus to a true conception of man's destiny.[11]

What follows from this victory in the doctrine of Epicurus, however, is that the knowledge, once gained, is to be handed down in the same fixed and unalterable form and that further study or elaboration of science is not called for. (Fr. 227–30 [Usener].) The wise man, withdrawn from the world, is to live a life which, though not devoid of intellectual pleasure, is in its material aspects almost as simple as the existence of primitive people. (Fr. 459–82; especially 472 [Usener].)[12] "Free yourselves from the prison of the liberal arts and political life" (*Gnomologicum Vaticanum*, 58) is the admonition of the new gospel.

The attitude of Epicurus' principal rival, the founder of Stoicism, was not much different. In Zeno's opinion mankind was born late in the process of divine creation, for the age of the human race, he held, must coincide with the age of the arts and crafts. Not only is man a rational being, by his very nature given to methodical

[11] That Lucretius' *laus inventoris* praises not Epicurus but the Greek inventor of philosophy I tried to show in "Primum Graius Homo," *Transactions and Proceedings of the American Philological Association*, LXXI (1940), 78 ff. Against this Bailey (*Lucretius* II *ad* I, v. 66) again argued that Lucretius was referring to Epicurus. Yet the latter's own insistence on the Greek origin of philosophy, a fact that I should have mentioned in my article, seems to corroborate the thesis that the *laus inventoris* was meant to refute those who traced philosophy to the Orient (see *Epinomis* above, pp. 86 f.). The position of Epicurus resembles that of Herodotus (see above, chap. II, p. 48) and differs from that of Eratosthenes (see below, pp. 152 f.). For Taine cf. E. Cassirer, *The Logic of the Humanities*, trans, C.S. Howe (New Haven [Conn.], 1961), p. 13; and for Epicurus' theory of language and its difference from that of Democritus cf. G. Vlastos, *A.J.P.*, LXVII (1946), 51 ff.

[12] For Epicureanism and the simple life cf. e.g., Lovejoy and Boas, p. 152. From the agreement of certain passages in Lucretius (V, 999 ff.) with a later source (Tzetzes), supposed to be influenced by Epicurus, Norden concluded (*Jahrbücher für Classische Philologie*, Suppl. XIX [1892], 416 ff.) that Epicurus distinguished the arts necessary for the preservation of life and therefore useful from those that are the product of luxury and bring about moral decline and unwanted evils. This would make his teaching somewhat inconsistent, for, although it included no "Golden Age," it would ascribe a kind of superiority to early mankind, as being happier and free of other faults even though less civilized. If Lucretius echoes Epicurus, the difference between life in the beginning and later would still be only relative, other disadvantages having been eliminated by the progress made (cf. below, p. 161). To say that Epicurus bestowed "praise upon primitive beginnings" because men were then guiltless (Uxkull, *op. cit.*, p. 33) is unwarranted even on the evidence of indirect testimony.

investigations, but without the assistance of the arts and sciences human life would be impossible; and, if one scrutinizes the dates of the various inventions, disregarding the mythological stories adorned in the manner of tragic poetry, one sees that the arts and sciences were created rather recently. (Philo, *De Incorr. Mundi*, 24 = I, Fr. 106 [Arnim].)[13] There had not been in the distant past a "Golden Age," for according to Zeno man himself, born from the earth with the help of divine fire—i.e., divine providence (Censorinus, *De Die Nat.* IV, 10 = I, Fr. 124 [Arnim])—gradually built up an inhabitable world;[14] but again the instrument of that construction is discarded after it has served its purpose. Zeno's wise man is concerned not with the arts and sciences but with moral conduct and, though not unmindful of his social obligations, regards the things of this world as being without intrinsic value of their own, for they are at best "to be preferred." Moral improvement, progress of the individual on the road to virtue, is his aim.[15]

On the whole, then, early Hellenistic philosophy expressed less enthusiasm for the ideal of progress than did its classical counterpart, but whether its attitude adequately reflected the temper of the time is quite a different question. In the poetry of the age can be found many passages that set the simple life of nature above the life lived in the large cities and at court, and even curses upon those

[13] The assumption that Philo gives the opinion of Zeno has often been questioned (cf. J.B. McDiarmid, "Theophrastus on the Eternity of the World," *T.A.P.A.*, LXXI [1940], 239 ff.) but unjustifiably, I think: cf. M. Pohlenz, *Die Stoa* (Göttingen, 1948–49) II, 44 *ad* S. 77, 2, 28 and O. Regenbogen, *s.v.* Theophrastus, R.–E. col. 1540. If, as is not unlikely, Zeno gave a detailed account of the rise of the various arts (in the style of Plato's *Laws*), it is not preserved.

[14] Belief in a Golden Age is commonly attributed to Zeno and other members of the old Stoa; but, since Zeno assumed that the human race could not exist without the inventions of the arts, he cannot have been an adherent of the dogma of the Golden Age (cf. P. Barth, *Die Stoa*, ed. A. Goedeckemeyer [Stuttgart, 1946], p. 21). This is also likely on general grounds, even disregarding Philo's report, cf. G. Pasquali, "Das Prooemium des Arat," Χάριτες; *Friedrich Leo zum sechzigsten Geburstag dargebracht* (Berlin, 1911), pp. 118 f.; cf. also Hirzel, *op. cit.*, pp. 85 f.

[15] Zeno, of course, insisted on philosophical knowledge as a precondition of moral insight, and it was only in the construction of the ideal state that his "Cynicism" went so far as to exclude "the ordinary education." (Diogenes Laertius, VII, 32: τὴν ἐγκύκλιον παιδείαν.) The old Stoa did not require renunciation of the goods of this world but advocated their right, i.e., their moral, use. Ariston alone taught indifference to all things in the Cynic manner.

who had made inventions.[16] Aratus, not such a strict primitivist as Dicaearchus, sings the praises of a Golden Age in which men were farmers. Justice dwelt among them, and peace reigned supreme; but with the "silver race" justice was rarely to be seen, and it vanished from the earth with the "bronze race," people still worse than their fathers. Continual moral decline was the inseparable companion of the growth and refinement of civilization. (*Phaenomena* 96–136.) Such at least is "the story current among men," the poet says (100 ff.), thus bearing witness to the fact that cultural pessimism was widespread, although moral criticism and even despair do not imply that he rejected civilization himself or advocated withdrawal from it, for it must be remembered that his poem was meant to popularize the astronomical observations of Eudoxus and to teach how to watch the rising of the stars and the occurrence of weather signs important for navigation. (730, 765 ff.)[17]

Nevertheless, the historiography and the rational criticism of

[16] For these "curses" see Kleingünther, *op. cit*, p. 98. On Hellenistic poetry, M. Pohlenz, "Die hellenistische Poesis und die Philosophie," Χάριτες *Friedrich Leo zum sechzigsten Geburstag dargebracht* (Berlin, 1911), pp. 76 ff.; (esp. pp. 83 ff.: Callimachus; p. 86: Hellenistic fragment influenced by Dicaearchus; p. 103: Theocritus; pp. 109 ff.: the *Consolationes*). It is hard to decide whether the poets followed the teaching of the philosophers or independently expressed the same thought, inspired by their own time and perhaps by older poetry (Euripides, Frs. 892, 285 [Pohlenz, pp. 91, 96; cf. also pp. 101, 111]). In any case, the poems express interest in a life remote from the complexities of the present and the disillusionment of a highly cultivated society in the midst of plenty, attitudes not unrepresented in the new comedy either (Philemon, Fr. 92 [Pohlenz, p. 91, note 4]). For Onesicritus see above, chap. III, note 26. It should be observed that the commonplace, "Time teaches everything," is also echoed in Hellenistic poetry (e.g., Philemon, Fr. 96 f. [Lovejoy and Boas, *op. cit.*, p. 213] and Menander, *Sententiae* 13 and 839 [Jaekel]).

[17] Aratus' is the first poetical interpretation of the Hesiodic myth of the ages as a story of moral decay bound up with the vice of civilization (cf. Nilsson, *Geschichte der griechischen Religion*, p. 588), for Dicaearchus followed Hesiod in having the Golden race live on the bounty of the earth without arts and crafts, while Aratus assumes that they were farmers. Pasquali (*op. cit.*, p. 119) ascribes this less primitivistic view to the influence of Stoicism, but Aratus was not a full-fledged Stoic (cf. Pohlenz, *Die Stoa* II, 86; on the un-Stoic tenor of vv. 96–113 cf. Wilamowitz, *Hellenistische Dichtung in der Zeit des Kallimachos* [Berlin, 1924], II, 266). Moreover, the old Stoa did not defend the myth of the Golden Age (cf. above, note 14), nor is it attested that the school at first claimed a progressive deterioration of morals. It seems best to take Aratus at his word when he presents the myth as one commonly told. Cf. also below, note 26. For the various ancient versions of the story in general see Rohde, *Der griechische Roman und seine Vorläufer*, p. 216, note 2, and Christ–Schmid, *op. cit.*, I, 1, 275, note 2.

mythology elaborated at this time express definite approval of the world as it is. Philochorus in his history of Athens sets forth Athens' merits in the development of civilization, eliminating what seem to him to be irrational stories. Hecataeus, presenting the history of Egypt, which in his opinion was the cradle of civilization, reads into it an account, largely drawn from Democritus, of the origin of man and of the most ancient forms of life. Experience and need, the human hand and human reason, are the teachers that led the race out of its animal-like existence and established communal life. (Diodorus, I, 8.)[18] As to the gods, he distinguishes the celestial deities who represent the elements from those who were mortals and were deified after their death because they had benefitted their fellow men by inventing the arts. (I, 13.) The same kind of theology appears in the writings of Euhemerus and others. It interprets the history of religion largely as the history of civilization, which evolves gradually because of the "service to mankind" rendered by great individuals. Such Euhemerism, diametrically opposed to philosophical quietism and skepticism, may justifiably be regarded as the typical form of religious belief current among the educated.[19]

What is more important still, the early Hellenistic period was in fact an age of great productivity and originality. In poetry it developed new forms and a new language, it created a new prose style and a new rhetoric, and it inaugurated a corresponding change in the fine arts. What Callimachus said of his own poetry is characteristic of all the work being done. Apollo advised him to "walk on the path where the carriages do not journey, not to drive his car in the

[18] That Diodorus here and in later chapters of the first book of his *History* follows Hecataeus is generally agreed upon. That the views given in chap. 8 ultimately go back to Democritus was argued by K. Reinhardt, *Hermes*, XLVII (1912), 492 ff.; cf. G. Vlastos, *A.J.P.*, LXVII (1946), 57 f. (but cf. contra W. Spoerri, *Späthellenistische Berichte über Welt, Kultur und Götter* [Basel, 1959], with A.D. Nock, "The Sources of Diodorus: Review of W. Spoerri, *Späthellenistische* . . . ," *Classical Review* N.S. XII [1962] 50–51). For Philochorus, see 328 Fr. 2; 93–8; 103 f., Jacoby and his *Commentary*.

[19] Paul Wendland (*Die hellenistisch–römische Kultur in ihren Beziehungen zu Judentum und Christentum* [2. Auf.; Tübingen, 1912], pp. 115 ff.) emphasized the importance of the rationalistic and pragmatic interpretation of mythology and stressed its acceptance by the intellectuals (p. 118). According to Nilsson (*loc. cit.*, above, note 17) the story as told by Aratus prevailed immediately, but this cannot be true.

tracks of others, and to travel not the highway but a road of his own, though it be a strait one." (*Aitia*, Fr. I, 25–28 [Pfeiffer].) [20] The new vitality was most obvious, however, in the natural sciences and in the humanities. In pure mathematics the theory of conic sections advanced from elementary beginnings to considerable perfection, and trigonometry was successfully begun and systematized. Upon the hypothesis that the earth rotates on its axis followed the planetary theory later proposed by Tycho Brahe, then the heliocentric hypothesis, and finally that form of the geocentric model of the cosmos that continued to be accepted until the Copernican revolution. In geography the calculation of the circumference of the earth first made by Dicaearchus was reduced by Eratosthenes to an estimate that was approximately correct, and latitudes and longitudes of cities were fixed by astronomical means. Distant countries that had hitherto been known only by hearsay were explored. Pytheas sailed to Britain and Norway and to the Arctic sea, and his voyage was important for the notions about the earth elaborated by Eratosthenes and Hipparchus. Anatomy based on the dissection of the human body opened an entirely new field of study and made medicine scientific in the modern sense. Philological and historical research were put on a solid basis, and work was begun in archives and on the collection of epigraphical material. Historiography extended its range and with Polybius became universal in its scope and undertook to delineate not only types of character but also the development of character. Last but not least, technical ingenuity performed such feats as to justify the boast: "vanquished by nature, we became masters by technique." (Aristotle, *Mechanics* 847 a 20.) In fact, the Hellenistic period laid the foundation of all the research that was to be done in antiquity, and its achievement proved to be the starting-point of modern science in the Renaissance. During approximately a hundred and fifty years from the death of Theophrastus to the time when Hipparchus was writing there was, as has truly been said, a growth of true science such "as

[20] See H.J. Rose, A *Handbook of Greek Literature from Homer to the Age of Lucian* (2d ed.; London, 1942), p. 318, and also below, p. 149. The inventor of the new prose style was Hegesias, the leader of the Asianists (Christ–Schmid, *op. cit.*, p. 207); and the originator of the new rhetoric was Hermagoras.

the world was not to see again for very many centuries; the supremacy of this period till quite modern times is unquestionable." [21]

It is not surprising, then, that in the Hellenistic age even the great accomplishment of the fourth century was regarded as having been surpassed and even rendered obsolete. About the middle of the third century Eratosthenes in an epigram announcing his new method of finding the proportional between two given lines defied those who had preceded him in such investigations during the fourth century: "Do not seek the cumbersome procedure of Archytas' cylinders or to make the three Menaechmian sections of the cone; seek not the type of curved lines described by god-fearing Eudoxus, for with these plates of mine you could readily construct ten thousand means beginning with a small base." (Eutocius, Commentary on Archimedes' *Sphere and Cylinder*, p. 96, 16–21 [Heiberg].) [22] Early in the second century, when Philo of Byzantium described the success "recently achieved by the Alexandrian engineers" in the construction of artillery (Belopoeica [*Mechanics* IV], 3, 5 [Diels–Schramm]), he did not fail to add: "The ancients, directing their attention solely to the shape and arrangements [of the parts], had scarcely any success in securing an effective discharge of the missile because of their failure to employ the proper ratios; but their successors by making some parts smaller and other parts larger produced engines that were correctly proportioned and effective." (*Ibid.*, 30.) Polybius too, believing that "at the present

[21] Tarn, *op. cit.*, p. 295. A survey of the sciences is given *ibid.*, pp. 295 ff.; cf. also W.C. Dampier, *A History of Science* (3d. rev. ed., Cambridge, 1943), pp. 40 ff. For human dissection see L. Edelstein, "The Development of Greek Anatomy," *Bull. Inst. Hist. Med.*, III (1935), 238. For Hellenistic biographies e.g., Dicaearchus, Frs. 25–46 (Wehrli). For Peripatetic history see C.O. Brink, "Tragic History and Aristotle's School," *Proceedings of the Cambridge Philological Society*, N.S. VI (1960), 14 ff.

[22] Though the letter in which the epigram is preserved is spurious, the poem itself is genuine, cf. Wilamowitz, "Ein Weihgeschenk des Eratosthenes," *Nachrichten von der Königl. Gesellschaft der Wissenschaften zu Göttingen, Phil.–Hist. Klasse* (1894), 15 ff. (Christ–Schmid, *op. cit.*, p. 250, note 2). An attitude similar to that assumed by Eratosthenes is taken by Apollonius of Perga (general Preface to *Treatise on Conic Sections* and Preface to Book IV, Morris Cohen and I.E. Drabkin, *A Source Book in Greek Science* [New York, 1948], 76 f.). A third-century writer on the *Luxury of the Ancients*, Aristippus (Diogenes Laertius, V, 3), included Aristotle and other fourth-century philosophers among the ancients (Wilamowitz, *Antigonos von Karystos, Philologische Untersuchungen*, IV [Berlin, 1893], 48 ff.).

day the progress of the arts and sciences had been so great that the love of learning had been provided as it were with a method for dealing with any contingency that may arise" (IX, 2, 5), decided to write his book because, written in a scientific way as was now possible, history could be more useful than ever.[23]

Confident as these men were of their contributions and their success, they nevertheless had the firm belief that more could and should be done in the future. Thus Archimedes writes, "I am myself in the position of having first made the discovery of the theorem now to be published [by the method indicated before], and I deem it necessary to expound the method partly because I have already spoken of it [in another book] and I do not want to have been thought to have uttered vain words, but equally because I am persuaded that it will be of no little service to mathematicians, for I apprehend that some either of my contemporaries or of my successors will by means of the method, when once established, be able to discover other theorems in addition, which have not yet occurred to me." (*Method*, Introduction, p. 430 [Heiberg].) Archimedes felt sure that his discoveries were only the beginning of further inquiry, and he published his results with a view to the cooperation of his successors as well as of his contemporaries.[24]

Polybius, the historian, in the second century took the same attitude to the future in a more general way. What interested him in the sciences and their progress was not primarily how much had been accomplished already but how much remained to be done in the future if and when there would appear to be advantage in doing it. Certain military techniques were in his opinion still quite imperfect (X, 43, 1); and after explaining how they could be refined (43,

[23] Cf. Bury (*The Ancient Greek Historians*, p. 199), who says that the statement made in IX, 2, 5 and referred to by Polybius in X, 49 is "one of the rare passages in which an ancient writer betrays a sense of progress" (p. 199, note 2).

[24] See also Hero, *Pneumatics* I, Introduction II, 11 (Cohen–Drabkin, *op. cit.*, p. 249) and Apollonius, Preface to Book II, *Treatise on Conic Sections*. Such an appeal as Archimedes makes to the future is, to my knowledge, not found in earlier literature (Xenophon's hope, expressed at the end of his Greek history, that someone would continue where his story ends is quite a different matter). For the resemblance of the passage of Archimedes to those assertions by Dürer and other Renaissance artists in which E. Zilsel, "The Genesis of the Concept of Scientific Progress" (*J.H.I.*, VI [1945], 328), finds the first inkling of the modern concept of scientific progress cf. my remarks *ibid.*, XIII (1952), 575.

chap. 47, 10) he adds: "we should not abandon anything useful owing to the difficulties that appear in the beginning, but we must call in the aid of practice through which all good things fall into the hands of man" (47, 11), for "in our time all arts and sciences have advanced so much that knowledge of most of them may be said to have reached a point where a kind of methodical approach to problems has become possible." (47, 12.) Obviously, he wished and expected further efforts to be made; and, when elsewhere he states that certain regions are "up to now unknown and will remain so unless the curiosity of explorers should lead to some discoveries in the future" (III, 38, 2–3), it is implied that such curiosity will one day lead to such discoveries.

The work of Hipparchus, the younger contemporary of Polybius, testifies to the fact that belief in future progress determined even the way in which specific problems were approached, for, dissatisfied with the available maps of the earth and also with the data available for drawing new ones, he called for a combined research-project by means of which the necessary material could gradually be brought together. Outlining the approach to the task and laying the foundation for it, he advised the retention of the old maps without premature changes, "until we shall know something more reliable." (Strabo, p. 69.)[25] In the same spirit he prepared a list of the fixed stars observed in his own time in order that "future astronomers" might compare the stars seen by them with the stars known before, and thus perhaps decide whether the fixed stars themselves are variable, as he had been led to suspect by the rise of a constellation hitherto unknown (Pliny, II, 26, 95); and he recorded observations of the course of the planets which he trusted might later be of value for the formulation of a theory of planetary movements. (Ptolemy, Almagest, IX, 2.)[26]

[25] H. Berger, Die geographischen Fragmente des Hipparch (Leipzig, 1869), pp. 14 and 75; Berger, Geschichte der wissenschaftlichen Erdkunde der Griechen (2. Auf.; Leipzig, 1903), pp. 458 ff.
[26] For a short summary of Hipparchus' work, cf. Manitius in his edition of Hipparchi in Arati et Eudoxi Phaenomena Commentarii (Leipzig, 1894), pp. 282 ff. O. Neugebauer, "Notes on Hipparchus," The Aegaean and the Near East, Studies Presented to Hetty Goldman (Locust Valley [N.Y.], 1956), pp. 292 ff., much as he detracts from Hipparchus' glory, does admit that "wherever we are confronted with facts, we see Hipparchus at work to provide observations and to arrange them for proper analysis by later generations." (p. 296)

These few statements are the only ones preserved among the scanty remnants of scientific literature, but two facts show that they indicate a general trend. First, the followers of Chrysippus, the Stoics of the second century B.C., seem to have been fond of invoking the law of scientific progress in their debate with the skeptic philosophers; and, when the latter countered the Stoic teleology with the objection that many animals and plants in this world have no usefulness whatever, the Stoics retorted that the usefulness of many of them had not yet been discovered but would surely be found "as time progressed," just as necessity and experience had previously discovered many data unknown to earlier generations. (Lactantius, *De Ira Dei*, p. 13 = II, Fr. 1172 [Arnim].) In the same way apparently the Stoics met the general skeptic argument that dissension among philosophers precludes the possibility of the truth's ever being known. What is not now agreed upon, the Stoics said, may one day come within the ken of human knowledge. In fact, this assumption that the truth will probably be discovered in the future was taken to be the mark distinguishing a Stoic from a Skeptic. (Galen, *Adv. Iulianum* 5 [XVIII A p. 260 K] = II, Fr. 120 [Arnim].) [27]

Now, belief in future progress was professed by Xenophanes, who first formulated the idea of progress, and by many writers after

[27] The two late statements refer only to the Stoics in general but are rightly attributed by Arnim to the Chrysippean Stoa, for II, frag. 1172 identifies the Skeptics with the "Academics" and the debate between Stoa and Academy was especially characteristic of Chrysippus and his followers. Furthermore, the fragment identifies teleology with usefulness to men in the typical manner of Chrysippus (cf. P.H. DeLacy, "Lucretius and the History of Epicureanism," *T.A.P.A.*, LXXIX [1948], 16; Pohlenz [I, pp. 98 ff.] seems to ascribe such a teleology even to Zeno, but I, Fr. 172 [Arnim] differs considerably from II, Frs. 1152 ff.). A further indication of belief in progress is to be found in Aratus, who, speaking of weather signs, says: "For not yet do we mortals know all from Zeus; but much still remains hidden, whereof he will reveal even hereafter whatever he may wish, for openly he aids the race of man, manifesting himself on every side and showing signs on every hand" (*Phaenomena* 768–772). Aratus speaks in the mythological language that befits the poet, but what can the versifier of Eudoxus' theories mean except the further progress of astronomical or meteorological investigations? The resemblance between Aratus' verses and the statement of Xenophanes (Fr. 18) was observed by H. Diels, *Poetarum Philosophorum Fragmenta*, p. 41; and the importance of the passage in connection with Aratus' faith in Providence was stressed by Pasquali (*op. cit.*, p. 121), who saw in it an indication of the "*mehr religiösen als philosophischen Weltauffassung des Dichters*" (*ibid.*). It certainly confirms the inference that the story of the Golden Age was, as Aratus says, the one commonly told rather than the one he believed (see above, note 17).

him; but they usually asserted in a general way the probability or necessity of further advance, and their interest was concentrated on the past and present, their notions about the time to come remaining vague. Even Aristotle, when formulating the idea of scientific progress apart from all general historical considerations and though stressing the indissoluble unity of past and present, did not dwell upon the fact that future generations would carry the torch of learning still further. There is this difference in the evidence extant from the Hellenistic age. Archimedes, well aware how much one owes of one's own discoveries, novel though they may be, to one's predecessors (*Method*, p. 430 and *Quadrature of the Parabola*, Preface, pp. 262–64 [Heiberg]), and Hipparchus, who credited earlier investigators with "having labored as individuals for the common good" and expressed his gratitude to them on that account (*Commentaria*, p. 4, 21–23), were both fully conscious of doing their work for the future and keenly aware that the present is nothing but a moment in the forward movement and a preparation for better things to come.

This new feeling is epitomized in the new word used by Hellenistic authors to denote the advance of mankind. Instead of the "augmentation of knowledge" (ἐπίδοσις), the favorite term of the fourth century, the Hellenistic age preferred "cutting one's way forward" (προκοπή), Zeno's word for the unending striving for self-improvement (I, Fr. 234 [Arnim]) and the word which in its Latinized form (*procedere, progredi, processus, progressus*) became the archetype of the modern word "progress."[28] While the older metaphor emphasizes the additions made to science, an increase in magnitude produced by the efforts of past, present, and future, the new metaphor looks not to what has been achieved and its mere

[28] For προκοπή see Polybius X, 47, 12 and IX, 24. The noun seems to appear only in Hellenistic language, but the verb was used earlier (see Thucydides, VII, 50 and IV, 60; also above, chap. III, p. 92, note 79). Cicero translates προκόπτειν as *procedere* (e.g., *De finibus* III, 14, 18) and *processum habere* (*Brutus* 272), but he also uses *progredi* and *progressus*. In translating an Aristotelian fragment (53 [Rose]), he has *accessio*. That "we owe [to Lucretius] the blessed word Progress in the modern sense" (Inge, *op. cit.*, p. 276, with reference to V, 1453) is incorrect. The older expression, ἐπίδοσις, of course, continued to be used (e.g., Polybius, I, 20, 2; Philodemus, *Rhetorica* II, p. 51 [Sudhaus] [but προκοπή, p. 54]). Προκοπή like ἐπίδοσις is also an ethical concept.

increase but to what lies ahead. Man, marching on from the place where he finds himself and laying out his own path, faces forward and not backward. He fixes his eye not on the distance already covered but on the ground still to be conquered. About three centuries after Xenophanes language itself thus gave expression to that aspect of the "advancement of learning" which has been prominent ever since in the minds of the "progressivists," the notion that the advance is a continuing process, that today is followed by tomorrow as surely as it follows yesterday, that, as Leibniz said, the present is filled with the past and pregnant with the future.[29]

The available evidence does not reveal how these Hellenistic thinkers came to recognize the fact that the scholar labors for truth that he will never fully know, nor does it indicate whether they thought that this would always be the case. They seem to be expressing a pragmatic conviction rather than a theory, and it is unlikely that in this they were influenced by any philosophical system. Archimedes and the others were not without philosophical learning, for each of them "studied" or adhered to one or the other of the systems of the time; but they were not philosophers,[30] and the differences of their backgrounds also makes a specific philosophical influence improbable. Both the resignation and the hope that they express are quite understandable as a pragmatic faith if one takes into consideration the scientific situation and the temper of the times.

[29] For this interpretation of the meaning of προκοπή , see Seneca, *Ep.* 33, 10–11 (see below, p. 171 and note 82); and for Leibniz see Cassirer, *The Logic of the Humanities*, trans. C.S. Howe (New Haven, 1961), p. 20.

[30] Hero expressed his disdain for theoretical philosophy. Polybius is called a Stoic by R. Hirzel (*Untersuchungen zu Cicero's philosophischen Schriften* [Leipzig, 1877–83], II, 841 ff.) but an Academic Skeptic by Heinemann (*Poseidonios' Metaphysische Schriften* [Breslau, 1921–28], I, 18 ff.) and is connected with the empirical physicians by K. Deichgraber (*Die griechische Empirikerschule* [Berlin, 1930], pp. 324 ff.); but it is characteristic of him that his famous analysis of the cycle of constitutions gives an over-simplified picture of the beginnings of mankind when compared with philosophical prehistory (VI, 5, 4–7; see also Täubler, *Tyche*, pp. 91 f.). Archimedes according to ancient tradition was a Platonist (Plutarch, *Marcellus* XVII, 4), and Eratosthenes studied in the Academy (and the Stoa; for his eclecticism see R.–E. VI, col. 360, 9–20). Hipparchus in his work rejected all theory, although his astrological doctrine at least indicates philosophical interests (Rehm, R.–E. VIII, col. 1680, 36 ff.). Erasistratus (see below, p. 150) was indebted to Democritus and Aristotle.

Expectation that the goal would soon be reached had been shaken even at the turn of the fourth century. Life is short and Art is long according to the skeptical wisdom of the opening sentence of the Hippocratic *Aphorisms*. Theophrastus, who was equally great and successful as a student of nature and of history, is said to have cursed nature when he was more than ninety years old because she gives animals a long life for which they have no use, while to men, to whom such long life would be of greatest value, she grants only a brief span of existence. Could men live longer, he complained, the arts and sciences might be brought to perfection and with them life itself; but, things being what they are, it would be his fate to die when he was just beginning to see the truth. (Cicero, *Tuscul. Disput.* III, 28, 69.)[31]

In the course of the third century it must have become increasingly clear that what remained to be done could be accomplished by no individual, even if he lived more than a hundred years. The very rapidity of the advance that was being made engendered humility. The work of the four or five generations to which Aristotle and Theophrastus looked back was still being corrected and supplemented by that of each successive day. The premature confidence of earlier generations that they were approaching the goal must have begun to be regarded as a warning against falling into a similar error. The closer and more direct contact with the Orient, where data had been collected for many centuries or even millennia, as Aristotle had already observed (292 a 7; cf. 270 b 14), must also have had an effect in intensifying the awareness of time and the importance of long protracted studies.[32]

There was, moreover, a growing awareness of the historicity of

[31] The anecdote may be apocryphal (for a different version cf. Diogenes Laertius, V, 41), but it is not out of character with the skepticism noticeable throughout the work of Theophrastus (cf. Regenbogen, *s.n.* Theophrastus, R.–E. Suppl. VII, cols. 1556 ff.). Seneca (*De brevitate vitae,* chap. 1) ascribes the same attitude to Aristotle himself (cf. below, note 79) and compares it with that expressed in the Hippocratic aphorism. From his statement it is clear that the saying, to whomever it belongs, had come to be a symbolic expression of the futility of life and study, an attitude that Seneca combats.

[32] This must have been true even if, as Rehm contended (*Exakte Wissenschaften,* p. 40, cf. 13), the positive influence of the Orient on scientific development was small. On the Aristotelian passages quoted see Simplicius' commentary *ad loc.;* and for some of the Oriental material cf. Tarn, *op. cit.,* pp. 295 f. Seneca quotes Berossus (*Nat. Quaest.* III, 29).

events. In literary criticism this still took a conventional form. Against the allegorizers of Homer Eratosthenes contended that the poet of old could not possibly have hidden in his fanciful stories all the knowledge that later generations had gained in the course of time, for conditions then had not yet been ripe for the insight that was available later and was merely projected back into the Homeric age (Strabo, VII, 3, 6; cf. I, 3, 3); and the school of Aristarchus took a similar position.[33] In the debate as to whether the style and form of the Homeric epic could be imitated and should be, while Apollonius Rhodius and others took the affirmative, Callimachus (Fr. 74 a) and Theocritus (16, 20) maintained that Homer could not be surpassed and should not be imitated, because to be a poet in contemporary circumstances was to go another way entirely. Whether these men believed that this was true of other occupations too or only of the arts (as later centuries did exempt the arts from the general law of progress), they felt that their own age could not do everything and that the tasks men have to do are prescribed or circumscribed by the situation and the circumstances.[34]

Finally, there was increased appreciation of the personal factor involved in the work done. Poetic theory instead of dealing exclusively or mainly with techniques began to distinguish the poem from the poet, the exigencies of the former from the gifts of the

[33] The historicism of Eratosthenes was observed by Bury (*The Ancient Greek Historians*, p. 189) and rightly connected by him with the "antiquarianism" of historical inquiry (*ibid.*). He also pointed out (p. 251, note 1) that the same principle underlies Thucydides' judgment of piracy, but he overlooked the influence of Aristotle, cf. above, chap. III, pp. 89 ff. Eratosthenes (in Strabo, 299) is credited with saying that those who come later are more experienced than those who are earlier. The Alexandrian critics "athetized" Homeric lines referring to letters because the heroes were analphabets, cf. K. Lehrs, *De Aristarchi studiis Homericis* (Leipzig, 1865), p. 95. According to Aristarchus Homer, as an ancient poet, could not have known that the morning star and the evening star are one and the same (Scholion A *ad Iliad.* XXII, 318) and did not understand anything about medicine (Scholion T *ad Iliad.* XI, 846 f.). For further material see Christ-Schmid, *op. cit.*, p. 266, note 5 (the Homeric language as an older form of Attic language) and note 7 (the difference of religion in old and modern times). While the Pergamene school relied upon allegorical interpretation of the texts, the Alexandrian school clung to a realistic and historical interpretation (see Dilthey, "Die Enstehung der Hermeneutik," *Gesammelte Schriften* V, 321 f.).

[34] For the Alexandrian debate cf. A. Couat, *Alexandrian Poetry*, trans. J. Loeb (London, 1931), pp. 518 f. and 572. Euphorion called Homer the one honored above all others, Fr. 118 (Powell, p. 50).

latter.[35] In scientific and scholarly research the individual effort required was distinctly discerned and appreciated. Plato had spoken in a general way of man's obligation to work like a slave for the truth (*Republic* V, 494 D); but Erasistratus, the great physician of the third century, said: "One who is accustomed to investigation, worming his way through and turning in all directions, is unrelenting in the search not only day and night but all his whole life long until he arrives at the solution of his problem." (*Apud* Galen, *Scripta Minora*, II, 17 [Müller].) So, even as an individual, the scholar progresses.[36]

All these considerations must have led to recognition of the insignificance of any single life. A man who knows that he must labor incessantly to acquire whatever shred of knowledge it may be his lot to grasp, who knows that his work is prescribed for him by the situation in which he finds himself, and who knows that many before him have failed to reach perfection, he must be willing to admit that he is himself only a link in the chain of generations. The wonder is that despite this fact he can have the courage to go on in his search for knowledge, if it is not merely a game but the search for truth, a goal that he knows must forever recede before his advance into the future, when others will know more than he can ever know. The eighteenth century still understood this tragedy in the life of the scholar. Recalling what Hippocrates and Theophrastus had said, Kant admitted that they well express the instinctive and natural reaction of the man who is aware of being precluded from knowing all.[37]

[35] The distinction between the "nature of the poet" and his art seems first to have been made by Aristotle (*Poetics* 1455 a 32), although earlier the Sophists had made a distinction between nature and training. In the second century Neoptolemus of Parion posed problems concerning "the poem," "poetry," and "the poet," but did not provide the solutions to them. Such solutions were proposed only later, in the first century after Christ. For the changing evaluation of the artist's personality see Schweitzer, *Neue Heidelberger Jahrbücher*, pp. 103 ff., and in general E. Zilsel, *Die Enstehung des Geniebegriffes* (Tübingen, 1926), chap. 1.

[36] For the development of professional ethics see my sketch in "Motives and Incentives for Science in Antiquity," *Scientific Change*, ed. A.C. Crombie (New York, 1963), pp. 1 ff. The individualism of the Hellenistic period (e.g., Tarn, *op. cit.*, p. 2) does not, however, exclude a certain universalism, see below, note 43.

[37] I. Kant, "Mutmasslicher Anfang der Menschengeschichte," *Sämtliche Werke* (Insel Ausgabe, 1921), IV, 200 n.

Kant consoled himself by believing that, whereas in relation to the physical order the individual existence is everything, in relation to the intellectual realm the individual lives in the future. Such a notion would have been incomprehensible to Archimedes; but even the third century B.C. would have agreed with that other contention of the eighteenth century which is often regarded as a rationalization of the Christian message of an afterlife, the notion that in "the uses of posterity, in a better world to come,"[38] the individual can find compensation for what is denied to him in the present. It is his solace that what he cannot accomplish himself others will accomplish with his help, help that they will gratefully acknowledge. To live on in the memory of future generations had always been a characteristically Greek wish. At the beginning of the Hellenistic era it was perhaps for the first time not a foolish fancy but a reasonable expectation that scholarly work would be continued and remembered.

The enterprise of science had begun as an adventure of a few, who worked in isolation or at best in a haphazard relation with one another; and, while even in the fourth century this had continued to be so, some steps, however halting, now began to be taken for the organization of science.[39] Institutes for research were founded in a number of places; communication among individual workers was facilitated by cheaper and easier production of books, which were assembled in public libraries; and schools with a tradition of learning and teaching began to take shape. Despite the fact that to a large extent research still depended upon the individual's resources and initiative, more of a common purpose in scientific matters was acknowledged. That scholars sought the collaboration of their fellows in the same field, as Archimedes or Apollonius (Preface to Book II, *Treatise on Conic Sections*) did in their theoretical investigations or Hipparchus did for his enterprises, is an indication of this sense of the common purpose that unites

[38] C.L. Becker, *The Heavenly City* . . . , chap. IV. The evidence cited shows that contrary to Becker's belief the eighteenth century could have learned about "the uses of posterity" from ancient authors and probably did so, no matter how strongly it was influenced by Christian ideas in the specific formulations of the concept, see also below, p. 172 and note 83.

[39] Cf. above, chap. III, p. 82.

those interested in learning and the growth of which was not unconnected with the institutionalization of science.[40] Conscious of being a member of the community of scholars and a contributor to an enterprise in which there were obviously many contemporary collaborators, the scholar or scientist now naturally assumed that posterity would carry on his work from the point at which he would leave it, for he could not imagine that there might no longer be scholars to take up the task. Scholarship was now a career and had a fixed place in society. The professor had gradually come to be a social type like the farmer or the soldier.[41]

Moreover, the Hellenistic age learned to think in categories that transcended the individual life. The particularism and parochialism of the old city-states were shattered; and the subjects of the Hellenistic monarchies shared the common interests of a large society, while even the free cities sought the protection of leagues. A capitalistic system of trade linked the various parts of the world together. In Egypt, where for the first time scientific institutions were supported by the state, a planned economy was directed by the government. Thus the organization or rationalization of daily life begun in the fourth century rapidly became more extensive and more complicated. After the conquests of Alexander had unified the physical world as it had never been before, the poet Lycophron in his *Alexandra* spoke of future political events in the voice of a prophet with the conviction that there is a balance between past and future and that the two are mysteriously bound together, while Polybius attempted to interpret at least all the past "systematically" or "organically." (I, 3, 41; cf. III, 32.)[42]

In every respect, then, the claim of the individual was merged into the claim made upon him by the greater unity of which he was only a part; and his thoughts were directed not to what was peculiarly his but to a common task. Practically it was not merely

[40] Cf. Edelstein, *J.H.I.*, XIII (1952), 598 and 604.

[41] Cf. Burckhardt, *Griechische Kulturgeschichte* IV, 598 ff. (following Rohde, *Der griechische Roman*, p. 17). E. Mach in his *Die Mechanik in ihrer Entwicklung* (7. Auf.; Leipzig, 1912), pp. 4 f. clearly recognized the connection between the rise of professional classes and the rise of tradition in the scientific interpretation of data. See L. Olschki, *Geschichte der neusprachlichen wissenschaftlichen Literatur* [Heidelberg, 1919–1927] II, 51 f.

[42] For Lycophron cf. A.W. Mair in the Introduction to his translation (Loeb Classical Library, 1921), p. 482 and Christ-Schmid, *op. cit.*, VII, 2, 1, 175.

fanciful to expect the shortcomings of the present to be remedied by a future, which is as much a part of the life of men as is the past, and the natural brevity of individual life to be compensated in some degree by the life span of mankind, a mankind comprised of Greeks and barbarians, since in the words of Eratosthenes the true distinction between men lies not in race but in virtue and vice. (Strabo, I, 66.)[43]

This new science and its ethos may at first seem to have had little influence upon laymen or people in general. Science in the fourth century had still been the concern of a few. A change occurred in the Hellenistic era, however, when there were written for entertainment or practical purposes many didactic poems on geography, drugs, poisons, medicine, agriculture, history, chronography, and philosophy, of which Aratus' *Phaenomena* and Lucretius' *On the Nature of Things* are the most famous examples extant.[44] Scholars now considered it their duty to keep the public informed and abreast of new discoveries. Hipparchus composed a commentary on Aratus' poems with the express intention of driving out antiquated opinions and preventing all "lovers of learning" from being misled about heavenly phenomena by the mistaken notions of Eudoxus. The authors of universal histories felt that they were entitled to thanks "because at the cost of their own troubles they benefit common life." (Diodorus, I, 1.)[45] Even highly technical subjects were made available to the general public. So, whereas earlier au-

[43] For Hellenistic universalism as the corollary of individualism see Tarn, *op. cit.*, p. 2. The hope of living on in the memory of humanity is only a transformation of the characteristically Greek hope for immortality by means of glory, most eloquently expressed in Plato's *Symposium*; see also above, chap. I, p. 5. For the remark by Eratosthenes see T. Mommsen, *Römische Geschichte* V, 569, note 1; this view, which was opposed to that of Alexander, may have influenced the policy of the Egyptian kingdom.

[44] For a survey of this didactic poetry see Couat, *op. cit.*, Book V. The rise of a class of lovers of learning is noticed by Burckhardt, *Griechische Kulturgeschichte*, p. 538. It should be observed that, if Aratus really expressed the concept of progress in mythological language (cf. above, note 27), then his poem was the source not only for the story of decay but also for that of the ascent of man.

[45] Cf. Hipparchus, *In Arati et Eudoxi Phaenomena Comment.* I, i, 5–8 (pp. 4–6 [Manitius]). Cf. G. Murray, *The Rise of the Greek Epic* (3d ed.; Oxford, 1924), pp. 1 f. for the fact that these scholars spoke of their work as "service to humanity," an attitude that was consistent with the rationalistic interpretation (Euhemerism) of the gods as human beings who were deified because of their benefactions to mankind (cf. above, p. 140). The ideal of service is not derived from Christianity, as it is said to be by C.L. Becker, *op. cit.*, p. 39, cf. pp. 41 and 34.

thors had addressed themselves to "experts," Hero composed a book on artillery for "all and sundry" (*Belopoeica*, I, 2), stressing throughout his account the common intention to make improvements (4; 8; 9) and leading up to the accomplishment of the present; and he introduced his enterprise in the following words: "The most important and necessary part of philosophy surely is that dealing with (the ideal of) calmness; this has been the subject of inquiry in the majority of philosophical treatises hitherto, and in my opinion the theoretical discussion of this problem will never come to an end. The theory of mechanics far surpasses the theory of ethics, however, for one small part of it is sufficient to teach men a love of calmness, I mean the doctrine concerning what is called 'manufacture of missiles,' for by means of this one is enabled in times of peace not to tremble at the thought of attack by adversaries and enemies and, if war has broken out, not to lose one's calm, being in the possession of that wisdom and philosophy which the theory of mechanics provides by providing artillery." (I, 1.)[46]

Bizarre and exaggerated as Hero's statement may sound, it shows that scholars had become popularizers of science, taking over the rôle of the sophists and acting very much in the spirit of Fontenelle, in whose celebrated *Conversations on the Plurality of Worlds* the new astronomy is explained to a lady in the park of a country house.[47] This would not have happened if the interest of laymen in the results of research had not been steadily growing. Obviously it was no longer enough to study rhetoric or philosophy, but one had to have at least a smattering of science and the humanities. Culture no longer meant simply rational wisdom as opposed to mythological fantasy, the free and unhampered enjoyment of the aesthetic experience as opposed to a life in conformity

[46] Hero's date is controversial, see Tarn, *op. cit.*, p. 301 and Neugebauer, *The Exact Sciences in Antiquity* (2d. ed.; Providence [R.I.], 1957), p. 178. I side with those who put him no later than the second century B.C., for the passage quoted would have little meaning after 150 B.C.

[47] For Fontenelle's rôle as a popularizer of science see Bury, *The Idea of Progress*, pp. 112 ff. Though his contribution was decisive for his time, the examples that I have quoted show that he was not so revolutionary as Bury assumes. In the late Middle Ages and in the Renaissance preachers had popularized science (cf. Olschki, *op. cit.*, II, 141), and the Renaissance also had "science-writers," for example Anton Francesco Dossi in the sixteenth century (Olschki, p. 135).

with traditional values, the rationalization of life, or a metaphysical orientation; it meant also an acquaintance with scientific facts gained through research, though the lack of such acquaintance did not yet disqualify a person for service in high positions. Polybius well illustrates the strongly anti-authoritarian and pragmatic temper of his time when, in discussing a problem of geography, he writes: "I must leave no point unelaborated and barely stated as is the habit of most writers but must rather give a description of the facts supported by proofs, in order that no doubt may be left in the reader's mind, for this is the characteristic of the present age, in which all parts of the world are being made accessible by land or sea, that it is no longer proper to cite the testimony of poets and mythographers regarding matters of which we are ignorant, as those before us did in most cases, 'offering,' as Heraclitus says, 'untrustworthy sureties for disputed facts,' but we should aim at laying before our readers a narrative resting on its own credit." (IV, 40, 1–3.) [48]

In the Hellenistic era the scientist became the expert to be consulted even by the philosopher. The mass of accumulated data had become too large and science too complicated to be mastered by an outsider; [49] and both the philosopher and anyone else who aspired to a knowledge of scientific methods and particular results had to seek the advice of the scientist. It is not rash to maintain that, this being so, the belief in progress held by the scientist was accepted and cherished by many. Despite the philosophical and poetic praise of the simple life or the preoccupation with moral

[48] Cf. *J.H.I.*, XIII (1952), 600, where I described the general situation but failed to point out that, though the state did not pay attention to scientific results, philosophers and the educated public did.

[49] For the changing rôle of the expert see L. Edelstein, *Bull. Hist. Med.*, XL (1966), 201–204. The relation of the sciences to philosophy is hard to estimate, but it is dangerous to speak of independent, positive sciences in the modern sense of the word as existing in the Hellenistic period (Jaeger, *Aristoteles*, p. 432; L. Robin, *La pensée grecque et les origines de l'esprit scientifique* [Paris, 1923], pp. 433 ff.; L. Edelstein, "Platonism or Aristotelianism" *Bull. Inst. Hist. Med.*, VIII [1940], 766 and *ibid.*, XXVI [1952], 303 ff. [cf. also above, note 30]). In ancient times methodological problems and questions such as those about the nature of life or the structure of matter always remained within the domain of philosophy. The sciences, therefore, were on the whole still influenced by philosophical systems, even though because of greater specialization the investigation of facts had been largely freed from any metaphysical bias.

questions that is apparent in Stoicism as well as in Epicureanism and in the more popular literature of philosophical diatribes, a great number of intellectuals must have been imbued with the hope that the future would know more and more about this world.[50]

In the period after the Roman conquest a decline of intellectual life at least in Greece proper might have been expected, for the loss of independence, the devastation wrought by the wars, and the consequent deterioration of moral standards might well have broken men's spirits and made all talk of progress sound empty; but this did not happen. Even in the motherland, work was continued. Athens remained the home of philosophical schools; and in Rhodes, the last free Greek city, a new center of research and of art developed which rivaled Alexandria. Polybius had tried to teach his contemporaries how the domination of Rome and the loss of political freedom might be borne with the aid of historical insight, "the most obvious help to the correction of life" (I, 1). He had tried to convince them that the time had come when, relieved of political cares, they could take on the duty of studying and learning (III, 59);[51] and they and their successors acted as if they had heeded his words. The lovers of great deeds, who could no longer find satisfaction in military success or in political careers of international or even local importance, became lovers of learning, to use Hipparchus' expression, amateurs in the original sense of the word, and especially teachers first of the Romans and through the Romans of the world. The movement that had begun in the fourth century had now reached its climax. A meaningful life was identified with a life for culture, and henceforward Greek history was not political but cultural history. Thus the idea of progress and progress itself were saved, and what might well have been the end proved to be a new beginning.[52]

[50] See above, pp. 135 ff.; for the influence of the diatribe in Hellenistic times, see Dudley, *op. cit.*, chap. V.

[51] For the significance of the Polybius passage cf. Burckhardt, *Griechische Kulturgeschichte* IV, 538 and 587, who also observed that Polybius considered retirement from active politics an advantage for historical understanding (XII, 28) and believed history written for the sake of glory instead of personal reward to be more objective (XVI, 14, 1–7 [p. 533]).

[52] Burckhardt (*op. cit.*, pp. 286 f.) insisted that Greek cultural history at a given point becomes "Greek history as such"; but this point in my opinion is not at the

To judge the value of the work that was now done is extremely difficult because of the literature of this period even less has survived than is extant from the period before it. Names of poets, littérateurs, artists, scientists, and scholars are known; but writings completely preserved are rare, and even fragments are extremely scarce. Poetic creativity and imagination seem to have been taken from the Greeks and given to the Romans, for the poets excepting the epigrammatists were probably inferior to their predecessors; but rhetoric and linguistic studies and history and the sciences still were provinces of the Greeks, and the claim of novelty was still made and still made good.

Even among the poets there were followers of Callimachus who rejected Homer's authority (*Anthol. Palat.* VII, 377), and a late didactic poem on philosophy seems to have inveighed against the mistakes of the ancients, Empedocles and Plato.[53] Hermagoras' rhetoric "goes its own way" (Quintilian, III, 1, 16; cf. Cicero, *De invent.*, I, 6, 8); it was not Isocratean or Aristotelian or Stoic, as rhetorical art had been before. (III, 1, 15.) Didymus prided himself on his novel interpretation of the mythological aspect of poetry.[54] In medicine Asclepiades attacked the dogma of the healing power of nature and stigmatized earlier medicine, especially that of Hippocrates, as mere "concern with death," denying that it had brought any succor to its patients. Sextus Empiricus, arguing that in questions concerning truth no attention should be paid to age, cited Asclepiades as having said "that the old fall far short of the young in intelligence and mental acumen, although the opposite was supposed to be the fact owing to the false opinions held by most people." (*Adv. Math.* VII, 323.)

Asclepiades in this argument reported by Sextus did little more than expand the old maxim that it is not age or experience that

---

end of the Peloponnesian war but in the fourth century (see above, chap. III, p. 132), and the development after 150 B.C. was more important than Burckhardt thought. Even in the states of the Diadochi the Greeks had not been reduced to the level of the Greeks under Roman domination, for in the states of the Diadochi they belonged to the ruling class.

[53] Cf. the two lines preserved from the work of Demetrius of Troizen (Diels, *Poetarum Philosophorum Fragmenta*, p. 224).

[54] For Didymus' historical importance see Wilamowitz, *Einleitung in die griechische Tragödie* I (Berlin, 1921), 162 ff. Although Didymus was not an original thinker, he solved the problems of his time by collection of material, text criticisms, and commentaries. See also Christ–Schmid, *op. cit.*, pp. 305, 427, 432.

teaches wisdom; but in his medical doctrine, which was based on atomism, he was revolutionary and laid the foundation for the teaching of the Methodists, the third great medical sect of antiquity, whose influence was almost as great in later ages down to the Renaissance as was that of Galenic Hippocratism.[55] Didymus greatly advanced grammatical investigations in general, and the work of all later commentators draws on his; nor was it a slight achievement for Dionysius Thrax to have written the first Greek grammar. Much was being done in mathematics too, the debate about the foundation of which in reason or experience was renewed by the Epicurean Zeno.[56] The greatest accomplishment, however, was that of the scientist and philosopher, Posidonius.

The work of Posidonius was Aristotelian in scope. Questions of meteorology, astronomy, geography, mathematics, history, and military science were of equal concern to him. About all these matters he pronounced his own opinion and recorded his own observations, sometimes made during years of travel that took him to the ends of the world then known. Critically evaluating older material (even Polybius, whose work he continued, did not escape strictures) he integrated the accumulated data into a system and thus gained a new insight into the subjects investigated. Explanation was his main concern in all that he studied: meteorological phenomena, the formation of clouds, the appearance of comets, the ocean surrounding the inhabited world, or the earth and its circumference, for which he gave a measurement more exact than that of his famous predecessor, Eratosthenes. In historical research physical factors that determine the course of events were taken into account as much as moral considerations and traits of character that determine man's reactions to what happens.

Posidonius did more than advance research in the various scientific fields, however. He investigated the relation of the sciences to philosophy and, following in the footsteps of Aristotle, denied their

[55] See s.n. Asklepiades, R.–E. II, col. 1632, 61 ff. and 2te Reihe V, cols. 1633, 63 ff., s.n. Themison.
[56] Concerning the Epicureans see also below, pp. 162 f. I do not here assemble names that are no more than names, for my purpose is merely to emphasize the significance of the scientific movement between 150 and 30 B.C. which, so far as I can judge, is usually underestimated.

claim to independence. He clearly recognized the hypothetical character of scientific explanations and reserved to the philosopher the right to judge their value. Planetary motions, for example, had been investigated by astronomers on the assumption that the sun is at rest, but it is not their business according to Posidonius to decide whether this assumption is preferable to the assumption that the earth is at rest, for here insight of quite a different kind is needed. Thus he assigned the scattered scientific data their proper place in a total view of the world, which influenced all later writers down to the time of Galen, when largely because of the latter and of Ptolemy the scientific approach was radically altered.[57]

It must be remembered that in the time of Posidonius and the others mentioned the hope of obtaining new insight was challenged by some. The teaching of the empirical physicians, beginning at the end of the third century and perfected in the first half of the second, tended to stabilize medicine, for these physicians were satisfied for the most part with the knowledge transmitted by their predecessors and were content to suspend judgment in all questions of theory and of "hidden" causes. What is worth knowing, they believed, had mostly been explored. New diseases of which earlier physicians had not yet known could be mastered, they held, without new investigations by relying on analogies drawn from previous observations. Their medicine tended to be bookish, for books contain the experience of others; and like all merely empirical research of that period it acted as a barrier to scientific research rather than as an impetus to further investigation, and it was in principle antiprogressivist.[58] More general criticism came from other quarters, however. Agatharchides, for example, a Peripatetic or perhaps a Pythagorean and a scholar himself who wrote a lengthy treatise on the Red Sea, was inclined to praise the primitives because

[57] For the historical and geographical investigations of Posidonius see 87 F 1 ff., Jacoby with his *Commentary*.

[58] Cf. K. Deichgräber, *Die griechische Empirikerschule*, esp. pp. 298, 301. For the relation of the empirical school to the academic Skepsis, see Edelstein, *Quellen und Studien zur Geschichte der Naturwissenschaften und Medizin*, III (1933), 253 ff. The view that the Skepsis is a precursor of the "positive spirit" (Robin, *La pensée grecque*, p. 386) is certainly wrong. The empirical geography of Polybius, for example, was opposed to all mathematization of the subject, see *J.H.I.*, XIII (1952), 601.

among them could be found better morals than among highly cultured people in large cities. The aesthetic bias of this writer was classicistic. He condemned the new prose style and not only evinced little appreciation of progress but apparently believed that the future would bring more decay and that things were gradually getting worse.[59]

Despite such reaction and romanticism scientific research and its fruitfulness were generally taken for granted, and the public apparently was as much interested in science as it had been before. Geminus in his *Introduction* to astronomy, composed early in the first century, included among "the ancients" Cleanthes, the Stoic philosopher of the third century (p. 172, 12 [Manitius]); and these "ancients" he mentions not infrequently to emphasize the mistakes that they had made (pp. 28, 26; 30, 17; 42, 13; 44, 19; 96, 5). His book, written mainly from the point of view of Hipparchus, reads as if its purpose was to initiate the educated into the current astronomy, just as Hipparchus had tried to keep them from accepting the mistakes of Eudoxus.[60] The belief in progress must still have been prevalent, for the subject of progress was a main issue for all philosophers of the period, Epicureans, Skeptics, and Stoics alike.

In the Epicurean system as Lucretius presents it the ascent of the human race through the course of history is a central theme (*On the Nature of Things*, V, 925–1357); and yet progress is not given unqualified approbation, for primitive life despite all its shortcomings is represented as having been less troubled than life is now. Then people were not killed in warfare and did not perish in dangers which beset the traveller on "the stormy waters of the ocean" (1000) or by the sophisticated torments devised by civilization. Intellectual improvement and the organization of states have

[59] The Pythagorean leanings of Agatharchides were emphasized by O. Immisch, "Agatharchidea" (*Sitzungsberichte der Heidelberger Akademie der Wissenschaften, Phil.–Hist. Klasse*, Vol. X [1919], Abh. 7). If he was a Peripatetic, he was in opposition to his own school which after having been reconstituted by Critolaus about 150 B.C. again showed an interest in scientific problems, especially in the history of culture written after the Aristotelian pattern; see R. Harder, *Ocellus Lucanus* (Neue Philologische Untersuchungen, I [Berlin, 1926]), 151–153.

[60] Geminus, it is now generally agreed, wrote about 70 B.C. (R.–E. VII, col. 1028, 8 ff.); his dependence on Hipparchus seems to be certain also (*ibid.*, col. 1031, 20 ff.), but the supposition that he was influenced by Posidonius, his contemporary, is refuted by K. Reinhardt (*Poseidonios* [München, 1921], pp. 178 ff.).

created ambition and greed (1120–23), and the advancement of life to its high plane has "stirred up from the lowest depths the great seething tide of war." (1434 f.) On the other hand, the advantages of primitive life are said to have been outweighed by disadvantages, which only the rise of civilization has overcome; and, if despite the gains that have been made "the race of man toils fruitlessly and in vain forever," it is "because, we may be sure, it has not learned what are the limits of possession nor at all how far true pleasure can increase." (1430–33.) It is men's own fault that they are unhappy and all the more their fault now that Epicurus had pointed out the true way of life. No longing for the distant past diminishes Lucretius' admiration for the great individuals "who excelled in understanding and were strong in mind" (1107) and who by their efforts brought men to the point where they are now.[61] Lucretius is on the side of progressivism too when he approves the forward strides taken recently and in his own time; and it is with a kind of jubilation that he announces: "Our whole world is in its youth and quite new is the nature of the firmament, nor long ago did it receive its first beginnings. Wherefore even now certain arts are being perfected, even now are growing; much now has been added to ships; but a while ago musicians gave birth to tuneful harmonies. This nature of things, this philosophy, is but lately discovered, and I myself was found the very first of all who could turn it into the speech of my country." (V, 330–336.)[62]

The outlines of the story told by Lucretius are not new. He

[61] According to L. Robin (*Revue de Métaphysique et de Morale*, XXIII [1916], 697 ff.) Lucretius believed in the superiority of primitive existence; and according to Lovejoy and Boas (*op. cit.*, p. 239) the evidence taken as a whole at least implies that for him the second stage of civilization was the happiest. Norden (*Jahrbücher für Classische Philologie*, Suppl. XIX [1892], 416) contended that the myth of the Golden Age was accepted by Lucretius and by Epicurus. These inferences were proved erroneous by E. Reitzenstein, *Theophrast bei Epikur und Lucrez* (Orient und Antike, II [Heidelberg, 1924]), 71 ff. and by M. Taylor, A.J.P., LXVIII (1947), 184 ff. Ancient progressivism was seldom as consistent in its optimism as modern progressivism is (see also below, note 84).

[62] The statement about the advance of the arts and crafts "within living memory" is attributed to Epicurus by E. Bignone, *L'Aristotele perduto e la formazione filosofica di Epicuro* II (Firenze, 1936), 463 ff. and F. Solmsen, "Epicurus and Cosmological Heresies," A.J.P., LXXII (1951), 11; but it is unlikely that Epicurus, who was so little concerned with the arts (cf. above, p. 137), would have made such an assertion.

reproduced under the cloak of Epicurus' doctrine the traditional picture that had been elaborated since the days of the Pre-Socratics;[63] but Epicurus had dealt with the subject in passing and in general terms, and the loving care with which the poet of the first century describes in detail how man "step by step" has reached the level of civilization and the poet's passionate sympathy with the accomplishment are hardly in keeping with the early dogma of the "life in seclusion" and are understandable only from the point of view of the Epicureanism of his time.

From the second century B.C. onwards the Epicureans evinced a greater interest in the arts and sciences than had Epicurus himself or the first generation of his pupils. Mathematical investigation began to be cultivated, and historical research in the form of doxographical surveys began to be favored. In the circle around Philodemus, a contemporary of Cicero, the principles of empirical research were worked out in detail. Thus the master's disdain for a life of learning was gradually toned down by his later followers. None of them was so eager as he had been to free himself from the prison of the liberal arts, and concessions were made even to the art of politics, the validity of which at least some of them were willing to acknowledge. All this happened, I believe, because progress was an accepted fact in their time.[64]

Philodemus and his pupils have left no written evidence of their opinion about the continuation of progress, and Lucretius in his poem never states explicitly that there will be progress in the future. He has been supposed to commit himself to it, however, by saying that some of the arts are even now growing and being perfected (332–34); and it has even been contended that he envisaged continuous progress and that in his opinion progress as it was

[63] Cf. Robin, *Revue de métaphysique et de morale*, XXIII (1916), 697 ff.; Norden had already noted Epicurus' indebtedness to the Peripatos, *Jahrbücher für Classische Philologie*, Suppl. XIX (1892), p. 414, note 3. Lucretius' divergence from Epicurus' teaching is most notable in his discussion of the origin of language which does not mention "the differences of the languages of different nations" or "the later stages in which words were invented θέσει" as did other later Epicureans (Bailey, *Lucretius* III, p. 1488; cf. also Diogenes of Oinoanda, Fr. 10).

[64] For Philodemus and his circle, see P.H. DeLacy and E.A. DeLacy, *Philodemus: On Methods of Inference* (American Philological Association, Philological Monographs, X [Philadelphia, 1941]), pp. 148 ff. A connection between Philodemus and Lucretius was suggested by Bruns (cf. Norden, *Jahrbücher für Classische Philologie*, Suppl. XIX [1892], p. 417, note 1).

in the past and is in the present "presumably will continue as long as man exists."[65] To me, the assumption that the poet is the champion of such doctrines appears to be in disagreement with his final verdict on the course of human civilization and with the whole tendency of the Epicureanism he professes.

Lucretius in summarizing his long account of man's history says: "Ships and the tilling of the land, walls, laws, weapons, roads, dress (and) all things of this kind, all the prizes and luxuries of life, one and all, songs and pictures, and the quaintly wrought polished statues, practice and therewith the inventiveness of the eager mind taught them little by little, as they went forward step by step. So, little by little, time brings out each thing into view and reason raises it up into the coasts of light. For things must be brought to light one after another and in due order until they have reached their highest point." (1448–57.) Whatever text or interpretation is adopted, the last sentence can mean only that all arts have a measure of perfection beyond which it is impossible to go;[66] and so Lucretius cannot have believed in a general law of progress, in the continuous advance of the arts and sciences throughout the ages to come.

Moreover, it is certain that in many fields in which especially the

[65] M. Taylor, *A.J.P.*, LXVIII (1947), 184; T. Frank, *Life and Literature of the Roman Republic* (Berkeley [Calif.], 1930), pp. 237–242; also Jean M. Guyau, *La Morale d'Épicure* (6th ed.; Paris, 1917), p. 167. Lovejoy and Boas speak of a "strain in Lucretius in which he appears as an *Aufklärer* of the first century B.C. and even a precursor of the enthusiasts for the idea of progress in the seventeenth and eighteenth centuries " (*op. cit.*, p. 240); but see below, note 70.

[66] In the translation of lines 1456 f. I follow H.A.J. Munro, *Lucretius, De Rerum Natura* (3rd ed.; London, 1873), as do Lovejoy and Boas (p. 237). The upshot of the statement is, as Munro puts it (p. 630), that "by degrees experience taught men all the useful and graceful arts, one advance suggesting another, till perfection was attained." The word used here to denote the high point in the growth of the arts (*summum acumen*) is the one that Lucretius uses elsewhere to designate the high point in the growth of the cosmos (II, 1130; cf. F. Solmsen, "Epicurus on Growth and Decline of the Cosmos," *A.J.P.* LXXIV [1953], 44, note 38). Bailey translated the lines in question differently: "For they saw one thing after another grow clear in their mind, until they reached the topmost pinnacle of the arts." (For the manuscript tradition and the various changes proposed, cf. III, pp. 1549 f). According to Bailey's understanding of the text, then, Lucretius would say that in the cases enumerated man has already advanced as far as possible. This seems to conflict with 330 ff., however, where the art of ship-building in particular is mentioned as "still developing." According to both interpretations Lucretius would, of course, acknowledge a final end to the development; but he is more likely here to be formulating the principle underlying the development than to be stating its outcome.

ancient progressivists would have expected further progress to be made Lucretius must have ruled it out, for as an Epicurean he believed that philosophy had been perfected by the founder of the school, who not only had designated the right way of life but also had revealed the truth concerning nature and had taught that any understanding of specific natural phenomena based on observation and mathematical analysis is out of the question. Even Philodemus and his associates did not abandon the opposition to astronomy and the other sciences, which follows from the epistemological principles of Epicurus.[67] The method of inference worked out by this group was applicable in different degrees of certainty only to painting, music, poetry, grammar, and rhetoric, and to medicine, navigation, and mathematics. Thus the possibility of progress in research was strictly limited for Lucretius as for every Epicurean, and limited to only a few of the arts and sciences as generally understood in antiquity.[68]

Finally, while Lucretius extols the strength of nature when praising his own time, he regards it as already exhausted when he speaks of the future in general terms. (II, 1150 ff.) Here his view is pessimistic rather than optimistic: "All things waste away little by little," he adds, "and pass to the grave foredone by age and the lapse of time." (1173 f.) Constant change throughout time, a law of growth and decay, was one of the fundamental axioms of his cosmology as it was of that of Epicurus. One would suppose, therefore, that the arts and sciences too after having reached the height of their development must decline, and with them civilization itself.[69]

The evidence is not sufficient to permit an unequivocal conclusion and is in part contradictory. It can scarcely be denied that Lucretius must have expected some improvement still to be made after his time in "certain arts that are now being perfected and even

[67] Philodemus spoke derisively of "wisdom's backward and forward progress" (τὰς ἐναντίας προκοπὰς τῆς σοφίας), Rhetorica, col. LI, 1–3 = II, p. 54 (Sudhaus).

[68] See DeLacy, Philodemus: On Methods of Inference, pp. 136, 152. Philodemus defended Epicurus' view that the sun is only as large as it appears (p. 170); astronomy is not regarded as a science any more than divination is (p. 136).

[69] For a reinterpretation of the biological theory of the decay of the cosmos advocated by Epicurus cf. Solmsen, A.J.P., LXXIV (1953), 34 ff. (The comparison of the cosmos to an animal is attested in Fr. 305 [Usener].)

now growing," but all the indications are against his having cherished great hopes for the future. Perhaps he was himself unable to resolve the conflict between the two views of the world to which he and his teachers were equally devoted. The progressivist tendencies of the third and second centuries had forced the younger Epicureans to alter their doctrine, and Lucretius took their part against the master; but, when he or the circle whose views he echoes tried to reconcile the new idea of progress with the system of Epicurus, the inherited dogma proved to be refractory. Epicurus himself had believed in progress during the past, and this belief could be stretched to cover the concession that to a limited extent progress was still possible in the future; but full confidence in man's ability to reach out beyond himself, to penetrate ever more deeply into the mystery of truth, to create ever new forms of human life, and to build a world of ever greater perfection was alien to Epicurus and remained alien to his followers.[70]

Upon the Skeptics the impact of the idea of progress was so strong as to be disruptive. Carneades, the head of the school about the middle of the second century, like his predecessor Arcesilaus and probably like Pyrrho, persisted in maintaining that the dissension among philosophers left no choice but to suspend judgment on all questions, for experience seemed to prove that man is incapable of finding the truth and can at best calculate probabilities and choose what seems to be more reasonable in practice. This was still the position of the Academy at the beginning of the first century.[71] It was challenged by Antiochus, a contemporary of Philodemus and his associates. Antiochus admitted that the first philosophers, dealing with problems then new and themselves being "newly born, as it were," had probably failed to discover the truth; but "should we really assume," he added scornfully, "that nothing has been discovered since, in the course of so many centuries, by men of great

[70] Lovejoy and Boas (*op. cit.*, p. 240) speak of a combination of "two incongruous moods" in Lucretius (see also W.M. Green, "The Dying World of Lucretius," *A.J.P.*, LXIII [1942], 51 ff. and M. Taylor, *A.J.P.*, LXVIII [1947], 183), but in my opinion the tension was between the spirit of the times and the traditional Epicurean teaching rather than between conflicting forces in the personality of the poet.
[71] For the development of Skepticism from Carneades to Philo see A. Goedeckemeyer, *Die Geschichte des Griechischen Skeptizismus* (Leipzig, 1905), pp. 91 ff. and L. Robin, *Pyrrhon et le scepticisme grec*, pp. 129 ff.

genius and their most earnest investigations?" (Cicero, *Academica* II, 16, 15.) Is not even the history of academic philosophy, he asked, a history of constant progress? (*Ibid.*, 6, 16–18; cf. II, 5, 3.) Antiochus consequently felt it necessary to renounce the argument basic to Skepticism, that the dissension of philosophers proves the impossibility of discovering the truth, and to regard this divergence of opinion as a phenomenon to be understood historically. Regarded in this way, the complicated problems of philosophy cannot have been resolved by a single stroke; it takes time to solve them.[72]

By insisting that man must have come nearer and nearer to truth in the course of time Antiochus threatened the very foundation of Skepticism. Philo, the head of the school, and his followers tried desperately to show that the dissension among philosophers was as great as ever and that this was true of all branches of philosophical investigation. (II, 42, 129 ff.; 46, 142 ff.) Nevertheless, while they thought it still possible to maintain that certainty in these matters is not to be attained, they did not dare to deny that some progress had been made, at least in formulating problems more succinctly (24, 77; 29, 93); and they even went so far as to admit that natural studies, despite the dissension about the truth of their results, have a certain charm of their own and may lead to a theoretical insight that is at least probable. (41, 127.)

These concessions did not satisfy Antiochus. He adopted Zeno's theory of cognition because he considered it superior to Plato's and Aristotle's (II, 1, 6 ff.), and, convinced of man's ability to advance in knowledge, he worked out a system of his own. This to a great extent was taken from the doctrine of the old Academy, i.e., from the teaching of Plato and Aristotle and the first generation of Platonists and Aristotelians (Cicero, *De Finibus* IV), for Antiochus held that according to these philosophers "all things are small in their beginnings but increase as they gain the advantages of the stages of progress through which they pass." (VI, 21, 58.) So mind too develops slowly; and it is the individual's task and the task of art to "supplement those mere beginnings by searching out the further developments which were implicit in them until what

[72] The interlocutor in the *Academica* who represents the attitude of Antiochus pretends to speak from recollection, but Cicero probably used a lost treatise of Antiochus, the *Sosus* (cf. J.S. Reid, *Cicero, Academica* [London, 1885], pp. 51 f.).

we seek is fully developed" (21, 60), even as in man written large, i.e., in humanity, nature developed gradually "with the assistance of the arts," as Xenocrates and Aristotle taught. (*De Finibus* IV, 6, 16; cf. 13, 34.) This theory is essentially the same as that professed by Cicero, the best known, though perhaps not the most original, of the Skeptics of the first century B.C. He assumes that in man "there is, as it were, hidden a certain divine fire of intelligence and reason" (*De Rep.* III, 1, 1), and he attributes the development of knowledge and of civilization to the power of human reason, thus putting an emphasis "lacking in Lucretius," as has been rightly said, "upon the differentiation of man by a trait approximating what in the eighteenth century was to be called his 'perfectibility.'"[73]

In the school of the Stoics the rigorous moralism of Zeno held sway for some time, and the followers of Chrysippus did not deviate significantly from Zeno and Cleanthes in their conception of the development of mankind;[74] but in the so-called Middle Stoa the doctrine of progress became part and parcel of the Stoic teaching. Perhaps Panaetius, with whom the reform of the school began, was the first to consider the cultivation of the arts and sciences the truly humanizing force. Posidonius certainly regarded the elaboration of civilization as the main task of man; and he taught that under the leadership of philosophy, i.e., of reason, the highest and lowliest kinds of knowledge, technical skills no less than juridical rules and political institutions, had been discovered. (Seneca, *Epistle*, 90, 6–7.) The development was regarded as a gradual ascent, a kind of education of the human race.[75]

For Antiochus see G. Luck, *Der Akademiker Antiochos* (Noctes Romanae, 7 [Bern, 1953]).

[73] Cf. Lovejoy and Boas, p. 244. Cicero, who was an admirer of Philo (Goedeckemeyer, *op. cit.*, p. 130), says that in his time Pyrrhonism was completely extinct (*De orat.* III, 17; 63). This is perhaps another indication of the strength of progressivism which may in addition explain the riddle of the philosophy of Aenesidemus, a younger contemporary of Cicero, who is reported to have treated Skepticism as an introduction to a dogmatic philosophy, cf. Goedeckemeyer, *op. cit.*, pp. 231 ff. (Sextus, *Adv. Math.* VII, 54, cf. 8).

[74] Cf. II, Fr. 739 and III, Fr. 705 ff. (Arnim). Chrysippus did attribute a greater value to the liberal arts, though (III, Fr. 738 [Arnim]); concerning his followers' views of progress see above, p. 145.

[75] Since only fragments survive from the works of Panaetius and Posidonius, it is difficult to determine exactly the position that each of them took in the matter; but none of the attested fragments states that Panaetius had a philosophy of culture (see

Cicero's writings provide at least an impression of the tenor and the content of this doctrine. According to it, although nature has not lavished upon the human being the loving care that she has bestowed upon animals, she has provided him, her "highest offspring," with reason, the divine spark within him; and by means of this he creates the arts and sciences and with their help and by his power and skill builds up a civilized world, "another nature, as it were, within the realm of nature." (*De natura deorum* II, 60, 152.) To the inventions of the spirit, the perception of the senses, and the hands of the craftsman and artist man owes everything. He "moderates" the violence of the elements and "reigns" over all the goods of the earth. (*Ibid.*) His is truly an *imperium in imperio*, to use Spinoza's phrase; he is, so to speak, the "caretaker of the earth," beautifying the land and preventing it from becoming a desert. (39, 99.) By the employment of reason, societies are built up. (*De officiis* I, 4, 12.) Without the multitude of the arts which are gradually established man would remain a mere animal, for there would be no order or morality and no life worthy of a human being. (II, 42, 15.)[76]

None of the fragments surviving from the Middle Stoa expresses an opinion about the duration of progress in the future; but among later Stoics writing in the early first century after Christ and about the middle of that century and under the influence of Panaetius as well as Posidonius the law of endless advance is common property. Manilius appears to take it as a law that is self-evident. "Use is always finding the seeds of new things in old," he says in his anti-primitivistic account of human prehistory. (*Astronomica*, I,

below, note 76), while it is clear from Seneca, *Ep.* 90 that Posidonius did write copiously on the development of civilization. I therefore deal with his views rather than with those of Panaetius. In stressing the practical aspect of early philosophy Posidonius followed Dicaearchus (see above, pp. 134 f.).

[76] The unqualified enthusiasm for human progress expressed in this last passage is remarked upon by Lovejoy and Boas (*op. cit.*, p. 251). The preceding passage (*De officiis* I, 4, 12) is regarded by van Straaten (Fr. 98) as having been taken from Panaetius, and Pohlenz (*Die Stoa* I, 199) finds Panaetius' theory of culture in *De natura deorum*; but in *De officiis* (I, 4, 12) Panaetius is not mentioned, although it is true that Cicero admits to following him in general. Nevertheless, there are additions from Posidonius, e.g., I, 45, 159; cf. III, 2, 7–8 (Edelstein, *A.J.P.*, LXXI [1950], 78 f.). As for *De natura deorum*, this seems to agree with Posidonius' teaching more closely than with that of Panaetius. See in general K. Reinhardt, *s.n.* Poseidonios, R.–E. XXII, cols. 805 ff. and col. 722 on *De natura deorum*.

90.) Pliny the Elder, speaking of planetary motions, about which he had novel views, says in passing: "If in these matters we profess opinions different from those of earlier thinkers, we nevertheless acknowledge that they too have merit who as the first showed the way to further inquiry—only let no one lose hope that the ages will always progress in knowledge." (*Naturalis Historia* II, 15, 62.) The same assertion of endless improvement in times to come is made by Seneca, who contends that every future generation will find some work to do. (*Naturales Quaest.* VI, 5, 31.) The agreement of these three writers, all of whom professed to be of the same school, can hardly be fortuitous but must reflect the common philosophy of the Middle Stoa.[77]

Before explaining how Panaetius and Posidonius came to accept the idea of endless progress and how it comports with their refashioning of Stoic teaching it will be well to put together occasional remarks of Seneca's which reveal the doctrine as Posidonius formulated it and the examples by which he illustrated it. This will make it easier to appreciate the rôle of progressivism in Stoic thought and will also be illuminating in itself, for Seneca gives a clearer and more comprehensive picture of what the ancients meant by progress than does any other author.[78]

Seneca takes it for granted that knowledge has not yet been perfected and is equally sure that what is still wanting will gradually be provided by those who live in later ages. "The time will

[77] Posidonius' influence on Seneca is obvious from the many quotations in the *Naturales Quaestiones* and in the *Epistles*. Pliny mentions Posidonius as one of his sources for Book II and later in the text itself (for his relation to Stoicism see Pohlenz, *op. cit.*, p. 360). Manilius depends, if not on Posidonius, then certainly on Stoic writers (Pohlenz, *ibid.*). According to Lovejoy and Boas (*op. cit.*, p. 377) no passage written before Pliny's "so definitely projects the notion of boundless progress into the future"; but even earlier Manilius introduced the term "always" that is missing in Lucretius. (The translation of Lovejoy and Boas, pp. 376 f., seems to me to be erroneous.) The passage of Pliny—"tantalizing in its brevity . . . how much is implied in this phrase it is impossible to determine"—can be clarified, I think, by the other testimony that I shall cite below.

[78] A reconstruction of Seneca's general views of progress is attempted by Delvaille and by Heinemann; but I confine myself to those statements that bear on the problem of endless progress. That Seneca was thoroughly familiar with Posidonius' theory of culture is clear from *Ep.* 90, where he gives a critical treatment of it. Posidonius may have written a treatise on the subject (Reinhardt, *R.–E.* XXII, cols. 805 f.). Seneca may also have drawn some material from the *Life of Hellas*, written by a pupil of Posidonius, Iason.

come when mental acumen and prolonged study will bring to light what now is hidden . . . the time will come when our successors will wonder how we could have been ignorant of things so obvious." (*Naturales Quaestiones* VII, 25, 4–5.) He is confident, moreover, that there will be no end to such progress. "Many things unknown to us will be understood by men of future centuries, many are reserved for ages yet to come, when our memory shall have perished. It is a petty world in which there would be no question worth asking for every generation." (VII, 30, 5.) What is done by the past and the present must inevitably fall short of the goal and must forever be supplanted by the work of the future; and, as if he were replying across the gulf of time to the disillusionment that oppressed Theophrastus when he recognized that he could not live long enough to attain the truth, Seneca calmly asserts: "A single lifetime, though it were wholly devoted to the heavens, is not enough for the investigation of problems of such complexity . . . it must therefore require long successive ages to unfold all." (VII, 25, 4.) [79]

These statements of Seneca's concern the study of natural phenomena, but he is careful to observe that the law is valid not only for natural science but for everything. "Nothing is completed at its very beginning. This is true not only of the matter with which we are dealing, the greatest and most involved of all (i.e., natural philosophy), where, even though much may be accomplished, every succeeding generation will still find something to do" (VI, 5, 3); and in particular he shows how for philosophical studies past, present, and future are interconnected. [80]

[79] Seneca (see above, note 30) ascribes the statement not to Theophrastus but to Aristotle. Bacon, who was familiar with Seneca's *Naturales Quaestiones* (cf. Bury, *The Idea of Progress*, p. 28), observed that Seneca believed in gradual progress; and it is in the Platonic and Baconian spirit (see above, p. 115) when Seneca, though rejecting the views of the ancients as crude, gives them some credit for the success of later generations because they were the first to start and the ones to raise hopes of success (VI, 5, 2).

[80] Lovejoy and Boas (p. 378) speak of Seneca's qualified faith in progress and point to primitivistic passages in his writings (e.g., *De providentia* IV, 14 ff. [p. 364]; *Medea* 301 ff. and 364 ff. [p. 279]); but the acknowledgment that early ages had a certain kind of superiority is not inconsistent with ancient progressivism (cf. above, note 61), and in any case the result of progress is regarded in the same light in the passage of the *Medea* and in the *Naturales Quaestiones*. A. Bonhöffer, *Die Ethik des Stoikers Epictet* (Stuttgart, 1894), connects Seneca's attitude in this latter work with

From the tradition inherited the philosopher chooses what seems right to him. Not bound by the dogma of one particular school or of one particular person, he judges for himself, and what his predecessors have left to him is not a "result" but a "problem." (*Epistula*, 45, 4; cf. *De Vita Beata*, 3, 2.)[81] Only those who "have never come of age" follow the ancients not only where nobody would differ with them, in matters for which they have provided the solution, but even where there are questions still unanswered. How would it be possible to discover more if one were content with what had already been found? He who simply treads in the footsteps of another cannot make any discoveries, for he does not even pose any questions. The right attitude is rather to "make use of the old road," to continue along it, but, if one sights another more appropriate and more convenient, to make it passable and to extend it. The ancients are "not our masters but only our leaders and guides. The truth is open to all; it has not yet been usurped. Much of it will be left even to the future." (*Epistula*, 33, 10–11.)[82]

Progress in understanding, then, depends on reasoned freedom from authority as well as on reasoned acceptance of it. Only so does knowledge become the common possession of mankind, a treasure to which the succeeding generations make their contributions, changing and rechanging it ever anew, sharing in it and enriching

his "conversion to science in his old age" (p. 125; see also Pohlenz, *Die Stoa* I, 313 f.); but the ethical writings (*De beneficiis* VII, 1, 5; especially 58, 25) recommend a *Lebensphilosophie* just as do the scientific ones, and, if their attitude is more consistent, it is because in them Seneca followed Posidonius throughout.

[81] F. Ogerau (*Essai sur le système philosophique des Stoïciens* [Paris, 1885], pp. 277 ff.), one of the few to raise the question at all, says that for Seneca philosophical progress meant the application of Stoic principles to new circumstances (p. 279). This is true of passages such as *Ep.* 95, 29 ff. and 64, 7; but Seneca insists on originality in others (*Ep.* 104, 16). Knowing that he stands in a tradition (*Ep.* 80, 1), he is not concerned only to make the doctrine his own (*Ep.* 33, 8; cf. *Ep.* 80, 1 ["*adsentior non servio*"] and 33, 8 [*meminisse-scire*]). Posidonius, whom Seneca follows, also respected tradition despite his love for what was new (see above, p. 158). Ogerau's general thesis (pp. 275 ff. and 300) that the Roman Stoa is not original is no longer tenable (cf. Edelstein, A.J.P., LXXII [1951], 429). Lovejoy and Boas, (p. 264), taking an attitude similar to Ogerau's, point to Seneca's insistence (*Ep.* 90, 34 ff.) that, contrary to the opinion of Posidonius, the essential moral truths are already known; but stress on "agreement" is characteristic of the time and of progressivism (cf. below, p. 178), and in another context Seneca speaks of the necessity of "adding" to the truth (64, 7).

[82] These are the passages on which I have based my interpretation of the meaning of "progress," above, p. 146 and note 29.

it. "I marvel at wisdom," Seneca exclaims, "as I marvel at the world itself which, no matter how often I contemplate it, seems always new. I revere the discoveries of wisdom and its discoverers. It pleases me to approach the subject as a legacy left to me by many men. For me they have gathered up, for me they have labored. May an even greater legacy be left by myself to posterity. Much remains to do; much will remain; and no one born after thousands of centuries will be deprived of the chance of adding something in addition." (*Epistula*, 64, 7–8.) This is what was to be said by Dante in his *De monarchia*, in "a sentence that implied more perhaps than he would willingly have conceded, that implied in fact all that the eighteenth century had to say on the subject. 'All men on whom the Higher Nature has stamped the love of truth should especially concern themselves in laboring for posterity, in order that future generations may be enriched by their efforts, as they themselves were made rich by the efforts of generations past.' "[83]

Envisaging the progress of knowledge in all future generations, Seneca remains undaunted by the evils which in his opinion do accompany the ascent of civilization. The inventions of ships spread war to all the far corners of the world. (V, 18, 6.) Luxury increases and moral decay appears to be inevitable. Man, born at the beginning of the world "under better auspices," as it were, and "without knowledge of crimes," will eventually become "like the beasts." (III, 30, 7 f.; cf. 28, 7.) Yet, this is so because man misuses the "gifts of nature"; and "nothing can be found, useful as it may be, that human fault does not turn into its opposite" (V, 18, 1; 5 f.; cf. 13, 24), Seneca asserts in the spirit of Aristotle. The value of progress is not diminished by human shortcomings, however, any more than is that of all the other goods that god has given the human race.[84] Seneca remains equally undisturbed by the prospect

[83] Becker, *op. cit.*, p. 130, who quotes *Naturales Quaestiones* VII, 25, 4–5 in order to show that the ancients dimly perceived the uses of posterity. The statement referred to in the text above proves that they were fully familiar with the concept (see also *De otio* 6, 4).

[84] For Aristotle (*Rhetoric* I, 4) see above, chap. III, p. 121. The same idea is expressed in the post-Aristotelian tradition by the saying that man is most harmed and most helped by man (see Dicaearchus Fr. 24 and Wehrli's commentary; cf. also Lucretius, V, 988 ff. and Cicero, *De officiis* II, 3, 11 ff.). Seneca gives as an example of this thesis the winds (18, 1–16), which Providence created for the purpose of

of the annihilation of the world and all the progress it has seen. This end, he believes, has been prepared from the beginning (*Naturales Quaestiones*, III, 30, 1) and cannot be far off (5); but with complete detachment he analyzes the events that will occur when that "fatal day" comes (27, 1) which will see "the burial of all mankind." (*Ibid.*) "All that the long forbearance of fortune has produced, all that has been reared to eminence, all that is famous, and all that is beautiful, great thrones, great nations, all will descend into the one abyss and will be overthrown in one hour." (29, 9.) Not after a period of decay but in its full flowering the world will be destroyed, and there will arise another destined to witness the same greatness and the same doom.[85]

What, then, can be the meaning of progress beset by human evil in a world doomed to destruction? What use can rightly be made of it? There is, first of all, the advantage it has for the individual. Participating in the search for knowledge, he is rewarded by increasing understanding, "a reward than which there is none greater." (VI, 4, 2.) He is also elevated above himself. "How contemptible a thing is a man if he does not reach beyond his human bonds" (I, Preface, 5), if he does no more than live a moral life, purging his soul of evil passions, of ambition and greed. Virtue's greatness is that "it prepares man for insight and makes him worthy of entering

---

sailing and exploring the world but which man uses for the purpose of conquests. Posidonius held man responsible for the evils resulting from civilization (Fr. 46–48 [Jacoby] = Strabo, III, 2, 9; Athenaeus, VI, 23–25), though like Plato (see above, chap. III, p. 112) he admitted that civilization engenders a tendency to greater evil (*Ep*. 90, 6).

[85] Posidonius considered the destruction of the universe to be at least a possibility, whereas Panaetius had doubted it (L. Edelstein, *A.J.P.*, LVII [1936], 295). The terms are Posidonian in which Seneca describes the beginning of a new and better world to replace the present one and its moral decay (III, 17 ff.; especially 28, 7; 30, 1; 5). The initial states of the world are the "Golden Age"; vice is "only gradually creeping in" (Posidonius in Seneca, *Ep*. 90). (Like Posidonius, Seneca [contrary to what is said by Lovejoy and Boas, p. 379, 18 and Bury, *The Idea of Progress*, p. 15] never espouses a theory of hopeless degeneration and corruption, as Le Roy and Holbach correctly concluded from *De beneficiis* I, 10, 1 and *Ep*. 124 [see Bury, *op. cit.*, pp. 46 and 170].) Whether the various worlds are identical in kind or in number is difficult to decide. From the time of Chrysippus the Stoa seems to have believed in their absolute identity, but the opinion of Posidonius is not attested. One should not overlook the contrast between Seneca's serenity in contemplating the end of the world and Lucretius' horror, between the suddenness of the end as envisaged by Seneca and the Epicurean belief in the death of the aged cosmos.

into communion with god." (Preface, 6.) Man finds the perfection of his nature in progress because the theoretical activity of the mind is the highest human activity.[86]

Such striving for individual perfection is not selfishness, however, for, although it does constitute the happiness of the individual, it is at the same time service to others in that it enables one to help guide others to their true goal. Man belongs to two cities or states, the one comprising gods and mankind and the other being that into which he happens to be born. By cultivating the theoretical virtues he serves the great and truly universal city (*De otio*, 4, 1–2), helping posterity (6, 4) and bestowing law and order upon future generations, not upon a few men only but upon all men of all races who are alive and who will live hereafter. (*Ibid.*) That is why wisdom lives on forever, why it receives more and more honors, and why the wise man "alone is absolved from the law that holds humankind in bondage; all centuries pay tribute to him as if he were god." (*De brevitate vitae*, 15, 4–5.)[87]

Of this wisdom, which is the virtue of man in so far as he belongs to the "heavenly city," the most important consequence for the "earthly city" is that man becomes aware of his true place in this world. Through knowledge and progress in the understanding of the universe he begins to comprehend the truth that in the larger scheme of things the earth is only "an infinitesimally small point." (*Naturales Quaestiones* I, Preface, 11.) So he looks upon human affairs in proper perspective and understands the insignificance of political events, of war and fighting; and, when he sees "armies marching forth with floating banners . . . as if some grand design were toward, [he will feel] like exclaiming 'the ants are hurrying through the plains.' " (*Ibid.*, 9.) Consequently he begins to take an interest not "in what is foreign to [his nature] but in what is [truly] his own." (*Ibid.*, 12.) Instead of misusing the gifts of nature for the

[86] The praise of the theoretical activity of the mind is in agreement with the doctrine of Posidonius (and Panaetius); cf. below, pp. 176 f. It is also reminiscent of Euripides, Fr. 910 (see above, chap. II, p. 54.) and of Plato, *Theaetetus* 172 D and 176 A and *Republic* 500 C–D.

[87] For the Stoic conception of the two cities see J. Bidez, "La cité du monde et la cité du soleil chez les Stoïciens," *Academie royale de Belgique, Bulletin de la classe des lettres*, 5th series, XVIII (1932), 244 ff. Occasionally Seneca like Pliny and others connects progress with the reign of the *pax Romana*.

purpose of destruction and devastation (*Naturales Quaestiones* V, 18, 14; cf. 4 f.) he learns to apply himself to the construction of a world of peaceful intercourse and civilization.[88] He understands that he is born to explore the earth: "We would be unskilled animals and without great experience in things if we were imprisoned within the boundaries of our native soil." (V, 18, 14.) He becomes capable of making the world what it is destined to be, a community of people who have "the resources of each particular region in common" (*ibid.*) and who share in the goods of culture and of knowledge, a task still far from being completed. (VII, 25, 3.)[89]

For Seneca, then, the ideal of progress was an expression of the highest aspirations of man and of mankind, and in explaining it and defining its scope he argued very much in the manner of the thinkers in the eighteenth century who were preoccupied with the same ideal. If Condorcet, whose manifesto inaugurated modern progressivism, "takes advance in knowledge as the clue to the march of the human race," if for him "the history of civilization is the history of enlightenment," the same is true of Seneca; and with slight changes in language one could say of the latter as has been said of the former that "he insists on the indissoluble union between intellectual progress and that of liberty, virtue, and the respect for natural rights, and on the effects of science on the destruction of prejudice. . . . All errors in politics and ethics have sprung . . . from false ideas which are closely connected with errors

[88] All interpreters except Delvaille (*op. cit.*, p. 63), who follows Renan (p. 62, note 31) and Renouvier (pp. 60, 5 and 61, 5), seem to overlook the social implications of the Stoic idea of progress, which are in accord with its elaborate social ethics. See also Pliny, II, 117. Bury expressly denies all social consequences to Seneca's theory of progress (p. 14) and speaks of his concern with theoretical knowledge which is restricted to "a few chosen individuals" (*ibid.*); but according to Posidonius the earliest philosophers are both inventors and "teachers of the human race" (*Ep.* 64, 9). The insignificance of political action and fame is connected with the relative smallness of the earth in Cicero's *Somnium Scipionis* 16 (cf. Macrobius' *Commentary* II, 9, 9–10 = p. 216 [Stahl]).

[89] Observations like these of Seneca's gave rise to the doctrine of natural sites, first stated explicitly in the sixteenth century by Emery de la Croix and later by Thomas Paine (see L.T. Hogben, *Retreat from Reason*, Northampton [Mass.], 1937, pp. 33 ff.), according to which world commerce is the most efficient and cheapest means of satisfying the needs of the various regions of the world and will eventually replace warfare. The doctrine itself seems to be foreshadowed by Thucydides (II, 38, 2) and Ps.–Xenophon (*The State of the Athenians* II, 7).

in physics and ignorance of the laws of nature." Nor did Seneca fall far short of envisaging "equality among all the peoples of the earth, a uniform civilization throughout the world, and the obliteration of the distinction between advanced and retrograde races."[90] It is apparent also that in his exposition of the idea of progress the "illusion of finality" had been dispelled. He saw that, as Kant was to express it, while every other animal is fully realized in the individual, which therefore represents the whole species, this is not true of the human animal. All the characteristics of the human species are represented not by any one of its members but only by the species itself: "the human race struggles upward to its destination only by progressing in a series of infinitely many generations." (*Anthropologie*, II, Charakteristik, E. Der Charakter der Gattung.)[91] It may now be possible to see more clearly why Posidonius did accept the notion of endless progress which together with its interpretation Seneca took over from him. In part the reason must have been the same as for the Epicureans and Skeptics, that in the first century B.C. progressivism was a living force that could not easily be resisted by anyone who saw the world as it was. It would have been still more difficult for Posidonius to resist, because like Panaetius he was a scientist and scholar himself and with him had introduced into the teachings of their school the treatment of specific natural and historical problems and the concomitant concrete knowledge, the absence of which from the Old Stoa its critics had not failed to notice. (Cicero, *De finibus* IV, 5–12.)[92] The decisive reason, however, was that Posidonius following Panaetius in this also abandoned the supremacy of moralism that the earlier Stoics had professed. He defined the aim of life as "living in contemplation of the truth and order of all things, and fashioning

[90] Cf. Bury, *The Idea of Progress*, pp. 209, 210, 213.

[91] The passages quoted refute the assertion by K. Jaspers, *Vom Ursprung und Ziel der Geschichte* (Zürich, 1949) that modern science is distinguished from ancient science by its admission that all knowledge is *"unfertig"* (p. 112). The continuity of human history of which Seneca and other ancient progressivists were aware would not exist, as Burckhardt put it (*Weltgeschichtliche Betrachtungen*, p. 269), "if we did not know about it" and it is "an essential interest of human existence and a metaphysical proof of the significance of its continuation." (*Ibid.*)

[92] For Posidonius' scientific work see above, p. 158; and for Panaetius' research Edelstein, *A.J.P.*, LXXI (1950), 81 ff.

oneself as far as possible in accordance therewith." (Clement, *Strom*. II, 129.) He thus gave equal status to theoretical reason and to practical reason or rather made the former dominant, for it is taken to provide the leadership which, as Seneca puts it, guides the whole development of civilization.[93]

It must also have been easier for Posidonius to incorporate the idea of progress into his philosophy than it was for Lucretius to graft it on to Epicureanism, for Stoicism by its very nature was rather more amenable to progressivism than was its rival. From the very beginning it looked at human phenomena and moral data from the point of view of progress and emphasized creativity and development even in the realm of nature, where like a craftsman god, the active principle, is supposed to fashion everything out of matter, the passive principle. (Diogenes Laertius, VII, 134 = I, Fr. 85 [Arnim].) The actual, the Stoics held, is to be understood as the realization of the possible, while the Epicureans almost reverted to the mechanistic factualism of the Pre-Socratics.[94] Whether or not Posidonius succeeded in constructing a consistent system, it is certainly true that in his doctrine the belief in progress that looks forward to posterity and to the continuation of work past and present was made into a reasoned system. It was not a metaphysics like Platonism and Aristotelianism; but philosophy in its new rôle as "pilot of life," inventor of all law, and teacher of all virtue, was established upon the results of the arts and sciences and their progress and was made a philosophy of life.[95]

The doctrine of Posidonius was only the culmination of the progressivism that characterized the main philosophical systems of

[93] Cf. Edelstein, *A.J.P.*, LVII (1936), 315.
[94] Cf. Faust, *op. cit.*, I, 218 ff., 232 f., 241 ff.
[95] The term *"Lebensphilosophie"* was coined by Dilthey (*Gesammelte Schriften* V, 351) in order to characterize Hellenistic philosophy in contrast to earlier Greek thought. The connection between *"Lebensphilosophie"* and progress seems to me to confirm and strengthen Dilthey's analysis. Posidonius' importance in this movement is implicitly admitted by Dilthey when he quotes Cicero's definition of philosophy (*Tuscul. Disput.* V, 2, 5), which undoubtedly goes back to Posidonius (see Seneca, *Ep.* 90). While earlier ages had merely a theory of progress, the second half of the Hellenistic period had a philosophy of progressing culture; and this was its original contribution. It completed the process by which Greek cultural history became Greek history as such; and this is why the later development seems to me to be more important than it did to Burckhardt (cf. above, note 52), who for this period put almost exclusive emphasis upon the Romans' philhellenism (pp. 556 ff.).

the second half of the Hellenistic period. That it was so widely accepted proves for one thing that even in the first century B.C. "the ancients" were not yet regarded with such respect and awe as they were to be in later centuries. They had showed the way, and their example led men on to further studies; but all subsequent knowledge was not considered to be merely derivative from what they had possessed.[96] It can be said with reasonable assurance that adherence to the idea of progress gained from the conviction that a general agreement on the truth is possible, a conviction that from the beginning of the Hellenistic era had grown stronger and stronger. In regard to theoretical and practical problems people believed in "common sense," that is to say in the capacity of the human mind to reach results that no one can contradict. Truth, therefore, was considered to be within the reach of men;[97] and even those for whom the pursuit of knowledge meant endless search did not despair of knowledge itself. It had been said that the modern idea of progress by "placing truth in a vague tomorrow" has proved to be a dulling opiate to humanity; truth is what is true now and not what remains to be discovered in an undetermined future.[98] The Hellenistic thinkers like Plato and Aristotle assumed that it is truth itself that unfolds in time and that one can be farther from it or nearer to it but not wholly deprived of it, wherever one is situated in the historical process, for knowledge, as Seneca puts it, is a legacy inherited from one generation and enriched and handed on to the next.

Epicureanism, Skepticism, and Stoicism, the three dominant philosophical schools, all embraced progressivism in some form or

[96] It has become customary to speak of *"Ableitungsmanie"* even in regard to Posidonius (K. Reinhardt, *Kosmos und Sympathy* [München, 1926], p. 361 and I. Heinemann, *op. cit.*, II, 15); but this interpretation is not supported by the attested fragments. O. Gigon, on the other hand ("Zur Geschichte der sogenannten Neuen Akademie," *Museum Helveticum* I [1944], 47 ff., and "Die Erneuerung der Philosophie in der Zeit Ciceros," *Fondation Hardt*, Entretiens III, *Recherches sur la tradition Platonicienne* [Genève, 1956], 25 ff.), has tried to show that Cicero rediscovered the authority of the ancients; but in fact for him no less than for Seneca they were still only the guides pointing the direction that research should take and were not absolute authorities.

[97] Klaus Oehler, *Antike und Abendland*, X (1961), esp. pp. 107 ff.

[98] José Ortega y Gasset, "History as a System," *Philosophy and History*, ed. R. Klibansky and H.J. Paton (Oxford, 1936), pp. 292 f.

other; but there were still some people who dissented. Among these dissenters were Agatharchides, who has already been mentioned, and Nigidius Figulus, a contemporary of Cicero's, who revived Pythagoreanism and for whom abstruse arithmological and astrological speculations probably had an attraction greater than did the sound scholarship in which he engaged.[99] Mystery-religions exercised a strong hold on people and may have been gaining in strength during the first century, when bitter political strife ravaged the Roman state. Yet, on the whole, trust in reason and in the possibility of mastering one's fate by free decision of the will had not yet been questioned. The turn to irrationalism had not yet occurred.[100] The temper of the time was clearly expressed by its reinterpretation of the old saying, "Know thyself," which the Greeks always treasured as the epitome of wisdom. This had hitherto been taken to mean that man should recognize the limitations of his humanity which, whatever he may accomplish, still ensure his inferiority to the divine; but a new meaning was read into the Delphic maxim by Hellenistic rationalists. They interpreted it to mean that man is akin to god, that this kinship allows him like the divine demiurge to fashion the world, and that the performance of this task is the truly human obligation.[101]

[99] Dodds (*op. cit.*, p. 263, note 70) underestimates the scientific interest of Nigidius (Cicero, *Timaeus* 1, 1 and Aulus Gellius, IV, 9, 1, who ranks Nigidius second to Varro) and overemphasizes his concern with necromancy, of which only later sources speak. Cicero, who was bitterly opposed to such practices (*Tuscul.* I, 16, 36 ff.), does not even mention Nigidius in this context; and his friendship and respect for the man (*Ad Quint. Fr.* 1, 2, 16; *Ad Famil.* 4, 13, 2) would be difficult to understand if Nigidius had been given to errors which in Cicero's opinion had been overcome by his time (*Tusc. Disp.* I, 16, 37).

[100] There is a tendency among modern interpreters to date the decline of rationalism from the first century B.C. (A.J. Festugière, *La révélation d' Hermès Trismégiste* I [Paris, 1944], 4 f.; Dodds, *op. cit.*, pp. 247 ff. and *loc. cit.* [referring to Nigidius Figulus]; M. Nilsson, *Review of Religion*, XII [1947], 115 ff.); but the revival of the dualism of mind and matter cannot be used to justify such a verdict, for it is not irrational to make a philosophical distinction between the two. The first century's trust in progress refutes the contention that it relied on authority rather than on reason; and it should be recognized that the belief current at this time in sympathy as an occult cause sprang from unchecked empiricism rather than from irrationalism (see Edelstein, *Bull. Inst. Hist. Med.*, V [1937], 230 ff.).

[101] Cf. Wilamowitz, *Reden und Vorträge* (4. Auf.; Berlin, 1925–26), pp. 171 ff. He bases his interpretation mainly on Cicero, *De legibus* I, 58, 61; *De finibus* V, 44; and *Tuscul. Disput.* I, 50–75. (According to the Stoa the virtues of god and man are identical [I, Fr. 564, Arnim].)

Thus, the two periods of the Hellenistic era, so very different from each other for the political experience of the Greeks, were together a spiritual whole. In good and bad fortune men lived for progress, and what this meant for them was not unlike what it was to mean in the nineteenth century. When in that century the importance and uniqueness of the Hellenistic age were for the first time recognized, this age was named "the modern period of antiquity."[102] It was so named because of its attitude to science and its psychological ethics, but the justice of the appellation is confirmed by Hellenistic progressivism; and the analogy then drawn between past and present seems to hold even now.

[102] J.G. Droysen, "Theologie der Geschichte. Vorwort zur Geschichte des Hellenismus II" (1843), *Johann Gustav Droysen, Historik* (München/Berlin, 1937), pp. 379 and 384.

BIBLIOGRAPHY

Adam, James (ed.). *The Republic of Plato,* with critical notes, commentary, and appendices. 2 vols. Cambridge, 1902.

Allen, T.W., Halliday, W.R., and Sikes, E.E. (ed.). *The Homeric Hymns,* with . . . notes. 2d ed. Oxford, 1936.

Apelt, Otto. *Platons Gesetze,* übersetzt und erläutert. 2 vols. Leipzig, 1916.

Arnim, H. von. *Leben und Werke des Dion von Prusa.* Berlin, 1898.

Bailey, Cyril. *Epicurus, the Extant Remains.* Oxford, 1926.

———. *The Greek Atomists and Epicurus.* Oxford, 1928.

——— (ed.). *Lucretius, De Rerum Natura,* with translation and commentary. 3 vols. Oxford, 1947.

Baillie, John. *The Belief in Progress.* New York, 1951.

Barker, Ernest. *Greek Political Theory;* Plato and his predecessors. 5th ed. London, 1951.

———(trans.). *The Politics of Aristotle,* with introduction. Oxford, 1946.

Barth, Paul. *Die Stoa.* 6. Auf., von Albert Goedeckemeyer. Stuttgart, 1946.

Basset, E.O. "Plato's Theory of Social Progress," *International Journal of Ethics,* XXXVIII (1927–28), 467–477.

Becker, Carl L. *The Heavenly City of the Eighteenth Century Philosophers.* New Haven (Conn.), 1932.

Berger, Hugo. *Die Geographischen Fragmente des Hipparch.* Leipzig, 1869.

———. *Geschichte der wissenschaftlichen Erdkunde der Griechen.* 2. Auf. Leipzig, 1903.

Bernays, Jakob. *Theophrastos' Schrift über Frömmigkeit.* Berlin, 1866.

Berve, Helmut. *Griechische Geschichte.* 2 vols. Freiburg, 1931–33.

Bidez, J. "La cité du monde et la cité du soleil chez les Stoïciens," *Académie royale de Belgique, Bulletin de la classe des lettres,* 5ᵉ série, Tome XVIII (1932), 244–294.

Bignone, Ettore. *L'Aristotele perduto e la formazione filosofica di Epicuro.* 2 vols. Firenze, 1936.

Bloch, H. "Studies in Historical Literature of the Fourth Century B.C.," *Harvard Studies in Classical Philology.* Supplement I (1940), 303–376.

Boas, George. "The History of Philosophy," *Naturalism and the Human Spirit,* ed. Y.H. Krikorian, pp. 133–153. New York, 1944.

———. "Some Assumptions of Aristotle," *Transactions of the American Philosophical Society,* N.S. Vol. XLIX, Pt. 6.

Boll, Franz. "Vita Contemplativa," *Sitzungsberichte der Heidelberger Akademie der Wissenschaften, Philosophisch-Historische Klasse,* Vol. XI (1920), Abh. 8.

Bonhöffer, Adolf. *Die Ethik des Stoikers Epictet.* Stuttgart, 1894.

Bowra, C.M. "Xenophanes and the Olympic Games," *American Journal of Philology,* LIX (1938), 257–279.

Breasted, James H. *A History of Egypt.* 2d ed. New York, 1909 (reprinted 1951).

Bréhier, Émile. "The Formation of Our History of Philosophy," *Philosophy and History,* ed. R. Klibansky and H.J. Paton, pp. 159–172. Oxford, 1936.

———. *Histoire de la philosophie.* Paris, 1931.

Brink, Charles O. "Tragic History and Aristotle's School," *Proceedings of the Cambridge Philological Society,* N.S. VI (1960), 14–19.

Brown, Truesdell S. *Onesicritus.* Berkeley, 1949.

Bultman, R.K. *Presence of Eternity: History and Eschatology* (Gifford Lectures, 1955). New York, 1957.

Burckhardt, Jakob. *Griechische Kulturgeschichte,* ed. Jakob Oeri. Berlin and Stuttgart, 1898–1902.

———. *Weltgeschichtliche Betrachtungen,* ed. J. Oeri. Berlin and Stuttgart, 1905.

Burnet, John. *Early Greek Philosophy*. 4th ed. London, 1930.

————— (ed.). *The Ethics of Aristotle*, with introduction and notes. London, 1900.

—————. *Greek Philosophy, Part I: Thales to Plato*. London, 1914.

Bury, John B. *The Ancient Greek Historians*. New York, 1909.

—————. *A History of Greece to the Death of Alexander the Great*. New York: Modern Library, 1937.

—————. *The Idea of Progress*. London, 1920 (reprinted New York: Dover Publications, 1950).

Bury, R.G. "Plato and History," *Classical Quarterly*, XLV (1951), 86–93.

Bywater, I. "Aristotle's Dialogue 'On Philosophy'," *The Journal of Philology*, VII (1877), 64–87.

Campbell, Lewis (ed.). *The Sophistes and Politicus of Plato*, rev. text with English notes. Oxford, 1867.

Cary, M. "The Ascendancy of Sparta," *The Cambridge Ancient History* VI, chap. II. Cambridge, 1927.

Cassirer, Ernst. "Die Antike und die Entstehung der exakten Wissenschaft," *Die Antike*, VIII (1932), 276–300.

—————. *The Logic of the Humanities*, trans. C.S. Howe. New Haven (Conn.), 1961.

Cherniss, Harold F. *Aristotle's Criticism of Presocratic Philosophy*. Baltimore (Md.), 1935.

—————. "The Characteristics and Effects of Presocratic Philosophy," *Journal of the History of Ideas*, XII (1951), 319–345.

—————. "The History of Ideas and Ancient Greek Philosophy," *Studies in Intellectual History*, pp. 22–47. Baltimore (Md.), 1953.

—————. "Plato (1950–1957)," *Lustrum*, IV (1959) and V (1960).

—————. "Review of H. Saffrey, *Le Περὶ φιλοσοφίας d' Aristote*," *Gnomon*, XXXI (1959), 36–51.

Childe, V. Gordon. *Man Makes Himself*. The Thinker's Library, 87 [1948].

Christ, Wilhelm von, and Schmid, Wilhelm. *Geschichte der griechischen Literatur* (Handbuch der klassischen Altertumswissenschaft, Vol. VII). 6. Auf. München, 1912–1924.

Classen, C. Joachim. "Aristippos," *Hermes*, LXXXVI (1958), 182–192.

Cleve, Felix M. *The Philosophy of Anaxagoras*. New York, 1949.

183

Cochrane, Charles N. *Christianity and Classical Culture*. Oxford, 1940.

Cohen, Morris R., and Drabkin, I.E. *A Source Book in Greek Science*. New York, 1948.

Collingwood, Robin G. *The Idea of History*. Oxford, 1946.

Comte, Auguste. *Cours de philosophie positive*. 3d ed. Paris, 1869.

Cornford, Francis M. (trans.). *Plato's Cosmology*. The *Timaeus* of Plato, with running commentary. London, 1937.

————— (trans.). *The Republic of Plato*, with notes. Oxford, 1941.

—————. *The Unwritten Philosophy and Other Essays*, ed. W.K.C. Guthrie. Cambridge, 1950.

Couat, A. *Alexandrian Poetry*, trans. J. Loeb. London, 1931.

Curtius, Ludwig. *Die Antike Kunst*. 2 vols. Berlin, 1923–39.

Dampier, Sir William C. *A History of Science*. 3d rev. ed., enlarged. Cambridge, 1943.

Deichgräber, Karl. *Die griechische Empirikerschule*. Berlin, 1930.

—————. *Hippokrates, Über Entstehung und Aufbau des menschlichen Körpers*. Leipzig, 1935.

DeLacy, Phillip H. "Lucretius and the History of Epicureanism," *Transactions and Proceedings of the American Philological Association*, LXXIX (1948), 12–23.

DeLacy, Phillip H., and DeLacy, Estelle A. *Philodemus: On Methods of Inference* (American Philological Association, *Philological Monographs*, X). Philadelphia, 1941.

Delvaille, Jules. *Essai sur l'histoire de l'idée de progrès*. Paris, 1910.

DeWitt, Norman W. *Epicurus and His Philosophy*. Minneapolis, 1954.

Diels, Hermann. *Der antike Pessimismus* (Schule und Leben herausgegeben vom Zentralinstitut für Erziehung und Unterricht, I [Berlin, 1921]), 27 pp.

—————. *Poetarum Philosophorum Fragmenta*. Berlin, 1901.

Diels, Hermann, and Kranz, Walther. *Die Fragmente der Vorsokratiker*. 6. Auf. Berlin, 1951–52.

Diller, Hans. "Die Hellenen–Barbaren–Antithese im Zeitalter der Perserkriege," *Fondation Hardt*, Entretiens VIII (*Grecs et Barbares*), Genève, 1962. pp. 37–68.

—————. "Hippokratische Medizin und Attische Philosophie," *Hermes*, LXXX (1952), 385–409.

—————. "Review of K. Weidauer, *Thukydides und die Hippokratischen Schriften*," *Gnomon* XXVII (1955), 9–14.

184

――――. "Weltbild und Sprache im Heraklitismus," *Das Neue Bild der Antike*, I (1942), 303–316.

Dilthey, Wilhelm. *Gesammelte Schriften.* 12 vols. Leipzig, 1914–58.

Dodds, Eric R. *The Greeks and the Irrational.* Berkeley, 1951.

Doren, Alfred. "Wunschräume und Wunschzeiten," *Vorträge der Bibliothek Warburg*, 1924/25 (Leipzig, 1927), 158–205.

Droysen, Johann G. "Theologie der Geschichte. Vorwort zur Geschichte des Hellenismus II" (1843), *Johann Gustav Droysen, Historik*, ed. Rudolf Hübner, pp. 369–385. München und Berlin, 1937.

Dudley, Donald R. *A History of Cynicism.* London, 1937.

Dümmler, Ferdinand. *Akademika.* Giessen, 1889.

Edel, Abraham. "Levels of Meaning and the History of Ideas," *Journal of the History of Ideas*, VII (1946), 355–360.

Edelstein, Emma J. *Xenophontisches und platonisches Bild des Sokrates.* Berlin, 1935.

Edelstein, Emma J., and Edelstein, Ludwig. *Asclepius.* 2 vols. Baltimore, 1945.

Edelstein, Ludwig. "The Development of Greek Anatomy," *Bulletin of the Institute of the History of Medicine*, III (1935), 235–248.

――――. "The Distinctive Hellenism of Greek Medicine," *Bulletin of the History of Medicine*, XL (1966), 197–225.

――――. "Empirie und Skepsis in der Lehre der griechische Empirikerschule," *Quellen und Studien zur Geschichte der Naturwissenschaften und der Medizin*, III (1933), 253–261.

――――. "The Function of the Myth in Plato's Philosophy," *Journal of the History of Ideas*, X (1949), 463–481.

――――. "Greek Medicine in Its Relation to Religion and Magic," *Bulletin of the Institute of the History of Medicine*, V (1937), 201–246.

――――. "Motives and Incentives for Science in Antiquity," *Scientific Change*, ed. A.C. Crombie. New York, 1963.

――――. Περὶ ἀέρων *und die Sammlung der Hippokratischen Schriften* (Problemata, IV). Berlin, 1931.

――――. "The Philosophical System of Posidonius," *American Journal of Philology*, LVII (1936), 286–325.

――――. "Platonic Anonymity," *ibid.*, LXXXIII (1962), 1–22.

——. "Platonism or Aristotelianism," *Bulletin of the Institute of the History of Medicine*, VIII (1940), 757–769.

——. *Plato's Seventh Letter* (Philosophia Antiqua, XIV). Leiden, 1966.

——. "Primum Graius Homo," *Transactions and Proceedings of the American Philological Association*, LXXI (1940), 78–90.

——. "Recent Trends in the Interpretation of Ancient Science," *Journal of the History of Ideas*, XIII (1952), 573–604. (Reprinted in *Roots of Scientific Thought*, ed. P.P. Wiener and A. Noland, pp. 90–121. New York, 1957.)

——. "The Relation of Ancient Philosophy to Medicine," *Bulletin of the History of Medicine*, XXVI (1952), 299–316.

——. "Review of W. Jaeger, *Diokles von Karystos*," *American Journal of Philology*, LXI (1940), 483–489.

——. "Review of M. Pohlenz, *Die Stoa*," *American Journal of Philology* LXXII (1951), 426–432.

——. "Review of M. van Straaten, *Panétius*," *American Journal of Philology*, LXXI (1950), 78–83.

Ehrenberg, Victor. "Athenischer Hymnus auf Demetrios Poliorketes," *Die Antike*, VII (1931), 279–297.

England, E.B. (ed.). *The Laws of Plato*, with introduction and notes. 2 vols. Manchester, 1921.

Eucken, Rudolf C. *Geistige Strömungen der Gegenwart*. 4. Auf. Leipzig, 1909.

——. *Geschichte und Kritik der Grundbegriffe der Gegenwart*. Leipzig, 1878.

——. *Die Methode der Aristotelischen Forschung*. Berlin, 1872.

Faust, A. *Der Möglichkeitsgedanke*. 2 vols. Heidelberg, 1931–32.

Festugière, A.J. *La révélation d' Hermès Trismégiste*. 4 vols. Paris, 1944–54.

Field, Guy C. *Plato and His Contemporaries*. London, 1930.

Finley, John H. *Thucydides*. Cambridge (Mass.), 1947.

Fraenkel, E. (ed.). *Aeschylus, Agamemnon*, with commentary. 3 vols. Oxford, 1950.

Fränkel, Hermann. *Dichtung und Philosophie des fruehen Griechentums* (American Philological Association, *Philological Monographs*, XIII). New York, 1951.

——. "Review of J. Zafiropulo, etc.," *Classical Philology*, XLV (1950), 187–191.

——. "Die Zeitauffassung in der archaischen griechischen Literatur," *Beilageheft zur Zeitschrift für Ästhetik und allgemeine Kunstwissenschaft*, XXV (1931), 97–118.

Frank, Erich. "Mathematik und Musik und der griechische Geist," *Logos*, IX (1920–21), 222–259.

──────. *Philosophical Understanding and Religious Truth*. London/New York, 1945.

──────. *Plato und die sogenannten Pythagoreer*. Halle, 1923.

──────. "Review of W. Jaeger, *The Theology of the Early Greek Philosophers*," *American Journal of Philology*, LXXI (1950), 189–193.

──────. *Wissen, Wollen, Glauben: Gesammelte Aufsätze . . .* , ed. L. Edelstein. Zürich, 1955.

Frank, Tenney. "Changing Conceptions of Literary and Philological Research," *Journal of the History of Ideas*, III (1942), 401–414.

──────. *Life and Literature of the Roman Republic*. Berkeley, 1930.

Friedländer, Paul. *Platon*. 2 vols. Leipzig, 1928–30. (2. erweiterte und verbesserte Auf. 3 vols., 1957–60).

──────. Πολλὰ τά δεινὰ , *Hermes*, LXIX (1934), 56–63.

Friedlein, G. *Procli Diadochi in Primum Euclidis Elementorum Librum Commentarii*. Leipzig, 1873.

Fritz, Kurt von. "Quellenuntersuchungen zu Leben und Philosophie des Diogenes von Sinope," *Philologus*, Supplementband XVIII, Heft 2 (Leipzig, 1926).

Fritz, Kurt von, and Kapp, Ernst (trans.). *Aristotle's Constitution of Athens and Related Texts*, with introduction and notes. New York, 1950.

Gigon, Olof. "Die Erneuerung der Philosophie in der Zeit Ciceros," *Fondation Hardt*, Entretiens III (*Recherches sur la Tradition Platonicienne*), pp. 25–59. Genève, 1956.

──────. "Zur Geschichte der sogenannten Neuen Akademie," *Museum Helveticum*, I (1944), 47–64.

Gilbert, Felix. "Cultural History and Its Problems," *XIᵉ Congrès International des Sciences Historiques, 1960: Rapports* I, 40–58.

Ginsberg, Morris. *The Idea of Progress*. Boston (Mass.), 1953.

Goedeckemeyer, Albert. *Die Geschichte des griechischen Skeptizismus*. Leipzig, 1905.

Golden, Leon. "Zeus the Protector and Zeus the Destroyer," *Classical Philology*, LVII (1962), 20–26.

Gombrich, Ernst H. *Art and Illusion.* New York, 1960.

Gomme, Arnold W. *A Historical Commentary on Thucydides.* 3 vols. Oxford, 1945–56.

Gomperz, Theodor. *Die Apologie der Heilkunst.* 2. Auf. Leipzig, 1910.

——. *Griechische Denker.* 3 vols. Leipzig, 1896.

Gooch, G.P. *History and Historians in the Nineteenth Century.* Boston (Mass.): Beacon Press, 1959.

Green, William M. "The Dying World of Lucretius," *American Journal of Philology,* LXIII (1942), 51–60.

Grote, George. *A History of Greece.* New York: E.P. Dutton and Co., Everyman's Library.

Gudeman, Alfred. *Aristoteles,* Περὶ ποιητικῆς . Berlin, 1934.

Guthrie, William K.C. "Aristotle as a Historian of Philosophy," *Journal of Hellenic Studies,* LXXVII (1957), 35–41.

——. *In the Beginning.* Ithaca (New York), 1957.

Guyau, Jean M. *La Morale d'Epicure.* 6th ed. Paris, 1917.

Haase, Wolfgang. "Ein vermeintliches Aristoteles-Fragment bei Johannes Philoponos," *Synusia: Festgabe für Wolfgang Schadewaldt* (1965), 323–344.

Harder, R. *Ocellus Lucanus,* Text und Kommentar (Neue Philologische Untersuchungen, I) Berlin, 1926.

Hasebroek, Johannes. *Staat und Handel im alten Griechenland.* Tübingen, 1928.

Havelock, Eric A. *The Liberal Temper in Greek Politics.* London, 1957.

Heidel, William A. "Anaximander's Book, the Earliest Known Geographical Treatise," *Proceedings of the American Academy of Arts and Sciences,* LVI (1921), 239–288.

——. *The Heroic Age of Science.* Baltimore (Md.), 1933.

——. "The Logic of the Pre-Socratic Philosophy," *Studies in Logical Theory,* Decennial Publications of the University of Chicago, 2d Series, Vol. XI (Chicago, 1903), 203–226.

Heinemann, Isaak. *Poseidonios' metaphysische Schriften.* 2 vols. Breslau, 1921–28.

Heinimann, Felix. "Eine vorplatonische Theorie der τέχνη," *Museum Helveticum,* XVIII (1961), 105–130.

Heinze, Richard. *Xenokrates. Darstellung der Lehre und Sammlung der Fragmente.* Leipzig, 1892.

Hirzel, Rudolf. *Ἄγραφος Νόμος, Abhandlungen der Sächsischen*

Akademie der Wissenschaften, Phil.–Hist. Classe, XX, 1 (1900).

––––––. *Untersuchungen zu Cicero's philosophischen Schriften.* 3 vols. Leipzig, 1877–83.

Höistad, Ragnar. *Cynic Hero and Cynic King.* Uppsala, 1948.

Hoffmann, Ernst. "Die Sprache und die archaische Logik," *Heidelberger Abhandlungen zur Philosophie und ihrer Geschichte*, III, 1925.

Hogben, L.T. *Retreat from Reason.* Northampton (Mass.), 1937.

Hume, David. *The History of England.* 4 vols. New York, 1852–53.

Ilberg, J. "Die Ärzteschule von Knidos," *Berichte über die Verhandlungen der Sächsischen Akademie der Wissenschaften zu Leipzig, Phil.–hist. Klasse*, Vol. LXXVI (1924), Heft 3.

Immisch, Otto. "Agatharchidea," *Sitzungsberichte der Heidelberger Akademie der Wissenschaften, Phil.–Hist. Klasse*, Vol. X (1919). Abhandlung 7.

Inge, William R. *The Idea of Progress.* Oxford, 1920.

Jacoby, Felix. *Atthis.* Oxford, 1949.

––––––. *Die Fragmente der griechischen Historiker.* Berlin, 1923–58.

Jaeger, Werner W. *Aristoteles.* Berlin, 1923.

––––––. *Diokles von Karystos.* Berlin, 1938.

––––––. *Paideia*, trans. Gilbert Highet. Vol. I² (New York, 1945) and Vol. III¹ (New York, 1944).

––––––. "Review of H. Cherniss, *Aristotle's Criticism of Pre-Socratic Philosophy*," *American Journal of Philology*, LVIII (1937), 350–356.

––––––. *The Theology of the Early Greek Philosophers*, trans. by (1955), 573–581.

––––––. "Review of H. Merki, Ὁμοίωσις θεῷ," *Gnomon*, XXV E.S. Robinson. Oxford, 1947.

––––––. "Über Ursprung und Kreislauf des philosophischen Lebensideals," *Sitzungsberichte der Preussischen Akademie der Wissenschaften, Phil.–hist. Klasse*, Berlin, 1928, XXV, pp. 390–421.

Jaekel, Siegfried. *Menandri Sententiae. Comparatio Menandri et Philistionis.* Leipzig, 1964.

James, William. "Great Men and Their Environment," *Selected Papers on Philosophy by William James.* New York: Everyman's Library, 1918.

––––––. *Talks to Teachers.* New York, 1900.

Jaspers, K. *Vom Ursprung und Ziel der Geschichte*. Zürich, 1949.

Joël, Karl. *Geschichte der antiken Philosophie* I. Tübingen, 1921.

Kant, I. "Mutmasslicher Anfang der Menschengeschichte," *Sämtliche Werke* IV. Insel Ausgabe, 1921.

Kern, Otto. *Orphicorum Fragmenta*. Berlin, 1922.

Kerschensteiner, Jula. *Platon und der Orient*. Stuttgart, 1945.

Kirk, Geoffrey S. *Heraclitus, The Cosmic Fragments*. Cambridge, 1954.

Kleingünther, Adolf. "Πρῶτος Εὑρετής," *Philologus*, Supplementband XXVI, Heft 1 (1933).

Kock, Theodore. *Comicorum Atticorum Fragmenta*. 3 vols. Leipzig, 1880–88.

Kopp, J.V. *Das physikalische Weltbild der frühen griechischen Dichtung*. Diss. Fribourg, 1939.

Kranz, Walther. "Empedokles und die Atomistik," *Hermes*, XLVII (1912), 18–42.

Lang, Paul. *De Speusippi Academici Scriptis Accedunt Fragmenta*. Bonn, 1911.

Leaf, Walter (ed.). *The Iliad*, with apparatus criticus, . . . notes, and appendices. 2 vols. 2d ed. London/New York, 1900–02.

Lehrs, Karl. *De Aristarchi studiis Homericis*. Leipzig, 1865.

———. "Vorstellungen der Griechen über den Neid der Götter und die Überhebung," *Populäre Aufsätze aus dem Alterthum*. 2. Auf. Leipzig, 1875.

Leo, Friedrich. *Die griechisch–römische Biographie*. Leipzig, 1901.

———. *Plautinische Forschungen*. 2. Auf. Berlin, 1912.

Linforth, Ivan M. *The Arts of Orpheus*. Berkeley and Los Angeles, 1941.

Löwith, Karl. *Meaning in History*. Chicago, 1949.

Lovejoy, Arthur O. *Essays in the History of Ideas*. Baltimore, 1948.

———. *The Great Chain of Being*. Cambridge (Mass.), 1936.

Lovejoy, Arthur O., and Boas, George. *Primitivism and Related Ideas in Antiquity, A Documentary History of Primitivism and Related Ideas*, ed. Arthur O. Lovejoy, Vol. I. Baltimore, 1935.

Luck, Georg. *Der Akademiker Antiochos*. (Noctes Romanae, 7). Bern, 1953.

Mach, Ernst. *Die Mechanik in ihrer Entwicklung*. 7. Auf. Leipzig, 1912.

Mair, A.W. (ed.). *Callimachus and Lycophron*, with English translation. Loeb Classical Library, 1921.

Manitius, C. *Hipparchi in Arati et Eudoxi Phaenomena Commentarii.* Leipzig, 1894.

Mattingly, Harold. *Roman Imperial Civilisation.* New York: Anchor Books, 1959.

McDiarmid, John B. "Theophrastus on the Eternity of the World," *Transactions and Proceedings of the American Philological Association,* LXXI (1940), 239–247.

McKeon, Richard. "Plato and Aristotle as Historians," *International Journal of Ethics,* LI (1940–41), 66–101.

Mekler, S. *Academicorum Philosophorum Index Herculanensis.* Berlin, 1902.

Mewaldt, Johannes. "Review of J. Ilberg, *Die Ärzteschule von Knidos,*" *Gnomon,* III (1927), 139–145.

Meyer, Hans. "Zur Lehre von der ewigen Wiederkunft aller Dinge," *Beiträge zur Geschichte des christlichen Altertums und der Byzantinischen Literatur (Festgabe Albert Ehrhard),* pp. 359–380. Bonn and Leipzig, 1922.

Meyer, W. *Laudes Inopiae.* Diss. Göttingen, 1915.

Michell, Humfrey. *The Economics of Ancient Greece.* New York, 1940.

Minar, Edwin L. "Review of R. Höistad, *Cynic Hero and Cynic King,* and of F. Sayre, *"The Greek Cynics,"* *American Journal of Philology,* LXXII (1951), 433–438.

Misch, Georg. *Geschichte der Autobiographie.* 3 vols. 3. Auf. Bern, 1949–62.

Mommsen, Theodor E. "St. Augustine and the Christian Idea of Progress," *Journal of the History of Ideas,* XII (1951), 346–374.

Monodolfo, R. *La comprensione del soggetto umano nell' antichità classica,* trans. Livinia Bassi. Firenze, 1958 (published in Spanish: Buenos Aires, 1955).

Muller, Herbert J. *The Uses of the Past.* New York, 1952.

Munro, H.A.J. (ed.). *Lucretius, De Rerum Natura,* with notes and translation. 3d ed. London, 1873.

Murray, Gilbert. *Aristophanes.* New York, 1933.

———. *Five Stages of Greek Religion.* New York: Anchor Books, 1955.

———. *Greek Studies.* Oxford, 1946.

———. *The Rise of the Greek Epic.* 3d. ed. Oxford, 1924.

Nauck, A. *Tragicorum Graecorum Fragmenta.* 2d ed. Leipzig, 1889.

Nestle, Wilhelm. *Griechische Geistesgeschichte*. Stuttgart, 1944.

———. "Der Pessimismus und seine Überwindung bei den Griechen," *Neue Jahrbücher für das klassische Altertum*, XLVII (1921), 81–97.

———. *Vom Mythos zum Logos*. 2. Auf. Stuttgart, 1942.

Neugebauer, Otto. *The Exact Sciences in Antiquity*. 2d ed. Providence (Rhode Island), 1957.

———. "Notes on Hipparchus," *The Aegaean and the Near East, Studies Presented to Hetty Goldman*, pp. 292–296. Locust Valley (New York), 1956.

Newman, William L. (ed.). *The Politics of Aristotle*, with introduction and notes. 4 vols. Oxford, 1887–1902.

Nicolson, M.H. "Two Voices: Science and Literature," *The Rockefeller University Review* (June, 1963).

Nietzsche, F. "Philosophie im tragischen Zeitalter der Griechen," *Gesammelte Werke*. Musarion ed. München, 1920–29.

Nilsson, Martin P. *Geschichte der griechischen Religion*. Handbuch der Altertumswissenschaft, V, 1 and 2. München, 1941–50.

———. *Greek Popular Religion*. New York, 1940.

———. "The Psychological Background of Late Greek Paganism," *Review of Religion*, XI (1946–47), 115–125.

Nock, Arthur D. "The Sources of Diodorus: Review of W. Spoerri, *Späthellenistische Berichte über Welt, Kultur, und Götter*," *Classical Review*, N.S. XII (1962), 50–51.

Norden, Eduard. *Agnostos Theos*. Leipzig, 1913.

———. "Beiträge zur Geschichte der griechischen Philosophie," *Jahrbücher für Classische Philologie*, Supplement XIX (1892), 365–462.

Oehler, Klaus. "Der Consensus omnium als Kriterium der Wahrheit in der antiken Philosophie und der Patristik," *Antike und Abendland*, X (1961), 103–129.

Ogerau, F. *Essai sur le système philosophique des Stoïciens*. Paris, 1885.

Oldfather, W.A., and Pease, A.S. (eds.). *Aeneas Tacticus*, with English translation. The Loeb Classical Library, 1923.

Olschki, L. *Geschichte der neusprachlichen wissenschaftlichen Literatur*. 3 vols. Heidelberg, 1919–1927.

Ortega y Gasset, José. "History as a System," *Philosophy and His-*

tory, ed. R. Klibansky and H.J. Paton, pp. 283–322. Oxford, 1936.

Palm, Adolf. *Studien zur Hippokratischen Schrift* Περὶ Διαίτης, Diss. Tübingen, 1933.

Pascal, Blaise. *Fragment de Préface sur le Traité du Vide, Oeuvres de Blaise Pascal*, Vol. II. Léon Brunschvicg et Pierre Boutroux: Paris, 1908.

Pasquali, Giorgio. "Das Prooemium des Arat," Χάριτες *Friedrich Leo zum sechzigsten Geburstag dargebracht*, pp. 113–122. Berlin, 1911.

Pickard-Cambridge, Arthur W. *Dithyramb, Tragedy, and Comedy*. Oxford, 1927.

Pöhlmann, Robert von. *Geschichte der Sozialen Frage und des Sozialismus in der antiken Welt*. 2 vols. 3. Auf. München, 1925.

Pohlenz, Max. "Anonymus Περὶ νόμων," *Nachrichten von der Gesellschaft der Wissenschaften zu Göttingen, Phil.–Hist. Klasse* (1924), 19–37.

———. *Aus Platos Werdezeit*. Berlin, 1913.

———. "Die hellenistische Poesie und die Philosophie," Χάριτες *Friedrich Leo zum sechzigsten Geburstag dargebracht*, pp. 76–112. Berlin, 1911.

———. "Review of D. Tarrant, *The Hippias Major Attributed to Plato*," *Gnomon*, VII (1931), 300–307.

———. *Die Stoa*. 2 vols. Göttingen, 1948–49.

Popper, Karl R. *The Open Society and Its Enemies*. London, 1945.

Powell, John U. *Collectanea Alexandrina*. Oxford, 1925.

Rabinowitz, W.G. *Aristotle's Protrepticus and the Sources of Its Reconstruction* (University of California Publications in Classical Philology, Vol. XVI). Berkeley (Calif.), 1957.

Rand, Edward K. *The Building of Eternal Rome*. Cambridge (Mass.), 1943.

———. *Founders of the Middle Ages*. Cambridge (Mass.), 1928.

R.–E. = Pauly–Wissowa, *Real–Encyclopädie*.

Regenbogen, Otto. "Eine Forschungsmethode antiker Naturwissenschaft," *Quellen und Studien zur Geschichte der Mathematik*, B: I (1930), 131–182.

Rehm, Albert. "Zur Rolle der Technik in der griechisch–römischen Antike," *Archiv für Kulturgeschichte*, XXVIII (1938), 135–162.

Rehm, Albert, and Vogel, K. *Exakte Wissenschaften*, in *Einleitung in die Altertumswissenschaft,* ed. A. Gercke and E. Norden, II, 5. 4th ed. Leipzig, 1933.

Reid, James S. (ed.). *Cicero, Academica,* revised and explained. London, 1885.

Reinhardt, Karl. "Hekataios von Abdera und Demokrit," *Hermes,* XLVII (1912), 492–513.

——. "Herodots Persergeschichten," *Von Werken und Formen,* pp. 163–224. Godesberg, 1948.

——. *Kosmos und Sympathy.* München, 1926.

——. *Poseidonios.* München, 1921.

Reitzenstein, Erich. *Theophrast bei Epikur und Lucrez* (Orient und Antike, II). Heidelberg, 1924.

Reitzenstein, Richard. "Alt-griechische Theologie und ihre Quellen," *Vorträge der Bibliothek Warburg,* 1924/25 (Leipzig, 1927), 1–19.

Richter, Gisela M.S. *The Sculpture and Sculptors of the Greeks.* New Haven, 1950.

Riegl, Alois. *Stilfragen.* Berlin, 1893.

Robin, Léon. *La pensée grecque et les origines de l'esprit scientifique.* Paris, 1923.

——. *Pyrrhon et le scepticisme grec.* Paris, 1944.

——. "Sur la conception Épicurienne du progrès," *Revue de Métaphysique et de Morale,* XXIII (1916), 697–719.

Robinson, David M. "Bouzyges and the First Plough on a Krater," *American Journal of Archaeology,* 2d Series, XXXV (1931), 152–160.

Rohde, Erwin. *Der griechische Roman und seine Vorläufer.* 3. Auf. Leipzig, 1914. (1. Auf., 1876; 2. Auf., 1900.)

——. *Psyche.* 2 vols. 7.–8. Auf. Tübingen, 1921.

Rohr, G. *Platos Stellung zur Geschichte.* Berlin, 1932.

Rose, H.J. *A Handbook of Greek Literature from Homer to the Age of Lucian.* 2d ed. London, 1942.

Rose, Valentinus. *Aristotelis Fragmenta.* Leipzig, 1886.

Ross, William D. (ed.). *Aristotle's Metaphysics,* revised text . . . and commentary. 2 vols. Oxford, 1924.

——. *Aristotle's Physics,* revised text . . . and commentary. Oxford, 1936.

Rothacker, Erich. *Logik und Systematik der Geisteswissenschaften* (*Handbuch der Philosophie,* hrsg. von A. Baeumler und M. Schröter, Abt. II). Bonn, 1926.

Sampson, R.V. *Progress in the Age of Reason.* Cambridge (Mass.), 1957.

Schmid, Wilhelm, and Stählin, Otto. *Geschichte der griechischen Literatur* (Handbuch der klassischen Altertumswissenschaft, Vol. VII). München, 1929–48.

Schmidt, Leopold V. *Die Ethik der alten Griechen.* 2 vols. Berlin, 1882.

Schröder, O. *De laudibus Athenarum a poetis tragicis et ab oratoribus opidicticis excultis.* Diss. Göttingen, 1914.

Schwartz, Eduard. *Fünf Vorträge über den griechischen Roman.* 2. Auf. Berlin, 1943.

Schweitzer, Bernhard. "Der bildende Künstler und der Begriff des Künstlerischen in der Antike," *Neue Heidelberger Jahrbücher* (1925), 28–132.

———. *Plato und die bildende Kunst der Griechen.* Tübingen, 1953.

Shorey, Paul. "Note on Xenophanes' Fr. 18 (Diels) and Isocrates, *Panegyricus* 32," *Classical Philology*, VI (1911), 88–89.

——— (ed.). *Plato, The Republic,* with English translation. 2 vols. Loeb Classical Library, 1930–35.

Simmel, Georg. *Die Probleme der Geschichtsphilosophie.* 5. Auf. Leipzig, 1923.

———. *The Sociology of Georg Simmel,* trans. and ed. K.H. Wolff. Glencoe (Illinois), 1950.

Skemp, Joseph B. (trans.). *Plato's Statesman,* a translation of the *Politicus* of Plato. London, 1952.

Snell, Bruno. *Die Ausdrücke für den Begriff des Wissens in der vorplatonischen Philosophie* (Philologische Untersuchungen, XXIX). Berlin, 1924.

———. *Die Entdeckung des Geistes.* Hamburg, 1946.

———. *Poetry and Society.* Bloomington (Indiana), 1961.

Solmsen, Friedrich. "Epicurus and Cosmological Heresies," *American Journal of Philology*, LXXII (1951), 1–23.

———. "Epicurus on Growth and Decline of the Cosmos," *American Journal of Philology*, LXXIV (1953), 34–51.

———. *Hesiod and Aeschylus.* Ithaca (New York), 1949.

Spencer, Theodore. "Review of A.O. Lovejoy, *Essays in the History Of Ideas*," *Journal of the History of Ideas*, IX (1948), 439–446.

Spoerri, Walter. *Späthellenistische Berichte über Welt, Kultur und Götter.* Basel, 1959.

Stahl, William H. (trans.). *Macrobius, Commentary on the Dream of Scipio*, trans., with introduction and notes. New York, 1952.
Stenzel, Julius. *Platon der Erzieher*. Leipzig, 1928.
Strauss, Leo. "The Liberalism of Classical Political Philosophy," *The Review of Metaphysics*, XII (1959), 390–439.
Sudhaus, Siegfried. *Philodemi Volumina Rhetorica*. 2 vols. Leipzig, 1892.
Susemihl, Franz. *Aristoteles über die Dichtkunst*, griechisch und deutsch. 2. Auf. Leipzig, 1874.
Täubler, A. *Tyche: Historische Studien*. Leipzig, 1926.
Tarn, William W. *Hellenistic Civilisation*. 3d ed. (rev. by author and G.T. Griffith). London, 1952.
Taylor, Alfred E. *A Commentary on Plato's Timaeus*. Oxford, 1928.
———. (trans.). *The Laws of Plato*, English translation. London, 1934.
———. *Plato, the Man and His Work*. 4th ed. London, 1937.
Taylor, Margaret. "Progress and Primitivism in Lucretius," *American Journal of Philology*, LXVIII (1947), 180–194.
Teggart, Frederick J. *The Idea of Progress*, rev. ed., with introduction by G.H. Hildebrandt. Berkeley, 1949.
Teichmüller, Gustav. *Aristotelische Forschungen*. 3 vols. Halle, 1867–73.
Theiler, Willy. *Zur Geschichte der teleologischen Naturbetrachtung bis auf Aristoteles*. Zurich, 1925.
Thomson, George D. *Aeschylus and Athens*. London, 1941.
Thorndike, Lynn. "Newness and Novelty in Seventeenth Century Science and Medicine," *The Roots of Scientific Thought*, ed. P.P. Wiener and A. Noland, pp. 443–457. New York, 1958.
Toynbee, A.J. *A Study of History* (abridgement of Vols. I–X by D.C. Somervell). 2 vols. New York/London, 1947–57.
Trüdinger, Karl. *Studien zur Geschichte der griechisch–römischen Ethnographie*. Basel, 1918.
Ueberweg, F. *Grundriss der Geschichte der Philosophie* I; *Die Philosophie des Altertums*. 12. Auf. by Karl Praechter. Berlin, 1926.
Usener, Hermann. *Epicurea*. Leipzig, 1887.
Uxkull–Gyllenband, Woldemar, Graf von. *Griechische Kultur–Entstehungslehren* (Bibliothek für Philosophie, XXVI). Berlin, 1924.
Vahlen, M.J. "Beiträge zu Aristoteles' Poetik," *Sitzungsberichte*

der Kaiserlichen Akademie der Wissenschaften, Phil.–Hist. Classe (Wien), L (1865), 265–317.

Van Straaten, Modestus. *Panaetii Rhodii Fragmenta.* Leiden, 1952 (editio amplificata, 1962).

———. *Panétius, sa vie, ses écrits et sa doctrine avec une édition des fragments.* Amsterdam, 1946.

Vlastos, Gregory. "Ethics and Physics in Democritus. Part II," *The Philosophical Review,* LV (1946), 53–64.

———. "On the Pre-history in Diodorus," *American Journal of Philology,* LXVII (1946), 51–59.

Wallis, Wilson D. "Progress and Power," *Journal of Social Philosophy,* II (1937), 338–346.

Wanner, Hermann. *Studien zu* Περὶ ἀρχαίης ἰητρικῆς. Diss. Zurich, 1939.

Weber, Alfred. *Das Tragische und die Geschichte.* Tübingen, 1943.

Wehrli, Fritz. *Die Schule des Aristoteles,* Text und Kommentar. 10 vols. Basel, 1944–1959.

———. *Zur Geschichte der allegorischen Deutung Homers im Altertum.* Diss. Zurich, 1928.

Weidauer, Klaus. *Thukydides und die Hippokratischen Schriften.* Heidelberg, 1954.

Weiher, Anton. *Philosophen und Philosophenspott in der attischen Komödie.* (Diss. München.) Nördlingen, 1913.

Weil, Raymond. *Aristote et l'histoire.* Paris, 1960.

Welcker, Friedrich G. *Griechische Götterlehre.* 3 vols. Göttingen, 1857–62.

Wendland, Paul. *Die hellenistisch–römische Kultur in ihren Beziehungen zu Judentum und Christentum.* 2. and 3. Auf. Tübingen, 1912.

Whitehead, Alfred N. *Adventures of Ideas.* New York, 1933.

Wilamowitz–Möllendorff, Ulrich von. *Antigonos von Karystos* (Philologische Untersuchungen, IV). Berlin, 1881.

———. *Aristoteles und Athen.* 2 vols. Berlin, 1893.

———. *Einleitung in die griechische Tragödie.* Berlin, 1921.

———. "Die griechische Literatur des Altertums," *Die Kultur der Gegenwart,* hrsg. von Paul Hinneberg, I, viii, pp. 1–236. Berlin and Leipzig, 1905.

———. *Hellenistische Dichtung in der Zeit des Kallimachos.* 2 vols. Berlin, 1924.

———. *Reden und Vorträge.* 4. Auf. Berlin, 1925–26.

————. *Timotheus, Die Perser*. Leipzig, 1903.

————. "Ein Weihgeschenk des Eratosthenes," *Nachrichten von der Königl. Gesellschaft der Wissenschaften zu Göttingen, Phil.–Hist. Klasse* (1894), 15–35.

Winter, Franz. "Griechische Kunst," *Einleitung in die Altertumswissenschaft*, ed. A. Gercke and E. Norden, II, pp. 73–187. 3. Auf. Leipzig, 1922.

Zeller, Eduard. *Die Philosophie der Griechen in ihrer geschichtlichen Entwicklung*. Vol. I, 1 and 2:5. Auf. 1892; Vol. II, 1:4. Auf. 1889.

Zilsel, Edgar. *Die Enstehung des Geniebegriffes*. Tübingen, 1926.

————. "The Genesis of the Concept of Scientific Progress," *Journal of the History of Ideas*, VI (1945), 325–349.

INDEX

Academicians, 145n, 165
Achilles, 15n
Adam, J., 36n, 106n, 108n, 113n, 117n
Aelian, 68
Aeneas, 131
Aenesidemus, 167n
Aeschylus, 25n, 35n, 43, 44, 55n
Aesop, 50n
Agatharchides, 159, 160n, 179
Agathon, 26, 80
Aglaophon, 79n
Agonistic culture, 4, 15, 16n, 52n, 99n
Aidos, 17
Alcmaeon, 73
Alexander the Great, 57, 133n, 152, 153n
Alexandria, 156
Alexandrian engineers, 142
Alexinus, 62
Allegory: in poetry, 149
Allen, T. W., 45n
Alphabet: introduction of, 34, 44
Anacharsis, 41
Analogies: use of, 119, 124
Anatomy, 141
Anaxagoras, 21–26, 29, 43n, 54, 73n, 74, 77, 80
Anaximander, 9n, 10, 46n, 77, 80
Ancestors: attitudes toward, 7n
Ancient traditions: attitudes toward, xvii, 34–35, 39, 73–76, 111
Animal communities: compared with humans, 19, 22, 24, 44, 50, 55, 85, 168
Animalitarianism, 50, 55, 62
Animals: praise of, 61–62

Anthropocentrism, 22n, 23
Antiochus, 165, 166, 167n
Antiphanes, 67n, 79
Antiphon, 53
Antiprimitivism, 51n
Antiprogressivism: rivalry with progressivism, 35–41
Antiquity: veneration of, xvii, 39
Antisthenes, 55n, 58–60, 61n, 62, 68n, 69n
Apelles, 79
Apelt, Otto, 27n
Apollo, 140
Apollodorus, 79n
Apollonius, 143n, 151
Apollonius of Perga, 142n
Apollonius Rhodius, 149
Aratus, 139, 140n, 145n, 153
Arcadia, 44n, 69n, 94n
Arcesilaus, 133n, 165
Archaeology, 35, 42
Archaic poetry: tenets of, 7–9
Archelaus, 22n, 55n
Archidamus, 82
Archimedes, 142, 143, 146, 147, 151
Architects: achievements of, 12, 26
Archytas, 142
Aristarchus, 149
Aristeas, 17
Aristides, 43, 67n, 80n
Aristippus, 58–60, 62, 142n
Ariston, 138n
Aristophanes, 36, 37n, 43n, 44, 45n, 50n, 51, 67n, 73n

199

Aristotle: on progress, xvi*n*, 69–70, 77, 102, 118–30, 170*n*, 172; on search for good, 13; on classical period, 22*n*, 41, 42; on philosophers, 26, 27*n*; on politics, 30, 108*n*; criticism of Hippodamus, 31; Diller on, 37*n*; on Golden Age, 43; on Greek learning, 48; on primitivism, 64; on ancients, 74, 75, 134; on Isocrates, 79; on comedy, 80; on Pre-Socratic logic, 81; on elections, 82*n*; on leisure, 83–84; on development of civilization, 87–92; conception of history, 93*n*; collecting historical material, 94–95; on history of ideas, 96; as historian, 97, 158; on achievement of truth, 98*n*; on rewards, 99, 101; on physical theories, 107*n*; on reforms, 115; criticism of Plato, 123; on poetry, 123, 150*n*; on infinity, 125; on medicine, 125*n*; empiricism of, 127; on sciences, 127, 146; on potentiality, 127–28; on technology, 141, 142*n*; influence on Erasistratus, 147*n*; awareness of time, 148, 149*n*; rhetoric of, 157; theory of cognition, 166, 167; metaphysics of, 177; on truth, 178
Aristoxenus, 70
Arnim, H. von, 79*n*, 138, 145, 146, 167*n*, 179*n*
Artemis: temple of, 12
Artillery: innovations in, 142, 154
Arts and crafts: development of, xxiii, 12, 22, 23, 86, 161; early religious estimate of, 6; status of craftsmen, 15; invention of, 25*n*, 45, 137–38; analogy with politics, 31; attitudes toward, 50; in fourth century, 71–72; innovations in, 77–78; technological theory of, 78; Plato on, 105–7, 109–13; Aristotle on, 118, 120
Asclepiades, 157, 158*n*
Asclepius, 56*n*, 132*n*
Asianists, 141*n*
Assyria, 16, 17*n*
Astronomy, 4, 60, 70, 76, 87, 139, 141, 144, 154, 158, 164
Athena, 44, 48
Athenaeus, 35, 42*n*, 54, 66*n*, 67*n*, 69*n*, 79, 101*n*, 132, 173*n*
Athenio, 66*n*
Athens, 14, 41–42, 44, 57, 67, 140
Athletics: value of, 14–15, 48
Atomism, 85, 158

Attic comedy, 42
Attic language, 149*n*
Augustine, xix, xxi
Augustus, Emperor, 133*n*

Babylon, 16, 17*n*
Bacon, Francis, xxxi, 18, 28, 66, 89, 91*n*, 98, 115, 129, 170*n*
Bailey, C., 136*n*, 137*n*, 162*n*, 163*n*
Baillie, John, xii*n*, xx*n*, xxi*n*, xxii*n*, xxiv*n*, xxvii*n*, 17*n*, 92*n*, 122*n*
Banking: development of, 81
Barbarians: compared with Greeks, 48
Barker, E., 30*n*, 88*n*, 103*n*, 104*n*, 119*n*, 122*n*, 123*n*
Barth, P., 138*n*
Bassett, E. O., 113*n*
Bassi, Livinia, xiv*n*
Becker, C. L., xxvii*n*, 88*n*, 151*n*, 153*n*, 172*n*
Belopoeica, 142, 154
Berger, H., 144*n*
Bernays, J., 33*n*, 91*n*, 121*n*, 135*n*
Berossus, 148*n*
Berve, Helmut, 11*n*, 57*n*, 81*n*
Bidez, J., 174*n*
Bignone, E., 161*n*
Biography: historical, 77
Biology, 76
Bloch, H., 77*n*
Boas, George, xi*n*, xxv*n*, xxvii*n*, xxxii*n*, 7*n*, 17*n*, 43*n*, 44*n*, 45*n*, 50*n*, 51*n*, 62*n*, 63*n*, 64*n*, 66*n*, 67*n*, 68*n*, 69*n*, 94*n*, 122*n*, 134*n*, 137*n*, 139*n*, 161*n*, 163*n*, 165*n*, 167*n*, 168*n*, 169*n*, 170*n*, 173*n*
Boeotia, 52
Boll, F., 54*n*, 114*n*, 128*n*
Bonhöffer, A., 170*n*
Books, production of, 151
Bowra, C. M., 4*n*, 16*n*, 36*n*
Brahe, Tycho, 141
Breasted, J. H., 17*n*
Bréhier, E., xxii*n*, 98*n*
Brink, C. O., 142*n*
Brown, T. S., 69*n*
Bruns, 162*n*
Bultman, R. K., xx*n*
Burckhardt, J., 5*n*, 6*n*, 15*n*, 49*n*, 67*n*, 82*n*, 83*n*, 99*n*, 131*n*, 132*n*, 152*n*, 153*n*, 156*n*, 157*n*, 176*n*, 177*n*
Burnet, J., 3*n*, 12*n*, 14*n*, 19*n*, 92*n*, 126*n*

Bury, J. B., xi*n*, xii*n*, xiv–xv, xix*n*, xvii, xviii, xxiv*n*, xxv*n*, xxvi*n*, xxix*n*, 6*n*, 7*n*, 11*n*, 16*n*, 39*n*, 40*n*, 46*n*, 57*n*, 76*n*, 77*n*, 81*n*, 92*n*, 106*n*, 107*n*, 108*n*, 124*n*, 143*n*, 149*n*, 154*n*, 173*n*, 175*n*, 176*n*
Bywater, I., 88*n*

Caesar, 116
Callicles, 52
Callimachus, 139*n*, 140, 149, 157
Campbell, L., 106*n*
Cannibalism, 65, 66*n*, 87*n*
Carneades, 165
Carthage: war with, 82
Cary, M., 58*n*
Cassirer, E., 75*n*, 137*n*, 147*n*
Catapults: use of, 82
Catholicism: and progressivism, xix*n*
Chaeremon, 66*n*
Change: attitudes toward, 33*n*, 34
Changes in ideas: processes of, xxvii
Cherniss, H. F., 3, 27*n*, 34*n*, 70*n*, 81*n*, 88*n*, 93*n*, 95*n*, 96*n*
Childe, V. G., 17*n*, 19*n*
Children: relationship with fathers, 36
Christ, W. von, 42*n*, 66*n*, 139*n*, 141*n*, 142*n*, 149*n*, 152*n*, 157*n*
Christianity: and progressivism, xii, xix–xxiii, xxxi, 153*n*; and belief in future, 151
Chrysippus, 76, 145, 167, 173*n*
Cicero, 26, 70, 125, 127*n*, 146*n*, 148, 157, 162, 166, 167, 168, 172*n*, 176, 177*n*, 178*n*, 179
Cimon, 74*n*
Cinesias, 36*n*
Cithara-playing, 79
City planning: invention of, 26*n*, 30
Civilization: studies of development of, 5, 21, 85–92; early explanations of, 9–11; philosophy of culture, 22; concept of, 24*n*; affiliation of cultures, 32; criticism of, 50, 58–59, 61–63, 160–61; and moral decline, 139
Classen, C. J., 58*n*
Cleanthes, 160, 167
Cleisthenes, 43*n*
Clement, 177
Clement of Alexandria, 136
Cleve, F. M., 29*n*
Cnidian school, 71*n*
Cochrane, C. N., 47*n*

Cognition: theories of, 166
Cohen, Morris, 142*n*, 143*n*
Coining of money: origin of, 4, 11
Collingwood, R. G., xvii*n*, xxii*n*, 94*n*
Colophon, 4, 5
Comedies, 42–43, 65, 67, 80
Comte, A., xii, xiv, xvi–xvii, xviii, xix, xxxi*n*, 40, 41, 84*n*, 91*n*
Condorcet, xiv*n*, 16*n*, 175
Conjecture: role of, 5
Copernicus, 141
Corinth, 42
Corinthians, 31, 32, 33
Cornford, F. M., xiv*n*, xxvi*n*, 85*n*, 106*n*, 107*n*
Corruption: Aristotle on, 72
Cosmos: origin of, 9; theory of decay of, 164
Couat, A., 149*n*, 153*n*
Crates, 62*n*, 133*n*
Cratinus, 42*n*
Critias, 23*n*, 25, 33*n*, 55*n*
Critolaus, 160*n*
Croix, Emery de la, 175*n*
Crombie, A. C., 150*n*
Cronus, 17, 18*n*, 35, 42, 43, 63, 134
Ctesias, 69*n*, 73, 74
Cult-legends, 6, 9*n*
Culture. *See* Civilization
Culture-heroes, 44–45
Curtius, L., 78*n*
Cyclical theory of world progress, 46
Cynicism, 58–63, 65, 68*n*, 69*n*, 83, 111, 121*n*, 133, 138*n*
Cypris, 25
Cyrenaics, 65

Dampier, W. C., 142*n*
Dante, 172
Darius, 50*n*
Decay of cosmos: theory of, 164
Deichgräber, K., 37*n*, 147*n*, 159*n*
DeLacy, P. H., 162*n*, 164*n*
Delphic Oracle, 100*n*
Delvaille, J., xii*n*, xiv*n*, xx*n*, xxvi*n*, 5*n*, 169*n*, 175*n*
Demeter, 6*n*, 44, 45*n*, 66, 132
Demetrius of Troizen, 157*n*
Democritus, 4*n*, 21–26, 28*n*, 29, 43*n*, 50*n*, 53, 54, 62*n*, 72, 73*n*, 74; 80, 83, 85, 114, 116*n*, 137*n*, 140, 147*n*
Demosthenes, 67, 131, 132

Destruction of works of men: periodic, 91, 105, 108
Destruction of world: belief in, 29, 172–73
DeWitt, N. W., 136n
Diadochi, 58, 157n
Dialogues: Platonic, 93
Dicaearchus, xxxi$n$, 94n, 134–35, 139, 141, 142n, 168n, 172n
Dice: invention of, 44
Didymus, 157, 158
Diehl, 15
Diels, H., 3, 4n, 5, 10, 14, 15, 21n, 22, 23, 24n, 25, 26, 27n, 29n, 30n, 33n, 34, 35, 53, 54, 55n, 62n, 65n, 73n, 85n, 92n, 116n, 142, 145n, 157n
Dietetics, 39
Diffusion theory, 87, 88
Dijon: Academy of, xxiii$n$
Diller, H., 37n, 47n, 48n
Dilthey, W., xii, xix, xx, xxvii$n$, xxxn, xxxi$n$, 90n, 91n, 149n, 177n
Dio Chrysostomus, 61
Diocles, 76
Diodorus, 22n, 24n, 41n, 82, 85n, 140, 153
Diogenes, 55n, 58n, 59, 60, 61n, 62, 65n, 133n
Diogenes of Apollonia, 21n
Diogenes Laertius, 10n, 59n, 60, 61, 62n, 68n, 69n, 133n, 136, 138n, 142n, 148n, 177
Diogenes of Oinoanda, 162n
Dionysius, 101n, 115n
Dionysius of Halicarnassus, 77
Dionysius of Sicily, 82
Dionysius Thrax, 158
Dionysus, 34, 42n
Diplomatists: appearance of, 81
Dissection: studies of, 141
Distinction: desire for, 99
Divine powers: and origin of cosmos, 9
Dodds, E. R., 15n, 56n, 132n, 179n
Doren, A., 9n, 45n
Dossi, Anton Francesco, 154n
Drabkin, I. E., 142n, 143n
Drama: innovations in, 80
Droysen, J. G., 180n
Dudley, D. R., 59n, 61n, 62n, 65n, 133n, 156n
Dümmler, F., 72n
Dürer, 143n
Duris, 78n

Eclipse of sun: explanation of, 4, 12, 26, 49
Economy: changes in, 81
Edel, Abraham, xxvii$n$
Edelstein, E. J., 9n, 56n, 60n
Edelstein, L., 9n, 56n, 71n, 76n, 83n, 93n, 107n, 117n, 120n, 126n, 132n, 142n, 152n, 155n, 159n, 168n, 171n, 173n, 176n, 177n, 179n
Education: criticism of, 58–59; development of schools, 83n; and transmission of knowledge, 91, 121, 153–54; Plato on, 117n; production of books, 151
Egypt, 16, 17n, 32, 87, 108–9, 140, 152, 153n
Ehrenberg, V., 132n
Eleatic philosophers, 21
Elections: Aristotle on, 82n
Eleusis, 44
Empedocles, 25, 38, 46, 73, 74, 132n, 157
Empiricism, 127, 132n, 159
Engineers: achievements of, 12, 142
England, E. B., 113n
Epaminondas, 131
Ephesus, 12
Ephorus, 67, 68, 77, 95n
Epic poets: concepts of, 7–8
Epictetus, 59
Epicureans, 69n, 156, 158, 160, 162–63, 164, 165, 173n, 176, 177, 178
Epicurus, 135–37, 161, 162, 164
Epistemology: importance of, 59
Erasistratus, 147n, 150
Eratosthenes, 92n, 137n, 141, 142, 147n, 149, 153, 158
Eschatology: historical aspects of, xx, 17
Eternalism, 92n, 98n
Ethics: importance of, 59, 60
Eucken, R., xiii$n$, 73n, 96n, 97n, 120n, 123n, 127n
Euclid, 70, 76
Eudemus, 4, 46n, 76n, 95n
Eudoxus, 76, 139, 142, 145n, 153, 160
Euhemerism, 153n
Euhemerus, 140
Euphorion, 149n
Euripides, 46, 48n, 54, 55n, 139n, 174n
Euryphon, 71n, 73
Eutocius, 142
Evolutionism, 25
Experts: belief in, 82n

Fame: contests for, 14–15; desire for, 99
Family relationships, 36
Fathers: attitudes toward, 7n, 36
Faust, A., 27n, 117n, 128n, 177n
Festugière, A. J., 179n
Field, G. C., xxxn, 57n
Fifth century: thoughts on progress, 21–56
Finley, J. H., 41n
Fire: discovery of, 55
Flutes: playing of, 48
Fontenelle, xxixn, 16n, 124n, 154
Fourth century: thoughts on progress, 57–132
Frank, Erich, 18n, 26n, 70n, 74n, 80n, 81n, 84n, 97n, 110n, 122n, 128n
Frank, Tenney, xvn, 163n
Fraenkel, E., 35n
Fränkel, H., 5n, 8n, 10n, 13n, 14n, 16n, 22n
Friedländer, P., 22n, 27n, 44n, 63n, 74n, 106n, 112n
Friedlein, 70, 76n, 101, 120
Fritz, K. von, 43n, 61n, 62n, 65n
Future development: attitudes toward, 5, 98, 145–46, 164–65
Futurism: political, 31

Galen, 145, 150, 158, 159
Galileo, 75
Gellius, Aulus, 179n
Geminus, 160
Generation: Aristotle on, 72
Genetic way of thinking, 10n, 11n
Genius: conception of, 78, 89n
Geocentric model of cosmos, 141
Geography: knowledge of, 12, 141, 155, 158, 159n
Geometry, 60, 69
Gercke, A., 72n, 77n
Gigon, O., 178n
Gilbert, F., xxiiin
Ginsberg, M., xxviiin
Glaucus of Rhegium, 36n
Gnostic theory, xxin
Gods: attitudes toward, 6–7, 153n; rejected by Xenophanes, 11; envy of, 45n; and recession of mythology, 49; Hellenistic views of, 140
Goedeckemeyer, A., 138n, 165n, 167n
Golden, L., 43n
Golden Age: belief in, xxv, xxvi, 7n, 8, 9n, 11, 17, 24, 64, 69, 106n, 114, 134,

Golden Age (continued)
139, 137n, 138, 145n, 161n, 173n; comic descriptions of, 42–43
Gombrich, E. H., 78n
Gomme, A. W., xvn, 31n, 47n
Gomperz, T., xiiin, 5n, 28n
Gooch, G. P., 58n
Gorgias, 25n, 46, 48, 54n, 72, 79, 116n
Grammar: advances in, 158
Greece: conquest of, 133
Greeks: concept of progress, xv; pessimism of, xxvii; attitudes toward ancient traditions, 39; concern with knowledge, 41; consciousness of history, 46–47; compared with barbarians, 48
Green, W. M., 165n
Grote, G., 12n, 13n, 42n, 48n
Growth: Aristotle on, 72
Gudeman, A., 89n, 124n
Guthrie, W. K. C., xivn, 95n
Guyae, Jean M., 163n

Haase, W., 88n
Harder, R., 160n
Hasebroek, J., 15n
Havelock, E. A., 130n
Hecataeus, 9, 13, 32, 33n, 34, 35n, 140
Hegel, 96, 97
Hegesias, 141n
Heiberg, 142, 143, 146
Heidel, W. A., 9n, 34n, 46n, 81n
Heinemann, I., 147n, 169n, 178n
Heinimann, F., 37n
Heliocentric theory, 70n, 141
Hellanikos, 33n, 73
Hellenistic age: definition of, 133n
Hellespont: bridge over, 12
Hepaestus, 44
Heracles, 61n
Heraclitus, 4n, 14, 21, 34n, 37n, 46n, 92n, 155
Hermagoras, 141n, 157
Hero, 143n, 147n, 154
Herodotus, 4n, 12, 13, 32, 34, 41, 42n, 46–47, 48, 50n, 51, 53, 55n, 64, 73, 77, 87, 137n
Hesiod, 4, 6–7, 8, 9, 17, 18n, 34, 42, 45, 49, 68, 99, 139n
Hiero, 101n
Highet, Gilbert, 16n
Hildebrandt, G. H., xin

203

Hipparchus, 141, 144, 146, 147n, 151, 153, 156, 160
Hippias, 21, 26, 33n, 34n, 35, 42, 72n, 86n
Hippocrates: contemporaries of, 73; fame of, 76; Kant on, 150; criticism of, 157
Hippocratic writings, 25n, 28, 33, 34, 37–39, 51, 54n, 71, 85n, 92n, 148, 150
Hippodamus of Miletus, 26n, 30, 31, 99, 118, 119
Hirzel, R., xiiin, 18n, 46n, 135n, 138n, 147n
Historians: of fourth century, 77
Historical biography, 77
Historical insight: and politics, 156
Historiography: ancient and modern attitudes toward, xxii; writers in, 71; development of, 141
History: Greek consciousness of, 46–47; and progress, 90–91; collection of material, 94–95, 141; views of Aristotle and Plato, 96; awareness of, 148–49
Hobbes, 84n
Hoffmann, Ernst, 81n
Hogben, L. T., 175n
Höistad, R., 59n, 60n
Holbach, 173n
Homer, 4, 6, 7, 8, 17, 33, 34, 35n, 44, 45n, 49, 68, 86, 89n, 110, 149, 157
Homeric Epic, 39n
Hope: connected with progress, 46
Horace, 40n, 41n
Howe, C. S., 137n, 147n
Humanism, 79n
Humanities: development of, 26
Hume, xxiiin
Humor: Plato on, 116

Iamblichus, 25n, 70, 100n, 120
Iason, 169n
Idealization of savages, 50
Ilberg, J., 37n, 71n
Illusion: conquest of, 78
Immisch, O., 160n
Immoralism, 131–32
India, 69n
Individualism, 82–83, 99, 130n, 131, 150, 153n, 174
Industry: development of, 81
Infinity: concept of, 26, 125
Inge, W. R., xiii, xiv, xxvin

Injustice: writings on, 8
Innovations: attitudes toward, 34–35
Institutes for research, 151
Intellectual class: rise of, 83
Inventions: concept of, 3–5, 32–33, 90n, 93–94; by individuals, 9; interest in, 11–12; origins of, 43n, 44, 85n; criticism of, 60–61; in social institutions, 88; rewards for, 99, 103
Ion, 36n, 73
Ionian literature, 42n
Ionian sculpture: development of, 12
Isocrates, 10n, 24n, 55n, 64, 67, 68, 69n, 72, 73, 79, 80, 83–84, 85, 92, 94, 95n, 98, 99, 101, 102, 129, 130, 132, 157

Jacoby, F., 9, 35, 44n, 47n, 62n, 67n, 68, 69n, 71, 77, 84n, 92n, 95n, 140n, 159n, 173n
Jaeger, W., xxxiin, 3n, 16n, 18n, 37n, 43n, 44n, 70n, 76n, 79n, 93n, 95n, 97n, 103n, 121n, 127n, 135n, 155n
James, W., 13n, 53n
Jaspers, K., 176n
Jeans, James, xxivn
Jews: and progressivism, xii, xivn, xix–xxiii; eschatological vision of, 17
Joël, Karl, 16n, 39n
Justice: writings on, 8

Kant, I., 19n, 98n, 150, 151, 176
Kapp, E., 43n
Kapp, J. V., 12n
Kepler, 75
Kern, 18n
Kerschensteiner, Jula, 87n
Kinkel, 17
Kirk, G. S., 37n, 46n
Kleingünther, A., xxxiin, 4n, 5n, 6n, 7n, 8n, 9n, 11n, 12n, 23n, 24n, 32n, 37n, 45n, 55n, 83n, 139n
Klibansky, R., 98n, 178n
Knowledge: individual search for, 150; transmission of, 91, 121, 131, 153–54
Kock, T., 66n, 67n, 79, 92n
Kranz, W., 3, 4n, 5, 10, 14, 15, 21n, 22, 23, 24n, 25, 26, 27n, 29n, 30n, 33n, 34, 35, 53, 54, 55n, 62n, 65n, 73n, 85n, 92n, 116n
Krikorian, Y. H., xxviin
Krug, W. R., 123n

Lacedaemonians, 12, 31, 33, 41
Lactantius, 127*n*, 136, 145
Lang, P., 128*n*
Language: studies of, xxx, 26, 34, 136, 162*n*
Lasson, 97*n*
Leaf, Walter, 7*n*
Legislation: attitudes toward, 28, 36; written and unwritten laws, 45–46; Plato on, 112; Aristotle on, 118
Lehrs, K., 45*n*, 149*n*
Leibniz, 147
Leisure: theories of, 83–84
Leo, F., 46*n*, 95*n*
Leroux, Pierre, xii*n*
Le Roy, 173*n*
Lessing, 128*n*
Leucippus, 73*n*
Linforth, I. M., 18*n*, 44*n*
Loeb, J., 149*n*
Logic: importance of, 59, 69, 72, 124*n*
Lovejoy, A. O., xi*n*, xxvi*n*, xxvii*n*, xxxii*n*, 7*n*, 11*n*, 17*n*, 43*n*, 44*n*, 45*n*, 50*n*, 51*n*, 62*n*, 63*n*, 64*n*, 66*n*, 67*n*, 68*n*, 69*n*, 94*n*, 96*n*, 99*n*, 122*n*, 134*n*, 137*n*, 139*n*, 161*n*, 163*n*, 165*n*, 167*n*, 168*n*, 169*n*, 170*n*, 173*n*
Löwith, K., xix*n*, xxii*n*, xxiii*n*, 47*n*
Lucretius, 84, 85*n*, 136, 137*n*, 145*n*, 146*n*, 153, 160, 161, 162, 163, 164, 165, 167, 172*n*, 173*n*, 177
Lycophron, 152
Lydians, 4, 5, 11
Lyric poetry: development of, 12, 18
Lysippus, 71, 72*n*, 77, 78

Macedonians, 57
Mach, E., 152*n*
Macrobius, 175*n*
Magic: revival of, 132*n*
Maine, H. S., xiii
Mair, A. W., 152*n*
Malthusianism, 86*n*
Man: nature of, 10–11, 18–19; compared with animal communities, 19, 22, 24, 44, 50, 55, 85, 168
Manilius, 168, 169*n*
Manitius, 144*n*, 153*n*, 160
Manual labor: attitudes toward, 50*n*
Maps: early use of, 12
Mathematics: 26, 64*n*, 70, 76, 81*n*, 107*n*, 141, 142, 143, 158, 159*n*, 162
Mattingly, Harold, xii*n*

Mausolus, 79*n*
McDiarmid, J. B., 138*n*
McKeon, R., 92*n*, 123*n*
Mechanical arts: progress in, 98
Mechanics: theory of, 154
Mechanism, 22*n*, 23
Medical writers, 33, 37–39, 71. *See also* Hippocratic writings
Medicine: attitudes toward, 27; ancient traditions discussed, 38; criticism of, 75, 157; rules for, 105; Aristotle on, 125*n*; anatomy and dissection, 141. *See also* Physicians
Megara, 42, 51
Mekler, 76*n*
Melampus, 34
Melissus, 73
Menaechmian sections, 142
Menander, 139*n*
Merchants: status of, 15
Merki, H., xxxii*n*
Meropians, 69*n*
Mesopotamia: achievements in, 16
Messianism: effects of, xx, 17
Meteorology, 158
Methodists, 158
Meton, 26*n*
Mewaldt, J., 37*n*
Meyer, H., 123*n*, 124*n*
Meyer, W., 43*n*
Michelangelo, 117*n*
Michell, H., 50*n*
Middle Academy, 133
Middle Ages: doctrine of progress in, xix
Middle Comedy, 80
Milesian school, 9
Miletus: tunnel near, 12
Military men: professional, 81
Mill, John Stuart, xii
Mimesis: conception of, 78*n*
Minar, E. L., 60*n*
Misch, G., 130*n*
Molière, 40
Mommsen, T. E., xxxi*n*, 153*n*
Mondolfo, R., xiv*n*, xxxi*n*
Moral decay: concepts of, 8, 131–32, 139
Moral progress: thoughts of, 52–53
Moral values: in lyric poetry, 13
Moralism: of Zeno, 167
Mosaic Law, xix, xxxi*n*
Moschion, 65–66, 88

Müller, H. J., 53n, 150
Munro, H. A. J., 163n
Murray, G., 43n, 48n, 58n, 67n, 69n, 135n, 153n
Music: discovery of, 23; innovations in, 26, 35, 36n, 37n, 48, 70, 79–80, 100, 161; criticism of, 60; Plato on, 108
Mythology: criticism of, 49, 139–40

Natural phenomena: studies of, 49, 60, 70, 164, 170
Naturalism, 22n, 27
Nature: Aristotle on, 84
Nauck, 66
Navigation, 105, 139
Neinze, 128n
Nemea: games in, 14
Nemesis, 17
Neoptolemus of Parion, 150n
Nestle, W., 11n, 18n, 21, 23n, 24n, 25n, 26n, 35n, 44n, 46n, 49n, 50n, 53n, 54n, 94n
Nestor, 7n
Neugebauer, O., 144n, 154n
Newman, W. L., 41n, 88n
Nicolson, M. H., 116n, 129n
Nicomachus, 88n
Nietzsche, xiii, 55n, 87n
Nigidius Figulus, 179
Nilsson, M. P., 18n, 44n, 45n, 139n, 140n, 179n
Noland, A., 76n
Nomadic life, 86
Norden, E., 23n, 35n, 72n, 77n, 137n, 161n, 162n

Odysseus, 8n
Oehler, Klaus, 178n
Oeri, J., 5n, 132n
Ogerau, F., 171n
Oldfather, W. A., xxxiin, 131n
Olschki, L., 142n, 154n
Olympia: games in, 14
Olympian religion, 132
Onesicritus, 139n
Oracles, 5, 49, 100
Oribasius, 75
Orient, 32, 87, 88, 132, 137n, 148
Origen, xxxin
Orpheus, 36, 44
Orphic movement, 18
Ortega y Gasset, José, 178n

Pagans: concept of time, xx–xxii; Christian interaction with, xxxi
Paine, Thomas, 175n
Painting: development of, 78–79
Palaephatus, 49n
Palamedes, 43, 44n
Palm, A., 37n
Panaetius, 167, 168, 169, 173n, 174n, 176
Pan-Slavism, 39n
Parmenides, 21, 73, 74, 75, 76
Parrhasius, 79n
Pascal, xvin, 40, 91
Pasicles, 89n
Pasquali, G., 138n, 139n, 145n
Past: longing for, 134
Paton, H. J., 98n, 178n
Pausanias, 44n, 94n
Pease, 131n
Pelopidas, 131
Peloponnesian War, 22n, 157n
Peloponnesians, 41
Perfection: Plato on, 117; striving for, 174
Pergamene school, 149n
Pericles, 44, 52n, 74n
Peripatetics, 46n, 77n, 94, 134, 142n, 159, 160n
Persian wars, 41
Persians, 13, 17, 50n, 100n
Pessimism: of ancients, xxiv, 17, 47, 53–54
Phaleas of Chalcedon, 30
Phanes, 18n
Pherecrates, 37n, 42n
Philemon, 139n
Philip: age of, 79
Philistus, 82
Philo, 138, 165n, 166, 167n
Philo of Byzantium, 142
Philochorus, 140
Philodemus, 146n, 162, 164, 165
Philoponus, 88n
Philosophers: status of, 15; dissension among, 165
Philosophy: growth of, 70; rivalry with rhetoric, 79; and politics, 82; Greek origin of, 137n; and science, 155, 158–59
Philoxenus, 26, 79
Phoenicians, 34
Photius, 71
Phrynichus, 26n

Phyrnis, 90
Physicians, 27, 71, 75, 159. *See also* Medicine
Physiocentrism, 22*n*
Pickard-Cambridge, A. W., 36*n*
Pindar, 36*n*
Piraeus, 30
Pisistratus, 43, 48
Planets: studies of, 70, 141, 144, 159, 169
Plato: on prehistory, 21*n*, 22*n*, 25; on arts and sciences, 27, 28, 34*n*, 78, 92, 105–13, 129; terminology of, 35; on music and poetry, 36*n*; Diller on, 37*n*; on experience, 46; on early mankind, 63–64, 85, 87; fables of, 68; on progress, 70, 72*n*, 102–18, 121–23, 170*n*; on Anaxagoras, 74*n*; modernity of, 76; on Isocrates, 79; on music, 80, 108; abstract reasoning of, 81; on service to state, 82; on leisure, 83–84; on rise of culture, 86; on time, 88; on civilization, 91, 173*n*; dialogues of, 93; as historian, 95; on history of ideas, 96; on reforms, 100*n*; on rewards, 101; on politics, 102–4; on poetry, 108; as lawgiver, 112–13; on virtue and vice, 113*n*; on contemplative life, 114; on possibilities and impossibilities, 115–16; Seventh Letter of, 115*n*, 117*n*; on perfection, 117; on education, 117*n*; criticized by Aristotle, 123; expectations of, 126, 127; and Pre-Socratics, 128*n*; on man's obligations, 150; on immortality, 153*n*; attacks on, 157; theory of cognition, 166; on theoretical activity of mind, 174*n*; metaphysics of, 177; on truth, 178
Pliny, 7*n*, 71, 76, 78, 79*n*, 144, 169, 174*n*, 175*n*
Plotinus, xxxi*n*
Plutarch, 10*n*, 43, 52, 61*n*, 80*n*, 147*n*
Poetry: archaic, 7–9; lyric, 12, 18; progressivism in, 35–37, 65–66; innovations in, 48; development of, 89*n*, 90; of fifth century, 98*n*; Plato on, 108; Aristotle on, 123; Hellenistic, 138, 140; knowledge contained in, 149, 153; and views on ancients, 157
Pohlenz, M., 25*n*, 74*n*, 138*n*, 139*n*, 145*n*, 169*n*, 171*n*
Pöhlmann, R. von, 7*n*, 42*n*, 45*n*
Poliorketes, Demetrius, 132*n*

Politics: plans for reform, 30–31; analogy with arts and crafts, 31; fourth century changes, 57–58, 67, 81; and philosophy, 82; Plato on, 102–8; Aristotle on, 119; and historical insight, 156
Polos, 25, 46
Polybius, 77, 141, 142, 143–44, 146*n*, 147*n*, 152, 155, 156, 158, 159*n*
Polygnotus, 79*n*
Popper, K. R., 104*n*
Popularizers of science, 153–54
Porphyry, 134, 135
Poseidon, 63*n*
Posidonius, 158–59, 160*n*, 167, 168, 169, 171*n*, 173*n*, 174*n*, 175*n*, 176, 177, 178*n*
Potentiality: Aristotle on, 127–28
Poverty: views on, 100, 101
Powell, 149*n*
Praechter, K., 23*n*, 26*n*, 58*n*, 59*n*
Praxagoras, 76
Praxiteles, 80
Prehistory: early treatises on, 21
Pre-Socratics, xiv*n*, xxxi*n*, 3, 6, 10, 22*n*, 24*n*, 26, 27, 28, 29, 43*n*, 46, 55, 74, 80, 81*n*, 83, 86–87, 89, 92*n*, 93, 97, 98, 106, 116, 118, 119, 126, 128*n*, 162, 177
Primitivism: theory of, xxviii, 24*n*, 50–51, 134–135, 159–61; analysis of, xxxii; and animalitarianism, 62*n*; Plato on, 63*n*; wane of, 69
Probabilism, 133*n*
Proclus, 76*n*, 101, 120
Prodicus, 21*n*, 25, 33*n*, 35, 53
Professional ethics: development of, 150*n*
Progress: definition of, xi, xxix–xxx; concepts of, xi–xxxiii, 173–174; fifth century views, 21–56; connected with hope, 46; fourth century views, 57–132; Aristotle on, 118–30; Plato on, 102–18; third century views, 133–78; Seneca on, 167–77
Progressivism: rivalry with antiprogressivism, 35–41
Prometheus, 7, 42, 43, 44, 61*n*, 65
Prophecies, 5, 49
Prose styles: new, 140, 141*n*
Protagoras, 21, 22–25, 28*n*, 50, 51, 56*n*, 79, 86*n*
Protestantism: and antiprogressivism, xix*n*

208

209

Vlastos, G., 22n, 23n, 27n, 137n, 140n
Vogel, K., 77n

Wallis, W. D., xxvn
Wanner, H., 37n
Warfare: changes in, 11, 12n, 49, 50, 82, 100, 142, 154; writings on, 33; professional soldiers, 81
Weber, A., 22n
Wehrli, 46n, 49n, 76n, 95n, 134, 135n, 142n, 172n
Weidauer, K., 47n
Weiher, A., 65n
Weil, R., 97n
Weiss, H., 110n
Welcker, F. G., 45n
Wellmann, 76
Wendland, Paul, 140n
Whitehead, A. N., 19n, 55n
Wien, 124n
Wiener, P. P., 76n
Wilamowitz-Möllendorff, U. von, 16n, 34n, 36n, 39n, 40n, 42n, 43n, 139n, 142n, 157n, 179n

Winter, Franz, 72n
Wisdom: views on, 174
Wolfe, K. H., 90n
World destruction: belief in, 29, 91, 105, 108, 172–73

Xenocrates, 128n, 167
Xenophanes, 3–18, 21–22, 29, 30, 31, 32n, 34, 35n, 41, 43n, 47, 48, 49, 51, 52, 55, 66n, 83, 88, 93, 99, 118, 125n, 130, 145, 147
Xenophon, 26, 54–55, 59n, 60, 69n, 92, 98, 99, 101, 102, 129, 130, 143n, 175n

Zafiropulo, J., 22n
Zarathustra, xiin
Zeller, E., 50n, 58n, 59n, 61n
Zeno, 137–38, 145n, 146, 158, 166, 167
Zeus, 7, 17, 35, 45, 63n, 145n
Zeuxis, 79n
Zilsel, E., 143n, 150n
Zoroastrianism, xxn, 17n

Designed by Gerard A. Valerio
Composed in Electra by Kingsport Press, Inc.
Printed letterpress by Kingsport Press, Inc., on Warren's 1854
Bound by Kingsport Press in Columbia Riverside and G.S.B.S/522